Sports Psychology

FOR

DUMMIES®

Sports Psychology

FOR

DUMMIES®

**by Leif H. Smith, PsyD, and
Todd M. Kays, PhD**

John Wiley & Sons Canada, Ltd.

Sports Psychology For Dummies®

Published by
John Wiley & Sons Canada, Ltd.
6045 Freemont Blvd.
Mississauga, ON L5R 4J3
www.wiley.com

For general information on John Wiley & Sons Canada, Ltd., including all books published by Wiley Publishing, Inc., please call our distribution centre at 1-800-567-4797. For reseller information, including discounts and premium sales, please call our sales department at 416-646-7992. For press review copies, author interviews, or other publicity information, please contact our publicity department, Tel. 416-646-4582, Fax 416-236-4448.

For technical support, please visit www.wiley.com/techsupport.

Wiley also publishes its books in a variety of electronic formats. Some content that appears in print may not be available in electronic books.

Library and Archives Canada Cataloguing in Publication Data

Smith, Leif H.

     Sports psychology for dummies / Leif H. Smith, Todd M. Kays.

Includes index.

ISBN 978-0-470-67659-2

     1. Sports—Psychological aspects. I. Kays, Todd M. II. Title.

GV706.4.S62 2010   796.01   C2010-902900-3

Printed in the United States
C10011813_062919

WILEY

About the Authors

Leif H. Smith, PsyD, is the president of Personal Best Consulting, a sports psychology and performance consultation firm located in Hilliard, Ohio. He has worked with hundreds of individual athletes from all walks of life — from amateurs and weekend warriors to professional athletes from Major League Baseball, the National Basketball Association, and the National Football League. Leif's company contracts with the Department of Athletics at The Ohio State University to provide counseling and performance consultation to its 36 sports and nearly 1,000 athletes. He has also worked with teams and athletes from The University of Iowa and Duquesne University, among others. Leif is an adjunct faculty member at the University of Dayton, teaching graduate courses in clinical assessment. He earned his doctorate in clinical psychology from The Chicago School of Professional Psychology and did his postdoctoral fellowship in applied sports psychology and counseling at The Ohio State University Sports Medicine Center. His work has been cited in publications such as *The New York Times, The Columbus Dispatch,* and *Entrepreneur* magazine, among others.

Todd M. Kays, PhD, is president of the Athletic Mind Institute, a sports and performance consulting firm in Dublin, Ohio. He is a licensed psychologist, devoted to helping athletes and people of all walks of life achieve peak performance on a consistent and frequent basis. He attended the University of Notre Dame for his undergraduate degree and earned his doctorate at the State University of New York at Buffalo. His training and guidance have helped hundreds of athletes eliminate the most common mental errors and breakdowns in sports. For five years, Todd was the sports psychologist for the Columbus Crew, the major league soccer team in Columbus, Ohio; he continues to work with numerous soccer players and coaches throughout the country. He has consulted with athletes and coaches from all different levels of sports, including Major League Soccer, USA Olympic Hockey, the Professional Golf Association, and the Ladies Professional Golf Association. He consults regularly with the athletic departments at The Ohio State University and Ohio University, both of which he serves as an adjunct faculty member. Todd was the first sports psychology fellow at The Ohio State University, training several athletes, coaches, and teams, including national champions, all-Americans, and Olympians. He has coauthored two books — *Positive Transitions for Student Athletes: Life Skills for Transitions in Sport, College, and Career* (Holcomb Hathaway Publishing) and *The Parent's Playbook: Developing a Gameplan for Maximizing Your Child's Athletic Experience* (Champion Athletic Consulting) — and produced *Peak Mental Performance in Golf: Sharpening the Mental Side of Your Game,* a CD, book, and video series addressing mental training for the sport of golf. Todd has appeared on radio and television and in newspapers and magazines, including ESPN, Fox Sports, the *New York Post,* and *NASCAR Illustrated.*

Dedication

This book is dedicated to Aiden and Gable Smith, my boys and my greatest teachers, and to Todd Kays, who shared my dream of getting this book in the public's hands.

—Leif H. Smith, PsyD

This book is dedicated to the numerous people who have inspired me in my journey, including my family, Kathy, Jake, Charley, Bill, Mark, Jenny, Jeff, Paul, Don, Tom, and Naomi. And to my coauthor, Leif — it has been a blast, and I look forward to many years of continuing to advance the field together. I would not be here without all of you.

—Todd M. Kays, PhD

Authors' Acknowledgments

Many thanks to all our clients over the years, who have inspired us and made it possible for us to write this book. We're humbled to have been afforded the privilege of sharing in your dreams.

Much gratitude to The Ohio State University Department of Athletics for continuing to entrust us with the care of its teams and athletes. The Buckeyes and The Ohio State University Sports Medicine Center continue to be leaders in improving the quality of psychological care for collegiate athletes. Thank you, also, to Ohio University for its vision and efforts to that end.

Many thanks to Robert Hickey for his vision on this project, to Elizabeth Kuball for her patience and tireless effort, and to Jack Lesyk for giving us his professional opinion and insight. Thank you, also, to Bernard Golden, who so generously offered his assistance to get this project off the ground. We couldn't have done this without you.

Publisher's Acknowledgments

We're proud of this book; please send us your comments at http://dummies.custhelp.com. For other comments, please contact our Customer Care Department within the U.S. at 877-762-2974, outside the U.S. at 317-572-3993, or fax 317-572-4002.

Some of the people who helped bring this book to market include the following:

Acquisitions and Editorial

Project Editor: Elizabeth Kuball

Acquiring Editor: Robert Hickey

Copy Editor: Elizabeth Kuball

Technical Editor: Jack J. Lesyk, PhD

Project Coordinator, Canada:
Lindsay Humphreys

Editorial Assistant: Katie Wolsley

Cover Photos: © bikeriderlondon/Shutterstock

Cartoons: Rich Tennant
(www.the5thwave.com)

Composition Services

Project Coordinator, U.S.: Lynsey Stanford

Layout and Graphics: Christin Swinford

Proofreaders: John Greenough, Leeann Harney

Indexer: Valerie Haynes Perry

Contents at a Glance

Table of Contents

Introduction

Sports psychology is a relatively new field, but it's one of the fastest-growing areas in sports performance. Professional sports are big money, and teams want a return on their investment in their players. So it should come as no surprise that every NFL, NBA, MLB, and NHL team employs someone trained in sports psychology to assist them with helping players work through mental blocks, slumps, and general decreases in performance.

We wrote this book because we want to get the information that we teach to elite athletes and teams to the general public. The services we provide as sports psychologists can be expensive, and most athletes who are just looking for a way to get the edge in their sports participation can't afford to fork over hundreds of dollars to meet with their own sports psychologist. With this book, you don't have to — you hold in your hands the same information we share with our clients, for a tiny fraction of the cost.

This book is packed full of information that can help you get more out of your physical talent. We've filled this book with techniques and skills that we teach to professional and Olympic athletes — skills that you can apply in your own training today.

About This Book

Most sports psychology books provide good stories and education on sports psychology concepts, but they don't take the next step and cover actual techniques and strategies that athletes can use. In this book, we do exactly that.

Plus, this book is organized for busy athletes who are on the go and don't have a lot of time to waste. The information is easy to access and written in plain English, without any psychobabble to bog you down. You don't need a PhD to understand this book. All you need is a thirst for knowledge and a willingness to work hard to reach your goals — we bring the rest.

Conventions Used in This Book

We don't use many special conventions in this book, but there are a few you should be aware of:

- When we want to share a story from our practice as sports psychologists, we refer to ourselves by our first names, so you can tell which of us is telling you the story. For example, we may say, "Leif was working with a pro soccer team . . ." or "Todd's client was a young tennis phenom. . . ." When you see the names Leif and Todd, just remember that's us.

- Whenever we define a new term, we put it in *italics,* and define it shortly thereafter, often in parentheses.

- When we give you a list of steps to take, we put the action part of the step in **bold** so that you can easily find out what you're supposed to do.

- When we give you a Web address, we put it in monofont. When this book was printed, some Web addresses may have needed to break across two lines of text. If that happened, rest assured that we haven't put in any extra characters (such as hyphens) to indicate the break. So, when using one of these Web addresses, just type in exactly what you see in this book, pretending as though the line break doesn't exist.

What You're Not to Read

To understand the subject at hand, you don't have to read any text preceded by a Technical Stuff icon (see "Icons Used in This Book," later in this Introduction, for more information). Also, sidebars (text in gray boxes) are asides and not critical to the text. Of course, if you *want* to read these things, we think you'll find them completely fascinating! But if you're short on time or you just want the information you absolutely need, you can pass them by.

Foolish Assumptions

In writing this book, we made some assumptions about you. One or more of the following should apply to you:

- You're an athlete with particular goals that you'd like to achieve, and you think that the mental aspect of your training and performance can benefit from further understanding and practice. You're willing to work hard to achieve your goals.

✔ You're a coach and you want to use sports psychology to help your athletes achieve their goals. You recognize that training isn't just physical.

✔ You're a parent of an athlete, and you want to support your kid's athletic career in all the right ways.

How This Book Is Organized

This book is conveniently divided into six parts. Here's what you find in each.

Part I: Getting the Winning Edge: Sports Psychology Fundamentals

In Part I, we introduce you to the important basic principles of sports psychology. We start off by telling you how to build your mental toughness, an essential skill for any competitive athlete. Then we turn to goal setting, because you're more likely to get somewhere you want to be if you know where you're going. Motivation is key to athletes of all levels, and it ebbs and flows throughout your season; we show you how to monitor your motivation and boost it when you need to. Finally, we give you the information you need to increase your confidence, because without confidence in your own skills and abilities, it doesn't matter how talented you are or how hard you've worked.

Part II: Your Mental Toolkit for Success

In Part II, we dig into some key concepts that you need to know in your pursuit of competitive greatness. These concepts include concentration, as well as mental imagery. We explain the basics of focus — what it is, how to do it, when to do it, and when not to do it. We fill you in on mental imagery — one of the tools the pros use to be their best. We tell you how self-talk can help or hurt your performance, and how you can use it to your advantage. Finally, we help you master the task-management principles of the best athletes in the world, which will allow you to do more in less time.

Part III: Staying Competitive: Sports Psychology in Action

In Part III, we fill you in on the power of routines in sports and show you how to create your own effective routines to kick your performance up a notch. We cover the keys to handling pressure in the big moments — how to keep your cool while taking that last-second jumper, how to you relax and drain that putt. We give you simple but effective ways to do both, and to remain poised, no matter the situation. We offer cutting-edge strategies for energy management, a key component to staying competitive. Finally, we share some key ways to bounce back from adversity — whether it's an injury or a slump or a losing season.

Part IV: Improving Team Performance with Sports Psychology

In Part IV, we show you how to improve communication on your team, because teams that communicate better perform better. We explain the importance of leaders in the team dynamic and help you become a better leader, regardless of your role on your team. We end the part by talking about teamwork — how to improve your team's chemistry and, in turn, improve your team's chances for success.

Part V: Sports Psychology for Coaches and Parents

We wrote Part V specifically with coaches and parents in mind. In this part, we offer concrete strategies you can use to improve your team's performance — from helping them focus to guiding them through playing under pressure to motivating them to succeed.

Sports are different today than they were when you were a kid, so we have a chapter specifically for parents of today's athletes. We tell you how you can support your kids without pressuring them, how to help them prepare for competition, and what to do if your kids say they don't want to play sports anymore.

Part VI: The Part of Tens

Part VI is chock full o' tips, in three brief chapters. We tell you how you can apply sports psychology principles and concepts in the business world — from mentally preparing for a grueling work day, to setting goals for advancing in your career, to dealing with difficult co-workers. We offer tips for mastering the art of competing like a world-class athlete. We give you specific strategies for managing stress — from using meditation and mental imagery to formulating an exercise plan. And we end this part with a chapter for parents, with ten tips for making your kids' athletic experience a positive and rewarding one.

Icons Used in This Book

Like all *For Dummies* books, this book's margins are sprinkled with icons to help direct your attention to certain concepts, definitions, and interesting information. Here's a key to what they mean:

This icon directs you to techniques that world-class athletes use to improve their performance.

This book is a reference book, which means you don't have to commit it to memory — you can come back to it when you need it. But when you see this icon, you're sure to find information that we think is so crucial that you need to remember it.

This icon alerts you to stories or examples of some of our work with athletes from all walks of life.

This icon is for people who can't get enough of sports psychology principles. You can skip reading these paragraphs without consequence — but if you really want the inside scoop, read on!

When you see this icon, you can be sure we're alerting you to a danger or pitfall of some sort — something you should avoid.

Where to Go from Here

This book isn't linear — you don't have to read it from beginning to end, like a novel. Each chapter is self-contained, so you can start anywhere you want, and skip around as you like. You can use the table of contents and index to guide you, but here are a few suggestions for places to begin: If you're new to sports psychology — you've only heard about it but you've never practiced any sports psychology techniques — start with Part I for a good foundation. If you want to improve in a specific area, like focus or managing your schedule, turn to the appropriate chapters in Part II. If you want to use sports psychology to win, make Part III your destination. If you're looking for ways to improve your team's performance, Part IV is for you. And if you're a parent or coach who wants to use sports psychology to help the athletes in your life, head to Part V. Finally, if you're short on time, Part VI is full of useful tips you can use today.

We hope you enjoy using this book to help you accomplish your goals. We also hope you share with us your success stories and accomplishments, and what you've found helpful in this book. Feel free to e-mail us directly at DrSmith@personalbestconsulting.com and DrKays@athletic mindinstitute.com.

If you want to work with a sports psychologist

Although this book offers many of the strategies and techniques that we provide to our clients as sports psychologists, no book can take the place of working one on one with a professional. If you find that you'd like to work directly with a sports psychologist to take some of these strategies farther, look for

- **Someone who has both sports psychology training and clinical psychology training:** Sports psychologists with training in both counseling techniques and sports psychology principles are able to understand both the person and the athlete.

- **A licensed psychologist:** If you have any questions about whether the person you're considering working with is licensed, you can contact your state's board of psychology. (Just search the Internet for your state and the term *board of psychology* to get that contact information.)

- **Someone who has extensive experience working with athletes and coaches, especially at your current level of competition:** Many people use exaggerated language on their Web sites and in their literature to make it seem as though they have more experience than they really do.

A good resource for more information on choosing a sports psychologist and sports psychology in general is the American Psychological Association Division 47 (www.apa47.org).

Part I
Getting the Winning Edge: Sports Psychology Fundamentals

In this part . . .

Success has a lot to do with your mind. You can accomplish as much as your mind will allow you to achieve. Don't believe us? Think about all the people who've faced tremendous obstacles — from physical disabilities to family problems to personal issues to limited resources — yet still exceeded and surpassed what most others believed was possible. This is the power of the mind. Unfortunately, many athletes don't allow their minds the freedom to pursue their ultimate goals. Even athletes who've experienced high levels of success often don't believe they ever reached their true potential.

In this part, we cover some traditional sports psychology concepts you've probably heard about in the past — concepts that you may never have known how to apply consistently and systematically in your life as an athlete.

We fill you in on mental toughness and tell you how you can develop and refine this skill so you can battle ferociously, no matter what your opponents throw at you.

We tell you about the importance of goal setting and show you, step by step, the best way to set goals, so that you can accomplish them and reach your full potential.

We also address motivation and answer some common questions athletes have: Where does it come from? How can you tap into your internal sources of motivation to achieve more in your sport? How do you set goals that are so motivating that you reach — and maintain — the highest levels of success?

Finally, we shed light on one of the most important states of mind for athletes and coaches: confidence. We explain the science and art of building true self-confidence in your sport — confidence that will catapult you toward success at a faster rate than you thought possible.

Chapter 1

Introducing Sports Psychology

In This Chapter

▶ Knowing what sports psychology can do for you

▶ Seeing your mind as a tool for success

▶ Using sports psychology to prepare for competition

▶ Putting sports psychology to work for your team

▶ Drawing on sports psychology as a parent or coach

*Y*ou've probably heard of elite athletes working with sports psychologists and pro teams having sports psychologists on staff. But what exactly is sports psychology, and is it limited to the pros?

Sports psychology is simply the practical application of psychological principles in a sports setting. It's used to help an athlete or team improve their performance — and it absolutely *isn't* limited to professional athletes. In fact, we're seeing sports psychology used at all levels of sport. The field of sports psychology provides benefits and knowledge to youth, high school, and college athletes, as well as to coaches, parents, administrators, sports medicine physicians, strength and conditioning coaches, dietitians, and physical therapists. It's used in the more popular sports — such as soccer, football, golf, and tennis — as well as in lesser-known ones — such as judo, snowboarding, fencing, and cricket. Sports psychology is even being used and applied in the non-sport realms, including medicine, education, business, politics, organizational development, and the military. Its benefits and uses are growing by leaps and bounds throughout the world. It's an exciting time to be tapping into the benefits of sports psychology!

The good news is that you don't have to pay hundreds or thousands of dollars to hire your own personal sports psychologist. With this book in your hands, you have an edge over other athletes and, most important, the ability to reach your highest potential.

Your Secret Weapon: Your Mind

The greatest tool that any athlete has is the mind. The brain — that wonderful organ that regulates your breathing, controls your beating heart, and manages the rest of your body — is at the core of all successful sports performances.

Everybody knows that talent and physical skill play an enormous role in every athlete's success, but not many people understand the importance of the mind and how we use it. In fact, your mind is one of the most powerful pieces of sports equipment you'll ever own. It can make or break you.

By understanding the power of your mind and being able to use it to your advantage, you can improve your performance. Sports psychology can help you to

- Manage performance anxiety
- Use visualization and imagery to improve your performance
- Increase and maintain your confidence
- Improve and maintain your level of motivation
- Relax under pressure
- Set and achieve goals
- Manage your energy levels
- Use routines to be consistent in your performance
- Bounce back from injuries and setbacks
- Manage and address conflicts with coaches and teammates
- Focus in critical moments and extend the duration of your concentration

Defining mental toughness

If you've spent much time in the sports world, you've probably run across the term *mental toughness*. Typically, mental toughness encompasses

- Resilience and the ability to bounce back or deal with adversity
- Motivation to do your best, regardless of the situation
- The ability to stay focused on the task at hand during important competitive moments
- The ability to remained poised when the pressure is on during competition

Mental toughness is predicated upon physical toughness. In other words, to be mentally tough, you first need to be physically tough and in shape. It's virtually impossible to be mentally tough when your body has given out on you and isn't fit. So, if you want to pursue mental toughness, start by getting your physical toughness in order and getting in the best shape of your life. For more information on building your own mental toughness, turn to Chapter 2.

Setting effective goals

To be an effective and productive athlete, you need to be able to establish a system for setting goals and achieving them. Goal setting may seem like a skill that's easily learned, but unless you've had a good role model or mentor in this area, you're probably like the rest of us: You use a trial-and-error approach to goal setting. Trial and error may be an acceptable way to do things if you aren't serious about being a top athlete, but the fact that you're reading this book tells us that that isn't the case.

So, here are some tips that you can use to do a better job of goal setting in your sport:

- ✔ **Begin with the end in mind.** Figure out what you want to accomplish, and work your way backward.
- ✔ **Set deadlines and timeframes to keep yourself motivated.**
- ✔ **After setting your goals, make sure you focus on your processes (how you intend to accomplish those goals).**
- ✔ **Make sure your goals are measurable.** For example, instead of saying you want to "get faster," say that you want to "improve my 40-yard dash time by 0.3 seconds."
- ✔ **Set both long-term and short-term goals.** Your short-term goals should lead you to your long-term goals.
- ✔ **Make your goals public.** The more people who are aware of your goals, the more people who will be there to support you and hold you accountable along the way.

For more tips on goal setting, turn to Chapter 3.

Understanding your motivation

As an athlete, you need to understand the driving force behind your participation in sports. Your reasons for playing are personal ones. Most competitive athletes will tell you that they play their sport because they love to compete. They love the fact that they get to measure their skills against other athletes. Whether they play basketball or badminton, the love of competition is what drives them.

The problem with being motivated by outside factors — such as money, or fame, or popularity — is that those things fade over time, and they only motivate you temporarily. External factors can certainly boost your motivation for short periods of time, but research shows that the single most powerful motivator is the love of the game.

Motivation ebbs and flows, so try not to feel discouraged when you find your motivation isn't where you'd like it to be. Lack of motivation happens to every athlete. Even the best athletes in the world go through periods when their motivation drops. The key is that they address their waning motivation head on. You need to know the common causes for drops in motivation, be able to recognize the warnings signs that your motivation is falling, and have some specific strategies to follow to get your motivation back on the rise. For all this information and more, turn to Chapter 4.

Building confidence in sports and life

One of the wonderful aspects of sports psychology principles and techniques is that they're applicable both on and off the field. They help you improve your confidence. And all improved performances — on and off the field — result from a gradual improvement in your confidence. The more confident you are, the more risks you'll take, and the more rewards and positive consequences you'll experience. All successful athletes know that when they're confident and comfortable, their chances for success are dramatically higher, even though their preparation and physical fitness may be the same. Confidence frees you to perform, compete, and reach your highest potential. And confidence is not an all-or-nothing game — it changes and develops over time.

In Chapter 5, we show you the art and the science of building true confidence. We take the guesswork out of the process of improving your self-confidence, and give you a solid framework from which to improve your performance in sports and in life. We also show you how best to address and manage those times when your confidence drops. Your goal is to maximize the times when your confidence is high and minimize the times when it's not.

Assembling Your Mental Toolkit

In developing your mind through sports psychology training, you want to develop your own personal "mental toolkit" that contains the techniques and strategies you need to strengthen your mental muscle. Just as you can use equipment to help you improve your physical fitness, there are tools you can use to do the same for your brain.

Focus is one of the most critical mental skills to develop for success in athletics. It's one of the most common assets of successful athletes, and a lack of focus is a primary reason for mental errors, mistakes, and the inability to perform under pressure. In Chapter 6, we give you the tools you need to take your focus up a notch.

Mental imagery can help you build confidence, manage pressure, recover from mistakes and poor performance, and prepare for practice and competition. In Chapter 7, we explain what imagery is and how it works, giving you specific steps to take to use imagery in your own life.

Your inner voice — your self-talk — and how effective, productive, and positive it is make or break your performance. Creating and practicing productive self-talk is important if you want to realize your athletic potential. In Chapter 8, we help you harness the power of self-talk, so that the messages you send yourself work to your advantage.

As an athlete, you're constantly working toward specific goals, and you're juggling all kinds of responsibilities at the same time — from work to school to family and friends. In Chapter 9, we introduce you to the task-management principles that help you stay on track so that you can accomplish the goals you've set for yourself.

Seeing Sports Psychology in Action

As you use your mental tools (see the preceding section), you'll see the direct benefits of sports psychology in action, both in practice and in competition.

You'll establish and maintain routines that will maximize your focus and create the conditions for great performances. No more of your mind drifting off or becoming distracted, resulting in poor performance. Routines help you keep your attention where it needs to be. (For more on developing effective routines, turn to Chapter 10).

As you practice and compete, you face all kinds of pressure. Being a great athlete is about being able to perform your best when the pressure is on. In Chapter 11, we give you strategies for improving your ability to do exactly that.

As an athlete, you have to manage your energy levels before a competition to harness the mental and physical energy you need when it counts. In Chapter 12, we explain how to calm yourself down and pump yourself up, so your energy resources are always there for you when you need them.

And, because mistakes are a regular part of the sports world, in Chapter 13, we give you lots of advice for bouncing back from them. From simple mistakes in competition to longer slumps, we show you how to move on from the mistakes of your past and focus on performing your best in the present.

Harnessing the Power of Teams

Sports psychology is beneficial not only to athletes individually but to teams as a whole. Anytime you get a bunch of people together, differences in personalities, priorities, and goals can lead to conflict. And any team in conflict will see a decrease in performance — if not in the short term, then over the long haul. You can use the principles of sports psychology to improve your communication, step into a position of leadership, or work together better as a team.

Teams aren't limited to team-based sports. Even athletes who participate in individual sports, like golf or tennis, are part of a team. They have swing coaches, strength and conditioning coaches, dietitians, parents, and maybe even a sports psychologist, all of whom are on their team.

Applying Sports Psychology as a Coach or Parent

Coaches are constantly looking for that extra edge that will put them over the top in the ultracompetitive sports world. With that in mind, they frequently turn to sports psychology to learn better ways to understand their players, motivate their teams, and get more from the talent they have at their disposal.

Every day, coaches see athletes with incredible talent who can perform in practice, but who can't carry that performance into competition. They know and understand that the mindset of their athletes is often what determines their success.

If you're a coach, you'll find plenty of advice throughout this book that you can use to help your athletes be their best. But we devote Chapter 17 in particular to you. There you find strategies for helping your athletes improve their focus and perform under pressure. We also give you strategies for motivating your athletes and helping them perform together as a team.

Don't limit yourself to Chapter 17 if you're a coach. The advice we give to athletes throughout this book is information you can share with your players individually or as a team, to help them reach their potential.

If you're a parent of an athlete, this book shows you the right ways to support your athlete — no matter how old she is or what level she's competing at. In Chapter 18, we help you understand your own reasons for pushing your kid to be his best, as well as identify when your encouragement crosses over into pressure and becomes detrimental.

Too often, parents don't know how to recognize burnout in their kids, not to mention how to prevent it from happening in the first place. In Chapter 18, we give you specific tips for dealing with burnout. We also help you help your kid manage the ever-increasing pressure of competitive athletics, from youth to collegiate levels.

Sports are supposed to be fun, and as a parent, you can help your kids get the most out of their sports participation.

Chapter 2

The Gladiator Mind: Strengthening What's Under the Helmet

* *

In This Chapter

▶ Knowing what mental toughness is and why it matters

▶ Setting a plan to improve your mental toughness

* *

When you think about what athletes have to do to be successful in their sports, you realize how important toughness is — you put your body through all kinds of challenges to succeed. But did you realize that mental toughness is every bit as important?

Mental toughness is talked about in athletics all the time, but many people have trouble defining it. It seems to be an almost abstract and intangible quality. Some people think an athlete either has it or doesn't. And, if you're lucky enough to be born with mental toughness, you'll have greater success and a longer career in sports — you'll win the praise of many people, most of all your coaches and teammates.

We're here to tell you that mental toughness is something you can develop, just as you develop your athletic skills and talents. We start this chapter by explaining what mental toughness is and why it matters. Then we help you set a plan for improving your own mental toughness so you can use it to achieve all your goals.

Defining Mental Toughness

You can't develop mental toughness if you don't know what it is, so we start this section by defining it. Then we explain why you want to do everything you can to develop your own mental toughness as an athlete.

What mental toughness is

We talk to athletes and coaches all day, and we asked some of them how they define *mental toughness*. Here's what they said:

- ✔ "Mental toughness is not letting anyone break you."
- ✔ "Mental toughness is not being affected by anything but what's going on in the game or competition, no matter what coaches, other players, or refs are doing. It's being able to block out what's not important."
- ✔ "Mental toughness is doing whatever is necessary to get the job done, including handling the demands of a tough workout, withstanding pain, or touching out an opponent at the end of a race."

Sports psychologist have their own definitions of the term. They say that *mental toughness* is about

- ✔ Coping extremely well with the many demands (competition, training, school, and lifestyle) that athletics places on you
- ✔ Consistently remaining determined, focused, confident, and cool under pressure

You could also say that *mental toughness* is

- ✔ Having an unshakable belief that you can do something
- ✔ Staying focused in big moments
- ✔ Maintaining persistence and commitment amidst challenges
- ✔ Coping well with pressure
- ✔ Controlling your emotions
- ✔ Never giving up
- ✔ Fighting back after a tough loss
- ✔ Looking fear in the face

We define *mental toughness* as the ability to fight and challenge yourself to become better, especially during tough times.

Mental toughness has nothing to do with talent. Many athletes have all the talent in the world but struggle to cope with adversity and pressure. We've worked with numerous athletes who have great skill, but when challenged with difficult circumstances, such as knowing what it takes to play at the collegiate level or fight for a starting spot, they won't pursue all avenues at all costs. Other athletes may not be as talented but have the resilience and determination to fight back and be successful no matter the odds or the roadblocks standing in their way.

The X factor

Mental toughness is the X factor when it comes to sports participation. When all else is equal on the playing field, the athletes who are tougher mentally will, more often than not, win in the end.

One of the toughest athletes to ever participate in any sport was a wrestler named Dan Gable. Dan finished his high school career with a record of 64-0 and went on to finish his amateur wrestling career at Iowa State with a record of 118-1. His only defeat occurred in the NCAA Final during his senior year. After suffering that devastating loss, Dan committed himself even more to his craft and set out to win the gold medal at the 1972 Summer Olympic Games. Amazingly, Dan accomplished this feat. He won the gold medal not only by defeating his opponents, but by destroying them: Dan didn't allow a single point in his drive to the gold medal, a feat that had never before been accomplished. He went on to become a coach at The University of Iowa, where his dominance in the sport continued, as his teams won 21 Big Ten team titles and 15 NCAA team titles in his 21-year career. His overall record was 355-21-5, an unheard of 94 percent winning percentage over his coaching career.

Dan's secret? His mental toughness. He was the hardest-working athlete in the sport. He was never content to merely win a match — he had to dominate. In college, when he would run out of challengers in his weight class in practice, Dan would wrestle guys in heavier weight classes, working his way up and down the lineup in a search of a better training experience. As an athlete, he said, "The obvious goals were there — state champion, NCAA champion, Olympic champion. To get there I had to set an everyday goal, which was to push myself to exhaustion, or, in other words, to work so hard in practice that someone would have to carry me off the mat."

Today, Dan Gable continues to pursue his passion for competing as an Assistant Athletic Director at The University of Iowa.

Mental toughness is a natural *or* developed trait. It isn't a static state — it ebbs and flows throughout your life. You can develop your mental toughness if you're aware of what it is and how to work on it.

Why mental toughness matters

Mental toughness is a requirement to be successful in sports. If being good in any sport were easy, you wouldn't need mental toughness. But, as you know, excelling at a sport requires weeks, months, and years of hard work. Without mental toughness, you wouldn't be able to pursue sports for years on end. They're just too difficult and require too much hard work, persistence, and resilience.

Think about your own athletic career. How many times have you had to face adversity? Maintain poise under pressure? Deal with distractions? How many times have you had to battle through both mental and physical turmoil?

What about pre-season conditioning — how much it hurts and how long two-a-days can be? What about facing the fact that you aren't skilled enough and you'll probably sit behind a starter until you get better or she graduates? What about making mistakes that have been costly to you or your team and having to bounce back? What about facing a long injury recovery and wondering whether it's all worth it anymore? These are just a small sample of the ways you have to battle through adversity and maintain mental toughness while competing in sports. Without mental toughness, you won't make it.

Brett Favre is one of the great examples of mental toughness in sport. Whether you're a Favre fan or not, you can't question his mental toughness. Through two decades in the NFL, he's faced all kinds of challenges, and he's met them with intense mental toughness every step of the way. He battled both physical and mental adversity with the death of his father, playing a Monday night game the day after his father died, leading the Green Bay Packers to victory over the Raiders. He faced tough criticism from his long-time team, the Packers, when he retired but then decided to play again, only this time for the New York Jets. He was scrutinized by the media and fans about his decision to retire and then come back. And finally he proved himself even more mentally tough in the 2009–2010 season, as he took the Minnesota Vikings all the way to one game short of the Super Bowl. The beating he took in the game against the New Orleans Saints (who went on to become Super Bowl Champions) showed his mental and physical toughness. Favre's mental toughness has enabled him to keep going past the age of 40 in the NFL, with most of his colleagues having long since retired.

Improving your confidence through mental toughness

Mental toughness has a direct relationship to your confidence. As your mental toughness rises, so does your confidence. These two qualities feed off each other and can make you a great athlete or block you from doing your best — if you don't address your mental toughness or confidence levels when they're low.

When you improve your toughness, your confidence automatically increases. If you know that you can go into the fire and be okay no matter what happens, your confidence rises to new heights. You believe that you'll be successful, even if the actual outcome isn't what you desire. You're still willing to put yourself out there and take risks to try to make things happen. You may feel fear and doubt, but they won't prevent you from trying.

Mental toughness also increases confidence because it helps you relax and go on autopilot. Many athletes struggle and worry about how they'll perform. If you feel confident, though, you'll worry less and focus more on things you can control, which will improve your athletic performance. Consistent optimal athletic performance is due to your ability to feel confident when going into competition. Confident athletes win more than less confident ones do, even if their skills and talents aren't as great. Confidence consistently carries over into positive performance — and one way to raise this critical component of athletic success is to sharpen and develop your mental toughness.

For more information on building confidence turn to Chapter 5.

Increasing Your Mental Toughness: A Plan of Attack

As an athlete, you know that having a plan and sticking to it is an essential part of athletic success. This is true whether you're focusing on skill development or mental toughness. You need a plan in place for how you're going to increase your mental toughness; odds are, it won't just happen on its own. In this section, we lead the way.

Knowing your starting point: Your mental toughness today

Before you can begin building your mental toughness, you need to know how mentally tough you really are. You do that by assessing your own mental toughness and then asking others to rate your mental toughness. This step involves a level of risk — you're not only looking inward (which is one of the most challenging things you can do) but you're asking others to give their honest opinion of you (which may not be easy to hear).

Assembling your feedback crew

Start by identifying five to ten people you trust to give you honest feedback. You don't want people who will only say nice things and who are afraid of hurting your feelings — you want people who will give you honest feedback so that you can improve.

Some people you may want to ask for feedback include the following:

- ✔ Current and former coaches
- ✔ Current and former teammates
- ✔ Family
- ✔ Sports psychologists

You want people who

- ✔ Know you and your athletic abilities
- ✔ Can be honest and pull no punches

Asking the right questions

A great way to get feedback is to e-mail a questionnaire to the people you've chosen. Here's a sample of the kinds of questions you want to ask:

- How mentally tough do you think I am?
- How well do I bounce back from mistakes?
- How well do I handle adversity and battle when the chips are down?
- How well do I accept feedback from coaches and teammates?
- How well do I handle the pressure involved in competition?
- How strongly do I believe in my ability to accomplish my goals?
- How well am I able to stay focused when the game is on the line?

Make sure you answer the questions yourself first. Then be sure to explain to your respondents what mental toughness is. You may want to give them a copy of this chapter to read. Regardless, think about what the term *mental toughness* means to you — what behaviors you want to change or improve when it comes to mental toughness — and then ask them to give you specific feedback about these areas or situations. They can also give you their own perspective about your mental toughness in addition to the specific situations you ask about.

If you want to ensure confidentiality and allow people to be as honest as possible, you can ask them to type their responses and mail them back to you without a return address. Some people will be honest with you if you talk to them face to face, but many people will feel freer to say what they need to say when they can do it anonymously.

Making the commitment

Now that you have a better understanding of your current level of mental toughness, you need to get to work improving it.

You know that excellence isn't easy — it takes dedication and commitment. You have to make a strong commitment to see improvements in your mental toughness. Think of improving your mental toughness as a gradual and long-term project. With proper and effective focus on specific objectives, your mental toughness can develop more efficiently and quickly.

Set a plan to improve mental toughness in all areas of your life, not just athletics. If you improve your mental toughness in your relationships, school, and work, you'll improve it in the realm of athletics, too. And when you increase your mental toughness in athletics, it'll spill over to all the other realms of your life.

Make a list of all the different ways that you have the opportunity to improve your mental toughness. Here are some examples:

✔ In athletics:

- Battling through an injury to make it back in the lineup

- Holding your teammates accountable to a high standard of excellence and performance

- Not giving up when you don't get a starting position

- Getting better despite not getting the minutes in games you would like to be getting

✔ In school:

- Battling back to raise your grades after a low mark on a test

- Getting it done in the classroom and in athletics at the same time

- Standing firm to your personal beliefs, such as not using drugs and alcohol in the face of peer pressure

- Seeking academic help when you need it

✔ In relationships:

- Saying something that's hard for another person to hear, but saying it with consideration and compassion

- Talking through your anger instead of ignoring it or repressing it

- Putting others first instead of being selfish

- Expressing your hurt or anger assertively and respectfully to your friend about what he did or said

Here are some ways you can improve your mental toughness:

1. **Answer the questions in the "Asking the right questions" section, earlier in this chapter, as honestly as possible.**

   If you did show mental toughness, what allowed you to so do? If not, what blocked you from doing so?

2. **Ask other people to answer those same questions and take their feedback seriously.**

   Choose people that give it to you straight.

3. **For each question, journal about or discuss at least three situations where you displayed that aspect of mental toughness in sports.**

   For example, describe three athletic situations where you bounced back from mistakes like a champion.

4. **For each question, journal about or discuss at least three situations where you did *not* display that aspect of mental toughness in sports.**

For example, describe three athletic situations where you didn't bounce back from mistakes like a champion. Then write about how you will do so in the future.

5. **For each question, journal about or discuss at least three situations where you displayed that aspect of mental toughness in non-sport situations (such as school, relationships, or work).**

   For example, describe three situations where you bounced back from mistakes like a champion in school.

6. **For each question, journal about or discuss at least three situations where you did not display that aspect of mental toughness in non-sport situations.**

   For example, describe three situations where you didn't bounce back from mistakes like a champion in school. Then write about how you'll do so in the future.

In addition, you can try the following strategies:

- ✔ At the beginning of each day, for the next 30 days, make a conscious effort every morning to be mentally tough in practice or the game.

- ✔ Create cue words that remind you of this focus point. For example, write M.T. (for mental toughness) on a piece of athletic tape and wrap it around your wrist.

- ✔ Rate yourself at the end of each day or practice using the questions earlier.

- ✔ Continually challenge yourself to get better in mental toughness every day in non-sport-related activities.

- ✔ Seek feedback once a month from a trusted individual who can offer you insight into the changes you're making. A good person would be one of those individuals who answered the questions originally.

- ✔ Seek out a sports psychologist to work with who can help you improve in this area.

- ✔ Tell coaches and/or teammates that you're trying to improve your mental toughness and ask them to continually challenge you in getting better in this area.

- ✔ Make a list of professional or high-level athletes who you see as mentally tough. Find books or articles on the Web about them. Read all about them and how they developed mental toughness. Imitate them.

- ✔ Challenge yourself to be physically strong — make a commitment to continue to work on your strength and speed. Seek out strength and conditioning coaches who demand that you give your all every workout.

ANECDOTE

Mental toughness: It's all around

For several years, Todd has worked with an athlete who learned a lot about mental toughness from a child. Angela was always seen as mentally tough by her teammates, but she discovered a new level of mental toughness after meeting a 9-year-old child, Jacob, who was dying of cancer. Angela says that her relationship with Jacob taught her what mental toughness is all about.

Jacob and Angela met when Angela had to do a hospital visitation to fulfill the requirements of a college class. Little did she know what she would learn that day. She saw a child who was smiling and enjoying the days he spent in the hospital, even though he was dying. Angela continued to visit Jacob in the hospital even after she had fulfilled her course requirement.

Jacob was taken from the earth too soon, but to this day, Angela says that she learned mental toughness from him. Any time she starts to complain about having to get up for early morning workouts, she remembers Jacob and that desire to complain goes away. Whenever she feels self-pity after a poor performance, she remembers Jacob and that feeling goes away. When she gets mad at her coach for yelling and gets negative and angry, she remembers Jacob and those feelings go away.

Examples of mental toughness are all around. When you're looking for role models, don't limit yourself to pro athletes — even a 9-year-old child can be an outstanding example of mental toughness.

You've already made a substantial commitment to this process if you've completed the first bullet above. Now, it's simply a matter of sticking with this program and staying the course in order for your mental toughness to improve.

Preparing for specific situations

As an athlete, you'll face numerous situations that can challenge and improve your mental toughness. In Table 2-1, we list a few of these situations. Rate your current mental toughness and then describe an ideal response — what a mentally tough response would be in this situation. We include blank lines at the end of the table for you to add your own specific examples.

By completing this table, you begin to understand and see what an ideal mentally tough response is all about. This exercise prepares you to address these situations long before they even happen. When they do — and they will — you'll be ready because you've already thought through what to do.

Table 2-1	Situations That Challenge Your Mental Toughness	
Situation	*Your Toughness (On a Scale of 1 to 5)*	*Description of an Ideal Response*
Suffering an injury		
Losing a position		
Not getting enough minutes		
Making a major mistake		
Making a minor mistake		
Getting yelled at by the coach		
Getting cut from the team		
Not making varsity		
Not getting an offer to play at your top-choice school		

Evaluating and measuring your progress

In order to improve your mental toughness, you have to stay focused on it and work at it every day. If you just take the steps in the previous sections and then never follow through and evaluate your progress, you won't get better. Evaluation — taking your own "toughness pulse" — is critical.

Make a six-month commitment to improving your mental toughness. Limit your focus to mental toughness during this time, instead of trying to tackle other issues as well.

One simple way to make sure you're getting better every day is to mentally prepare before every training session and game, and at the start of every day, to respond with mental toughness. You can do this by saying it out loud in the mirror, by writing it down, or even by telling someone else that you're going to be mentally tough. By doing so, you consciously place your focus on mental toughness, and your behaviors will follow in practice (you'll act tougher!) and then your confidence will grow even more. At the end of every day, rate yourself. Make a few notes about how you displayed mental toughness, or how you fell short. When you fall short, don't criticize and beat yourself up — just acknowledge it and move forward, wiser for the effort. Make a commitment to get better despite setbacks and obstacles.

How fitness affects toughness

The more physically fit you are and the more you trust your body, the greater your mental toughness. Think about it for a second: If you feel confident in your body — your muscles are strong, your cardio is at a peak level, and you're quick — you're tough mentally, too. You're able to stand face to face with your opponents and know that you'll outlast them. If the game runs long, you aren't worried — you're ready to go. You believe that you can do anything — all because you've trained your body to be ready to do battle. Strength and conditioning coaches may feel like your worst enemies, but they're improving your mental toughness and confidence every time they push you beyond what you believe you can do. Physical training can hurt, but you're doing much more than training your body — your mental toughness is improving as well!

You can also have key people in your athletic life track your progress and give you feedback. Have a coach or parent rate your mental toughness in a game or series of practices over a two-week period. Tell them what you're looking to improve so that they can rate you effectively.

Chapter 3

Setting Goals: Aiming High and Hitting the Bull's-Eye

• •

In This Chapter
▶ Setting effective goals
▶ Keeping track of your progress

• •

Most people miss the mark when it comes to goal setting, whether in sports or in life. The good news is, with this book in your hands, you won't be one of those people! So, why do most people fail at goal setting? Because they were never taught the simple secrets that comprise the art of making your dreams a reality, which is really all that goal setting is.

In this chapter, we introduce you to this art. We share with you the same information we've shared with thousands of other athletes who've come to us to work on setting and achieving goals. When you set goals correctly, your goals will allow you to achieve results that you never thought possible.

Goal setting and motivation: Two peas in a pod

Motivation is the fuel that powers your goals toward becoming a reality. If you're not motivated and inspired by your goals, you won't achieve them. And if you don't have goals, you won't be motivated to improve.

A simple way to measure your level of motivation is to use what we call the get-out-of-bed test. Do your goals make you want to get out of bed and hurry toward their achievement? Do they keep you up at night, excited, unable to go to sleep because you're too busy pursuing them? If so, your level of motivation is strong. If not, then you need to set better, more inspiring goals.

Many athletes tell us that they're losing their motivation to compete in their sports. They complain that it's no longer fun, that their coaches' demands annoy them, that their passion for training isn't what it used to be. When we ask these athletes what their current goals are, they usually say, "I don't know — I haven't thought about it." They're focused on the misery and pain and complaining. They've lost focus on their goals and the reasons they compete, and their motivation has declined because of it.

When you get into a car, you usually know your destination. When you start driving toward your destination, you're focused on making sure you reach it, which helps you adjust when you encounter obstacles, such as closed roads, traffic jams, and passing trains blocking the intersection. You're committed to reaching your destination, but you more than likely keep a flexible approach to getting there, depending on the circumstances and time of day. The same is true with goal setting in your sport. You need to know where you're headed. Then, after you've set inspiring goals, you need to stay flexible in your approach to making them come true. Obstacles will come in many forms — injuries, coaching decisions, sickness, and other unforeseen training issues. Your job as an athlete is to keep your mind focused on your goals, which, on occasion, requires that you take alternate routes to success.

Remember: Goal setting is both art and science. The key to good goal setting is outlining goals that inspire and motivate you. They should wake you up early and keep you up late at night!

Setting Effective Goals

Goal setting is really about being able to answer a couple simple questions:

- ✔ Where do you want to go in your sport?
- ✔ What will athletic success look like when you accomplish it?

In the following sections, we walk you through setting your long-term and intermediate goals, making sure your goals are specific and challenging, and setting timelines for your goals.

The difference between goals and priorities

What's the difference between a goal and a priority? A *goal* is an outcome around which you focus your attention — it's the purpose toward which your efforts are directed. A *priority*, on the other hand, is a goal that is more important to you than other goals. Priorities are simply the goals that are most important to your success.

All goals are important, but as an athlete, you need to set priorities to help shape your destiny. Which goals you've prioritized as most important will determine the magnitude of your success in your sport. Choose your priorities wisely — they're critical to your success.

Determining your goals

Goals can be divided into the following categories:

- **Long-term goals:** One to three years
- **Midterm goals:** Six months to one year
- **Short-term goals:** One to six months
- **Immediate goals:** One day to one week

In order to achieve your goals, each goal should build on the last. In other words, goals should be successive and cumulative. If you want to be an all-American, you have to start by being all-conference. Before that, you have to get enough playing time to be noticed. Before that, you need to earn a spot on the team. Start with the end in mind when you set about determining your priorities and goals in your pursuit of athletic success.

Work with specialized and trusted coaches to provide perspective and education. For example, when it comes to fitness goals, strength and conditioning coaches and exercise specialists are key. A skills coach would be helpful if you're a tennis player wanting to improve the speed of your serve. Getting to your long-term goal takes time and expertise. Use your support team to help you.

Long-term goals

You need to start by setting your long-term goal — this is the goal that will guide and inspire you to greater heights as an athlete. It's usually set at about one to three years out.

For most athletes (professional and Olympic athletes use different timelines), one year or one season is the perfect timetable for long-term goals. Anything longer, and you risk losing focus and motivation.

Here are some examples of long-term goals:

- ✔ Be the starting goalie on the team.
- ✔ Improve my national recognition among college coaches.
- ✔ Become all-conference.
- ✔ Be one of the mentally toughest players in the state.

Dream big. Make your goals big! Search within yourself for what you want to happen in one year. Don't place limits on yourself. Sure, you should be realistic (you aren't going to get a college scholarship if you decide to play football your senior year and you haven't played since the fourth grade), but too many people place limits on themselves before they even begin the goal-setting process.

Midterm goals

Next, set approximately three midterm goals that you intend to achieve in about six months (or half a season). These goals should be what we like to call *process goals,* or goals that deal with how you plan on going about doing things. For example, if your long-term goal is to become an all-conference athlete, your midterm process goals might include the following:

- ✔ Out-hustle every person on the field.
- ✔ Be the best-conditioned athlete on the field.
- ✔ Become more offensive minded.
- ✔ Immediately let go of mistakes and recover from poor performance.

There is a difference between outcome goals and process goals. Outcome goals are *what* you're pursuing, and process goals are *how* you're pursuing it. Outcome goals are usually not within your control, but they help guide you to greater heights in sports; process goals are completely in your control, and help increase the probability that you'll reach your outcome goals.

Short-term goals

Your short-term goals are ones that take one to six months and directly feed into your midterm goals. The accomplishment of the short-term goals is necessary for the success of the midterm goals. For example, if your midterm goal is to be the best-conditioned athlete on the field, you could set the following short-term goals:

- ✔ Run 2 miles in 12 minutes.
- ✔ Run the 40-yard dash in less than 5 seconds.
- ✔ Improve my leg strength.
- ✔ Practice my post-mistake mental-toughness routine every day in training.

Immediate goals

After you've set your short-term goals, your immediate goals take over. Immediate goals are actions you'll engage in to better the chances of your short-term goals happening. So, if you take the short-term goal of running 2 miles in 12 minutes, the following are examples of immediate goals:

- ✔ Meet with my strength and conditioning coach once a week.
- ✔ Time my 2-mile run at the end of every week.
- ✔ Perform a tempo run (set up by the trainer) four days a week.
- ✔ Do cross-training four days a week.

Making your goals specific

When you walk into a grocery store, whether you've written down a list of items to buy or you have that list in your mind, it's specific. It says more than just "food." You know you need milk, bread, cereal, bananas, and so on. If you do show up at the store without a list, you'll likely get home from the store, walk in the door, and realize you forgot something you needed.

The same is true for your goals in sports. The more specific you can be when you set your goals, the better your chances of achieving them. Clear and specific goals allow you to have laser-like focus in your pursuit of greatness. They leave little to chance or imagination, allowing you to channel your energy accordingly.

Here are some examples of specific and nonspecific goals:

Nonspecific Goals	Specific Goals
Get fit.	Run 2 miles in 12 minutes.
Serve well.	Have a first-service percentage of 60 percent.
Play hard.	Make three tackles per game.
Let go of my mistakes.	Follow my post-mistake routine in games.

When you say that you want to "play hard," what exactly does that mean? How are you going to measure it? Playing hard could be turned into a specific goal, but as it stands, it's broad, ambiguous, and lacking in clear direction.

Specific goals are better because they increase your motivation and focus — you know exactly what you're going after. You know what you're working toward, and your mind will have an easier time stayed tuned into that.

Setting goals that challenge you

In addition to being specific, your goals need to be challenging. They should push you beyond your comfort level and be slightly out of your reach. Setting your goals slightly out of reach, or slightly higher than you originally plan, ensures that you'll be motivated to chase them and improve along the way.

If you set goals that are too easy, you'll become bored, you'll lose motivation, and you won't improve. You may feel good for a while — "Wow, I'm good — I'm accomplishing so many things!" — but this feeling won't last.

Have you ever noticed how much better *you* play when you play against athletes who are better than you? Yes, it's difficult, and your ego may take a bruising, but look how much you improve.

At the same time, make sure you aren't setting unrealistic goals. A goal to become a state champion or make the national team may be challenging and realistic for some, but it may not be realistic for you where you are now. If you set this goal and expect it too soon, you may end up feeling frustrated and losing motivation. You're getting better — maybe *much* better — but you won't see it because you're focused on a goal that's beyond your reach.

You want to set goals that are challenging enough to motivate you, but not so unrealistic that they discourage you. For example, Leif challenges each athlete he works with to set goals slightly above what they think they can achieve. Instead of making the lineup, he has them aim to be a starter. Instead of performing well, he wants them working to become all-conference. The higher goals build confidence, and they also push the athletes to think and dream bigger in their pursuit of becoming better athletes.

Setting deadlines for each goal

When you've set goals that are specific and challenging, you'll want to add timelines to each goal. Doing so takes your goals from theory to actual practice — in other words, setting deadlines makes your goals more likely to become reality. Setting deadlines helps you remain focused on your goals, so that they don't exist simply as dreams — they become real.

Setting deadlines for your goals is one of the key factors that separates good athletes from elite ones. If you don't set deadlines, you'll likely allow other things to get in the way. Before you know it, the day, week, month, or even year has gone by and the goal is still sitting there unaccomplished.

Put your deadlines for accomplishing your goals on a calendar, and review that calendar regularly. You should know, every day, what you're doing to reach your immediate, short-term, midterm, and long-term goals.

Tracking Your Success in Reaching Your Goals

Make sure that you're tracking your success in reaching your athletic goals as you go. That way, instead of wondering how you became successful, you'll have a good idea of which strategies worked, and which strategies didn't work. You'll know what you did well, and what was effective. And you'll know what you didn't do well, and which tactics were ineffective.

You must keep track of your athletic skills, your fitness levels and physical strengths and weaknesses, and your mental toughness and abilities. If you don't track these, how will you know that you've reached your goal, or that you're even heading in the right direction? What if you need to make adjustments along the way? If you don't follow and track your success, you'll never know.

In this section, we show you how to hold yourself accountable to your goals and measure your progress. We also introduce the concept of adjusting your goals, and let you know that doing so is perfectly acceptable.

Holding yourself accountable

One of the defining characteristics of great athletes is the ability to hold *themselves* accountable for their own goals and progress — instead of requiring another teammate, athlete, or coach to hold them accountable. The best athletes place the responsibility for their goals, training, and results directly on their own shoulders. As an athlete, you want to do the same thing. Holding yourself accountable is key. Measuring your progress (see the following section) is one way to do that.

You can also hold yourself accountable by making your goals, expectations and action plans known to other people you trust, like your coaches, parents, or close teammates — your support network. Then they can help hold you accountable by inquiring about your progress. For more on support networks, see the nearby sidebar.

Enlisting a support network

A good support network is worth its weight in gold. A support network:

- Ensures accountability
- Keeps your ego in check
- Surrounds you with friends when things aren't going your way
- Allows you access to diverse opinions

Make sure that you build a support network to help you along the path of achieving your goals. Your support network should include a diverse group of four or five people, and could be made up of friends, family, current and former coaches, partners or spouses, medical doctors, chiropractors, nutritionists, sports psychologists, or teachers. The key is to enlist people whose values are similar to yours and whose support you'll need along the way. Be sure to include at least one person who's comfortable being controversial and contrary — you need someone who can tell you no from time to time.

Remember: No one accomplishes his goals and reaches high levels of success on his own.

Coming up with a way to measure your goals

How will you know when you've achieved your goals? That may seem like a simple question, but it isn't always. Goals need to be measurable. For example, you can easily measure a goal such as "I want to lead the team in tackles this season," but it's more difficult to measure a goal such as "I want to improve my confidence."

For every goal you set, you need a method of measurement. That way, when someone asks you whether you've achieved your goal for the season (or, better yet, when you ask *yourself* whether you've achieved your goal), you'll be able to answer yes or no and have the data to back it up.

If you don't measure your goals, you're plodding along a path without any course or direction in your journey. When you measure your progress, you get to see and feel success, make adjustments, and enable yourself to reach your goals more efficiently.

Sidestepping common goal-setting mistakes

Goal setting isn't easy. In fact, we've seen many athletes make the same mistakes when setting goals. Following are some of the most common mistakes — avoid them when you set your own goals:

✔ **Setting too many goals:** Athletes and coaches tend to set far too many goals, which results in their accomplishing none of them. All the goals you set may be motivating, and make sense, but too many at one time confuses the brain and diffuses energy. Instead, pick the goals that are most important or relevant for you and tackle them one at a time. Try to master one goal and then move on to the next one — instead of trying to accomplish four or five things at the same time.

✔ **Failing to set process goals:** Setting outcome goals is fun. You want to win the conference championship, hit a certain batting average, achieve a number of assists or goals, or obtain a college scholarship. Outcome goals go straight to our hearts and excite us! The next challenge is thinking about the *process* of how to make those goals become a reality. What will you have to do to make sure you give yourself the best chance of reaching those outcomes goals? Most athletes stop short of this, setting process goals because the task feels too overwhelming or too confusing. Just remember that if you don't put your primary focus on your process goals, your desired outcomes won't happen.

✔ **Leaving your goals in a drawer:** Many athletes spent a lot of time before the season setting both outcome and process goals. Some teams even take a one- or two-day team field trip just to focus on the goal-setting process. As the season gets going, however, these goals seem to fade to the background. As athletes and coaches get caught up in the day-to-day grind, they lose focus on their goals and why they want to accomplish them. Goals need to be living, breathing parts of your team mission. You need to tend to them, monitor them, and adjust them throughout the season. Remember to revisit your goals at least once a week, so you don't lose sight of what you're working so hard for.

✔ **Focusing too much on ego and not enough on mastery:** When we discuss *ego goals,* we're referring to outcome goals, like winning. *Mastery goals,* on the other hand are about improving skill and performance, regardless of the outcome. You can easily get wrapped up into thinking too much about ego goals and not enough about mastery goals. When you focus on the process of skill mastery and continual improvement, you're always getting better — even if it might not produce the win. You're still improving quantifiably and being successful. And when you're successful in this way, the wins will follow!

Don't limit yourself to goals that are easily measurable. You can set mental goals and measure your progress just as well. Throughout this book, we suggest rating yourself on a scale of 1 to 5, and tracking your progress in a performance journal throughout the season. You can read more about this in Parts II and III.

Giving yourself permission to adjust your goals

Think of your goals as living, breathing organisms — they can change as needed. Occasionally, you'll set a goal and then go out and achieve it sooner than you anticipated, or you may encounter obstacles (such as injuries or bad weather) that force you to adjust your goals.

Successful athletes adjust their goals when they need to, and they don't apologize for it. They realize that they aren't perfect and that life and the season or off-season can be unpredictable.

Adjusting your goals doesn't mean you've failed — it just means you're changing the course slightly or changing the timeline. Although having to adjust your goals can be frustrating, it's a natural part of success in athletics and life.

Chapter 4

Stoking the Fire in Your Belly: How to Fan the Flames of Motivation

* * *

In This Chapter

▶ Discovering the truth about motivation

▶ Identifying the different types of motivation

▶ Pinpointing your current level of motivation

▶ Increasing your motivation

▶ Sidestepping pitfalls on the journey to greater motivation

* * *

Motivation is one of the most important and most frequently discussed topics in athletics. Coaches and parents wonder why athletes aren't as motivated as they'd like, and athletes see their own motivation fall and wonder why. In this chapter, we explore the ins and outs of motivation.

We start by debunking some common myths about motivation — sometimes you get a better sense of what something *is* by finding out what it *isn't*. Then we introduce you to the two types of motivation: internal and external. We help you assess your current level of motivation. (Motivation levels aren't static — they rise and fall over time.) Then we give you some specific strategies for increasing your motivation, and warn you about some situations that can wreak havoc on your motivation.

Throughout your athletic career, your motivation will change. But one thing can remain constant: your ability to measure your motivation, increase it when you need to, and respond to the situations that make your motivation wane.

Debunking Common Myths about Motivation

Motivation has been studied and discussed for decades, but myths about motivation persist. In this section, we fill you in on some of the most common of these myths and explain why they're just not true. When you know what motivation is and isn't, you'll be better able to reach your full potential as an athlete, using motivation as a tool.

You can get your motivation from other people

There is only one type of "true" motivation and that's the motivation that comes from within yourself. Other people and experiences can motivate you in a variety of ways, but sustainable motivation will ultimately come from within. *Self-motivation* — your motivation and the choices you make that flow from that motivation — are completely up to you and within your control.

Many coaches and athletes look to sports psychologists to be outside motivators for teams — they see providing motivation as the primary responsibility of a sports psychologist. Many athletes believe that their coaches need to motivate them — and if they don't feel motivated, they blame their poor performance on the coach. The reality is that no one is responsible for motivating an athlete except the athlete himself.

People and experiences can assist you in motivating yourself. But you're responsible for your own motivation, and you have complete control over how motivated you are.

Fame and fortune are great motivators

Fame and fortune — what more could you want, right? These factors can definitely influence your motivation, but if motivation were as simple as fame and fortune, everyone would be motivated to be rich and famous and every rich and famous athlete would be motivated to perform his best all the time.

Think about yourself: Are you getting rich and famous playing your sport right now? Chances are, you aren't. Even if you're a pro athlete, you may not be making tons of money — for example, a typical rookie player in Major League Soccer may earn $25,000 to $40,000 per year. If you're still in school, you're playing for free, and even if you're a famous college athlete, when you first started out, nobody but your parents knew your name.

Fame and fortune can be motivating factors in sports (just as they are in other areas of life for most people), but they're never enough to sustain you to achieve and work hard all year. You need an internal passion that takes over in order for your long-term motivation to last.

Think about the unhappy rich and famous athletes you've read about. Research indicates that there isn't a huge difference in life satisfaction between people who make $50,000 a year and those who make over $1 million a year. When you achieve a certain level of money and fame, more money and more fame aren't going to do anything more for you. The best athletes don't play for financial security — they play for the love of the game.

Motivation alone can lead to success

Although motivation is critical to long-term success, by itself it isn't enough to make you successful. Numerous other attributes — including talent, fitness, discipline, knowledge, hard work, a support system, financial resources, and quality coaching — are important for success.

Talk to any coach and you'll hear about players who could have achieved so much more success if only they had been more motivated. At the same time, these same coaches can name players who are highly motivated but just aren't talented enough to perform as well as they'd like.

Defining Motivation

There are two types of motivation: internal and external. In this section, we explain the two types of motivation and tell you which type is best for your long-term success.

The two types of motivation: Internal and external

Internal motivation is associated with participating in sports for the joy and satisfaction of it. You play because you love the game and you love competing.

The flip side of internal motivation is external motivation, where your participation in athletics is driven by outside rewards — for example, the praise you get from your parents, or a potential scholarship offer to a prestigious school. You may not enjoy the activity for its own sake — you're more driven to compete by outside, external factors.

There is also a third type of motivation called *amotivation,* which is simply the lack of motivation to participate in sports at all. There's nothing wrong with feeling amotivated. In fact, most athletes have, at one time or another, experienced periods when they lost all motivation to play. Usually, amotivation is associated with burnout and exhaustion. If you've tried to participate in certain sports and found that you simply don't like them and lack motivation for them, you're better off finding what *does* motivate you — another sport or a non-sport activity — and pursuing that instead.

We cover internal and external motivation in greater detail in the following sections.

Internal motivation

Internal motivation is the type of motivation you need for sustained long-term success in athletics. It's characterized by the following:

- ✔ Enjoyment of the sport
- ✔ Enjoyment of practice and training for the sport
- ✔ A love of mastering technical aspects of the sport
- ✔ The ability to maintain motivation despite adverse conditions

If you want to compete at higher levels — or if you want to be highly competitive at *any* level — you need to love the process of competing. It has to be inherently rewarding on some level, or you won't be willing to put the time, energy, dedication, effort, and resources into it.

The top athletes in the world have high levels of internal motivation. They compete with themselves more than they compete with other athletes, and they want to be the best at what they do.

External motivation

External motivation is associated with outside rewards and benefits. Common characteristics of external motivation include the following:

- ✔ Participation in your sport for rewards, such as praise, fame, and trophies
- ✔ Peaks and valleys in motivation
- ✔ The need for greater or better rewards to sustain motivation
- ✔ The need for varied sources of external motivation in order to sustain motivation

External rewards can be motivating — there's no doubt about it. In fact, many coaches and parents use external rewards as a focusing strategy and reward system for young athletes, and that strategy is perfectly okay as long as it's not overused.

If you're engaging in sports for the sole reason of getting a scholarship, to keep your parents happy, or for other outside rewards, you'll find that your motivation is difficult to maintain over the long haul.

There is a place for external motivators, but they need to be used to *supplement* existing internal motivation and love of the sport. Otherwise, they lose their effectiveness.

Identifying which type of motivation is better

Most people think that internal motivation is the only type that matters, but the reality is, both types of motivation — internal and external — have benefits. If you want to maximize your motivation, use both: Start by participating in sports because you enjoy it. Choose a sport that you love and have some talent for. Then, when you need to, use external rewards to supplement your efforts.

Internal motivation is more important for your long-term success. External motivation can be effective in the short term — and it can be a *part* of your long-term success, but only if internal motivation is already present.

Assessing and Understanding Your Current Motivation Level

You can't improve your motivation unless you have a way of measuring where your motivation is currently and understanding why it is where it is. In this section, we give you the tools you need to assess your current motivation level, and give you some reasons your motivation level may be lower than you'd like.

Measuring your motivation

Measure and track your motivation over time by logging it in a performance journal. After every practice, simply assign a number from 1 to 5 (with 1 being low and 5 being high) to your level of motivation. If you notice many 4's and 5's, you're experiencing high levels of motivation. If you notice many 1's and 2's, your motivation is waning.

If your motivation drops, that isn't a *bad* thing — in fact, it's a part of life. It *is,* however, a signal to stop, figure out why your motivation is waning, and address the causes.

You can also ask your coaches and teammates if they've noticed any drop in your motivation during practice and competition. Try to take to heart their opinions, and keep in mind that they want what's best for you.

Making sense of your motivation

If you're consistently rating your motivation with 1's or 2's, you want to figure out why you're lacking in motivation. Start by considering your love of the sport. How much do you really enjoy your sport — not just hanging out with your teammates or making your parents proud, but actually playing the sport itself? Be honest with yourself.

If you really love your sport, you enjoy working hard to get better, and you want to play at higher levels, you're probably internally motivated.

On the other hand, if you're really doing it just to be part of the team or just to please your parents or coaches, and you don't really enjoy the sport itself, you'll be better off in the long run if you find an activity — another sport or a non-sport activity — that you're really passionate about.

If you have a high level of internal motivation and you're currently experiencing a drop in motivation, you need to explore potential causes, such as the following:

- **Physical fatigue:** You may be physically tired or just plain exhausted. Participating in sports requires tremendous physical exertion on a daily basis for most of the year. If you're run down, and your muscles and body are tired, that drop in energy can be the cause of your dwindling motivation. If you're in the middle of the season, try taking a day off; in the off-season, take off even more time. Give your body a chance to rest, and you may find your motivation increasing.

- **Lack of sleep:** Are you getting enough sleep? Believe it or not, something as simple as a lack of sleep can cause decreased motivation and performance. Keep track of how many hours of sleep you're getting each night and see how that corresponds to your motivation. You may find that you need a solid eight or nine hours to maintain the high motivation you're after.

- **Diet:** Are you eating right to fuel your body and mind for the exertion your sport requires? Changes in diet, especially an increase in fatty or sugar-filled foods, can dramatically affect mental alertness and motivation levels.

✔ **Overall health:** If you're sick — whether with a cold or flu, or because you're iron deficient or experiencing some other ailment — your motivation can decrease. If you're sure you're eating right and getting enough rest, and you've ruled out the other possible causes of waning motivation, make an appointment with your doctor for a checkup.

✔ **Confidence:** Maybe you're experiencing a crisis of confidence — you're struggling in your belief to perform certain parts of your sport. If so, accept that state of mind, and go back to basics where you can begin to develop confidence in yourself again. Start with very finite and specific skills — this strategy can build confidence, which, in turn, will increase motivation. (For more on confidence in sports, turn to Chapter 5.)

✔ **Burnout:** Because sports typically are year-round and athletes are specializing in one sport earlier in their lives and playing that one sport exclusively, it's natural for them to become bored and disenchanted occasionally. It may be time for you to get away from your sport, even just for a few days. Try playing another sport for a few days — run if you're a swimmer, swim if you're a runner, shoot hoops if you're a tennis player, play golf if you're a basketball player, and so on. Just getting some time away from your sport can help increase your motivation. (For more information on combating burnout, see "When you're burned out," later in this chapter.)

You may be experiencing a drop in motivation for some other reason. Maybe you aren't improving as you'd hoped. Maybe you aren't getting the playing time you want. Maybe your team is losing and the whole team is down. Or maybe you have a poor relationship with your coach. The solution to all these issues is to acknowledge them and then assess what you do and don't have control over, focusing on what you can control and setting aside what you can't.

If you can't pinpoint the cause of your lack of motivation, you may want to meet with a sports psychologist to explore potential causes.

Maximizing Your Motivation: How Fires Can Become Bonfires

Motivation is a complex mix of multiple issues, so you'll be addressing and adjusting it throughout your career. In this section, we give you some strategies for improving your motivation — you can pick and choose different strategies at different times, and see what works best for you.

Being completely honest with yourself

One of the most frightening but motivating tasks you can undertake is to be honest with yourself about your current level of motivation, why *you* are playing sports, what *your* goals are for your sport, how good you actually are, what skills need improvement, your mental toughness, areas in which you simply are not that good, and so on. Being completely honest may be painful, but motivation always increases when you clear away the excuses.

Don't limit the honesty to a conversation you have with yourself. Consult people you trust, and ask them to provide you with honest feedback. This feedback will help you understand your current athletic state and motivate you to improve.

Thinking about why you play the game

Throughout the season, revisit your reasons for participating in your sport. The season can be long, and it's natural to wonder why you're putting yourself through the physical and mental challenges.

Get to the core of why you're playing your sport. Is it to win a championship? To set a record? To be the best you can be? Then, when you know why you're playing, stay strongly connected to that purpose, especially when things are difficult. Remind yourself of this purpose every day. Some athletes post photographs of significant people in their lockers. Others tape up inspirational quotes.

Focusing on tasks, not ego

Sports psychologists like to talk about task orientation and ego orientation. If you're focused on the tasks of getting better — on those things over which you have control — your motivation will grow. Task orientation is common among people who have high internal motivation. Ego orientation, on the other hand, is more focused on the external rewards of competing, such as winning, money, success, fame, and media exposure. Most professional athletes have a combination of both ego and task orientation, with a greater emphasis on task orientation.

If you're struggling with motivation, ask yourself whether you're too focused on your ego fulfillment and not enough on the tasks of getting better and building your skill set in your sport.

As an athlete, you'll feel more motivated when you're confident in your skill set and believe in your ability to continue to improve. And you'll feel more motivated to practice and compete when you're performing well or when you feel confident in your athletic skills and potential. This confidence occurs regardless of whether you receive any external rewards, such as praise from your coaches or parents.

You'll feel more motivated when you're concentrating on aspects of competition within your control. What you do have control over — your attitude, your preparation, how much and how well you practice, your lifestyle decisions — determines how well you do. By keeping your focus on these things, you'll improve and, in turn, you'll maximize your motivation.

Finding ways to experience success

When you're successful, your motivation will typically go up. So, make sure to put yourself in situations where you can be successful. For example, if you're in a slump, work with your coach and break down complex skills into simple tasks. You can achieve success with these simple tasks, which will motivate you to get better. (For more on surviving slumps, turn to Chapter 13.)

Mixing up your training

Variety adds spice and energy to your training. Change your workouts and practice routines from time to time to keep your motivation up. Every sport involves some repetition, but you don't have to practice in the same way, or at the same pace and time every day. Working on a variety of practice drills can shake things up and keep you from getting bored and losing motivation.

Seek and find the new trends in physical and skills training in your sport. For example, more athletes are participating in yoga for both better flexibility and mind control.

Surrounding yourself with highly motivated people

If you're surrounded by others who are driven and achievement oriented, you'll pick up their energy and it'll buoy your confidence and motivation. These people are like the wind that helps to power your confidence sailboat.

On the other hand, if you're around athletes and coaches who are content at just competing and not succeeding, get away from them as quickly as possible — they'll sap your energy and motivation.

Being disciplined

With discipline comes freedom, so you need to discipline yourself to establish effective habits. Even though you may not feel like engaging in certain athletic tasks every day, your discipline will take over and build motivation. The goal is to establish strong, effective sports-related habits, and to make them subconscious and automatic. The habits require less mental effort the more you engage in them.

Seeking support

Surround yourself with emotionally supportive people who understand how hard sports participation can be. Express your thoughts and feelings to them — having people to talk to will lift the weight off your shoulders, allowing your motivation to return.

Sports psychologists are great at this because they're objective and supportive and allow athletes to vent and get things off their chest in a safe and supportive environment.

Moving on from your mistakes

You will experience failure and make mistakes in sports and in life. The best athletes in the world experience loss and imperfection every day. The key is to have a short memory when it comes to these failures. Learn from them, and then let them go. Nothing comes from obsessing about past mistakes except lower motivation levels and confidence. (For more on bouncing back from mistakes, turn to Chapter 13.)

Thinking positive

Thinking positive is a great way to raise motivation, which is why we devote an entire chapter to positive self-talk (see Chapter 8). Make sure that you're training your brain to respond positively in the face of adversity or failure.

No matter how bad something may seem, something good can always come out of it.

Overcoming Obstacles to Staying Motivated

Many challenging situations can get in the way of motivation. In fact, it's easier to *lose* your motivation than it is to maintain it. So, you need to be aware of these roadblocks and know how to address them when they come up. In this section, we lead the way.

When your role on the team has changed

Whether you're a high school athlete, a college athlete, or in the pros, your role on your team will change sometimes. Your coach may change you to a different position where she feels you'll be a bigger help to the team. Another player may come along and take your starting role. Or you may be traded to another team. Regardless of the reason, when your role on the team changes, staying motivated can be a challenge.

Stay focused on what you have control over. No matter what your role on the team is, focus on mastering the technical aspects of the sport. Even if you don't get playing time, you can stay motivated in practice by focusing on improving your performance. Make sure you're always ready to perform your best — you never know when you'll be called on to play another role on the team.

Talk with the coach about your concerns regarding your change in role. Don't go into this conversation with any expectations; keep an open mind. Listen to his reasons for making the change.

You may not agree with the coach, but he makes the decisions and you have to respect that fact while you're a member of the team.

When you're burned out

Burnout is one of the more common experiences among athletes today. Athletes are burning out earlier than ever before, and every year many athletes leave their sports as a result of burnout.

Why do athletes burn out?

✔ **They're expected to play sports year-round — there is no off-season.** Young athletes especially are not mentally or physically equipped to handle such demanding schedules.

- ✔ **Athletes are specializing in one sport younger than ever.** As a result, they play their sport year-round, without letting up, which takes a toll on their motivation.

- ✔ **The physical training in sports has become much more demanding and rigorous.** You're training longer and harder, and these physical demands weigh down not only your muscles, but your mental and emotional energy, as well as your motivation.

To stave off burnout, make sure to take care of your physical body with adequate diet and sleep. Getting enough rest and proper nutrition can have a strong influence on your emotional energy levels.

Take time off from your sport when you can. If it's during your off-season, you can afford to take more time off, maybe even a couple of weeks. The world won't end if you take some time off.

When burnout is knocking at the door, reach out to people you can trust — a family member, a friend, a mentor, or a sports psychologist. These people can help you get things out of your head and off your chest so that your motivation can return to its normal levels.

For more information on burnout and how to handle it, turn to Chapter 18.

When you're being pulled in different directions

If your life is out of balance, your motivation levels will be drained.

You aren't just an athlete — you're a person. And you have other aspects of your life that can be stressful, in addition to sports. When your emotional and physical energy resources are being drained by other things in your life outside of sports (like relationships, school, or financial difficulties), you won't have enough energy for your athletic training. When you're being pulled in many different directions, especially in a day and age where athletic competition is extremely demanding, your motivation can drop — not because you don't love your sport, but because you have a finite amount of energy.

To keep your motivation going strong when you have lots of outside commitments requiring your time and attention:

- **Make sure to take care of the physical basics: sleep and nutrition.** Stress drains energy, including motivation, and you need to replenish your body and mind often.

- **Build strong coping skills.** There are always going to be stressors in your life, but the most important thing is to have the tools to cope with them. The more tools you have, the less energy drain will occur and the less impact on your motivation level.

You can use the various skills we cover in this book (imagery, confidence building, goal setting, focus, bouncing back from mistakes, and so on) to cope better with life off the playing field as well. Don't limit their use to sports alone.

- **Talk to a sports psychologist about the reasons why your life is out of balance.** He can help you get it back.

- **Focus on task management.** Your life may be out of balance because you're overextended and not managing your time and priorities well. If you can get a handle on your schedule, you can prevent decreases in motivation that come with feeling overwhelmed. (For more on task management, turn to Chapter 9.)

When you're not seeing eye to eye with your coaches and teammates

Conflict with your coaches or teammates can drain your motivation. In fact, many athletes have left their teams or sports because of this kind of conflict.

The key is to realize that conflicts with coaches and teammates are part of the athletic experience. You just need to address any conflicts as quickly and as effectively as possible, to minimize their impact on your motivation.

You don't have control over your teammates and coaches, but you do have control over your own attitude and how you handle your relationships with them.

Here are some tips to keep in mind when dealing with relationship conflicts:

- **If there is a conflict, address it as soon as possible.** Holding onto anger, resentment, and bitterness, or simply being confused about why the conflict exists, drains your physical and mental energy and depletes your motivation.

- **Keep your focus on your own attitude and what you want to communicate.** Differences in opinions and personality styles are part of life. Focus on getting better as an athlete, and those conflicts won't hurt your motivation.

- **Try to understand the other person's point of view first.** You already know where you're coming from — if you understand how the other person feels, you'll be closer to resolving the conflict and moving on.

- **When you're in conflict with a coach, remember that you're ultimately in a one-down position.** The coach is the final judge and jury. Convey your opinion, but keep in mind that the coach's opinion takes priority.

- **Try not to take anything personally.** Although not taking things personally may seem impossible, you can do it. You may not like the behaviors or decisions of a coach or teammate, but you can choose to take it personally or to see it as unrelated to who you are as a person.

- **Consider the fit of the coach and/or team.** You may have to consider whether there are too many differences to remain on the team, at that school, or playing under that coach. Try to address your differences before you walk away. But if you're going to face a constant drain on your motivation by playing on this team under this coach, leaving may be the best choice.

When your priorities in life change

Your motivation will naturally ebb and flow over time, but if you notice that your motivation is dropping because of a lack of interest or because you're developing different priorities, pay attention.

If you're losing interest in your sport or you've developed an interest in another sport or another non-sport activity, keep in mind that this happens to athletes all the time. Just make sure that that your lack of interest or shift in interest is the true reason for your decline in motivation, and that some other issue — such as a lack of confidence, a conflict with a coach, or some other outside factor — isn't to blame. If you do have a lack of interest, talk to your parents, coaches, or other people you trust about what you're thinking and going through. This way, you'll be able to sort out your thinking more clearly and make a more informed decision.

For many athletes, admitting to a drop in interest in their sport or simply a greater interest in something else is extremely difficult. Especially if you've played your sport for a long time, much of your identity is tied to yourself as an athlete.

Admitting to your parents and coaches that you don't want to play your sport can be painful. You may find it helpful to talk with a sports psychologist — alone and/or with your parents. A sports psychologist can explain to your parents that goals change — and for good reasons. She can tell your parents that they can expect discipline, hard work, integrity, and commitment from you, but that expecting you to want to continue playing a sport you don't enjoy is unfair. Having the support of a good sports psychologist can help you make this transition more smoothly.

Chapter 5

Swagger: The Art and Science of Building Real Confidence

Lack of confidence is a common obstacle in many athletes' competitive lives. Confidence is also one of those concepts that many people talk about but few understand. Your parents probably told you, "Be confident!" or "Think like a winner to be a winner!" But, if you're like most people, you discovered that positive thinking can only get you so far. And if thinking positive doesn't get you the results you're after, it's easy to be frustrated.

The thing is, your parents weren't entirely wrong. Positive thinking *is* one piece of the puzzle — it's just not the entire puzzle. In this chapter, we give you *all* the tools you need to build and maintain confidence as an athlete. But we start by telling you why confidence matters.

What Confidence Is and Why It Matters

What is confidence? When it comes to athletics, we define it as the belief that you have a skill set related to your sport that helps you be successful in that sport. When you're confident, you believe that you can get the job done. Confidence is a nonrenewable resource — you have to be building confidence constantly, to buffer yourself from the harsh world of competitive sports. Even the best athletes experience the peaks and valleys of confidence throughout their careers. Where the best athletes differ from the rest is that they work to limit those peaks and valleys and level the landscape, which allows them to perform better.

We often see athletes who want to build their confidence, and they're surprised to learn that they can build confidence in many others ways, many of which don't require our help. Sports psychology can play a key role, especially when your confidence is low and you're out of solutions to build it up again, but other factors can assist in building confidence. For example, if a golfer is lacking confidence in her wedge, the best way to increase her confidence might be for her to hit 500 wedges in order to develop her skills. When a basketball player lacks confidence in his endurance, he needs to get more fit as a way to raise his confidence. If your lack of confidence has its root in your fitness or skills training, start there. Then, if you're still not satisfied with your confidence, after you've tackled all the physical aspects, consider working with a sports psychologist.

Confidence plays a big part in how often you win. In fact, it's one of the single most important ingredients to your success as an athlete. Sure, talent and preparation are important, but they go nowhere without confidence. Confidence is the fuel for your athletic success — it powers you and affects every other facet of competing.

Your opponent is battling his own self-doubts, insecurities, and weaknesses. Plus, he's battling against you and your confidence. Your opponent is constantly evaluating you and your confidence against his own. The higher your confidence is, the less likely it is for your opponent's confidence to remain high.

You need to stay on top of your confidence, not only for your own game, but for your opponent's game as well. The higher you can keep your confidence, the more difficult it will be for your opponent to match that level of confidence.

Debunking Myths about Confidence

You've probably heard some myths about confidence, like the following:

- ✔ You just have to believe in yourself.
- ✔ If you believe it, you can achieve it.
- ✔ Positive thinking is the secret to a good life.
- ✔ Either you're confident, or you aren't. There's no middle ground.
- ✔ If you stay positive and always look on the bright side, you'll become more confident.
- ✔ It's important to be confident — just don't be *too* confident, or people won't like you.

Any of these sound familiar? These myths often do more harm than good when it comes to building confidence.

What do *you* believe about confidence? How has your environment contributed to your confidence? Analyze your conscious and subconscious beliefs about confidence, and consider the impact those beliefs are having on your athletic performance. When you do that, you can move ahead and learn how to build real, lasting confidence.

Think about confidence on a continuum. Sometimes, your confidence will be through the roof; other times, not that much. Confidence isn't a static trait — it fluctuates. You can always improve and change your confidence level. The key is to develop habits that allow you to consistently perform and get better.

You can increase your confidence. No matter what happens in your athletic career or life, you can always improve your confidence. Be confident about that!

The difference between confidence and cockiness

Many people have trouble differentiating between what real confidence is and what cockiness looks like. They're afraid to get more confident, because they're worried that other people will think they're cocky. Here's the difference:

Confidence	Cockiness
You feel good about yourself.	You don't feel good, but you pretend to.
You're open to feedback.	You're afraid to get feedback.
You believe in your skills.	You doubt your skills.
You love to compete.	You shrink from true competition.
You don't need to brag.	You feel the need to brag about how good you are.
You're strong.	You're insecure.
You manage rejection.	You fear rejection.

Cockiness is not a confidence overload — instead, it's a genuine *lack* of confidence! Athletes who are cocky feel so fragile in their confidence that they try to mask it (to avoid detection) by putting on a front. They're hoping that this front will allow them to slip by, unnoticed. The problem is, the façade falls apart when they come up against another athlete who's truly confident.

Giving yourself permission to swagger

You can't feel confident in any aspect of your athletic performance if you haven't first given yourself permission to feel confident. You have to get out of your own way. As long as you work hard and control the aspects of athletic participation that you can control, you have every right to feel confident! When you realize that, you give yourself permission to swagger, or display your newfound confidence to the world. Swagger is the behavioral consequence of having a healthy level of confidence in yourself and your abilities as an athlete. It's that air about you that tells others that you expect great things from yourself, and that you expect to win every time you compete.

Your confidence is about you and you alone. Just because others may not have the same level of confidence doesn't mean you should be ashamed to show your skills in the heat of the battle. Many other athletes lack confidence, but that's not your problem. If you taunt them, you're displaying cockiness, but if you do what you worked hard and prepared to do, you're displaying true confidence.

Tapping Into the Confidence Cycle

The confidence cycle (shown in Figure 5-1) starts with a belief that you can do something. Let's say your belief is "I can win the starting job as quarterback." The next step is to go out and try to actually win the job. Work your butt off. Take chances and risks when appropriate. Every once in a while — hopefully, more often than not! — you'll succeed. Success may mean having a great practice — being in sync with your receivers, and hearing from your coach how nice your passes looked. Your risks are rewarded as your skills increase, which buoys your confidence, causing you to think, "I can do this! I'm going to try even harder tomorrow!" and so on.

You think positively, take the risks you need to achieve your goal, experience success, and then think even *more* positively. Success begets confident thinking, which begets more success. You think positively, take risks, and get rewarded. The development of confidence depends upon the ability to take risks in a graduated, successive manner until you experience some rewards.

In the following sections, we cover the three phases of the confidence cycle.

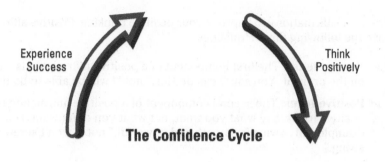

The Confidence Cycle

Experience
Success

Think
Positively

Take Risks

Figure 5-1:
The
confidence
cycle.

Thinking positive

To start, you need to believe that whatever you're pursuing is worth the effort, worth the pain, and worth the rewards that may come later. This is where the notion of positive thinking can be helpful. Positive thinking is characterized by optimistic, future-oriented, and solution-focused thoughts, like the following:

- ✔ I can do this.
- ✔ I'm determined to make this work.
- ✔ I'm willing to put the time in to be the best.

You may be thinking, "But how can I say these things when I don't believe them?" or "I haven't had success, so how can I believe these things?" It doesn't matter. You can still train yourself to think positive in order to get the cycle started.

Notice that these statements have nothing to do with outcome — they have to do with process. You can do all these things because they're within your control. The outcomes that you desire may or may not happen every time, but you can still gain confidence by starting to think positive about the process.

Try using affirmations to improve your positive thinking. Positive affirmations have the following three *P* qualities:

- ✔ **Present tense:** The first component of a positive affirmation is a focus on the present. You say "I can do this," not "I will be able to do this."

- ✔ **Positive focus:** The second component of a positive affirmation is a positive focus. Say what you want, not what you don't want. For example, "My swing is smooth and powerful," not "I won't screw up my swing."

- ✔ **Particular behavior:** The final component of a positive affirmation is a focus on one particular behavior, such as "I fight to the end, no matter the situation."

Write down positive affirmations for different situations pertaining to your sport. A golfer might make a positive affirmation about her tee shots, short putts, long putts, bunker play, getting up and down, approach shots, chips, and flop shots. Get as specific as you can, and write an affirmation for every situation you can think of.

Here are some examples of positive affirmations that meet all three of the criteria we list earlier:

- ✔ I am (present tense) one of the best defenders in the conference (positive focus). My hands are quick (specific) like lightning, and I make big defensive plays every game.

- ✔ I am (present tense) money in the 50 free (specific). I am known for my explosiveness in the water. I blast off like a rocket and swim as fast as I can (positive focus).

Taking risks

The next phase, after you're thinking positive, is to take appropriate risks. That means shooting more, driving to the hoop more, stepping in with the first team squad more, and being more aggressive on defense. These are all risks that you take to try to gain the associated rewards.

This is about taking *appropriate* risks — risks that fit into your everyday practice, and have good consequences. Inappropriate risks — like shooting the ball every time you get it or playing so aggressively that you're out of control — don't get you anywhere.

Taking appropriate risks requires courage. Many athletes play it safe — they may do many things well, but their success will always be limited. Successful athletes are willing to take risks. Sometimes these risks pay off and other times they don't, but these athletes are the ones who will eventually have more success and, therefore, more confidence.

It takes courage to pursue risks, and it takes risks to build confidence.

Experiencing success

The third phase of the confidence cycle is the easiest but sometimes most elusive part of the equation, because it relies solely on your doing the first two steps well. Frequently, arriving at this step can take the longest, because success tends to come on its own schedule.

Hard work doesn't ensure success and new skills, but it does increase the *likelihood* that you'll experience it eventually.

Success breeds confidence, but be careful with how you define *success*. You may have tremendous confidence in certain skills, but you may not have been doing it long enough to win or you may not have developed certain aspects of your sport to be successful consistently. For example, a tennis player may have tremendous confidence in her serve, but she may still not have as much success as she could because she lacks abilities in her ground strokes.

Success does wonders for your confidence. When you play with confidence, your true abilities and potential can be put on display. Think about a player on tour who wins his first tournament — it isn't uncommon for him to win or come close to winning more tournaments in the several weeks following that first big win. Why? Because his thinking improves, he starts taking better risks, and he experiences success. He becomes supremely confident.

Building Your Confidence

Confidence is like most other things in life: It requires effort. You can't be confident if you haven't changed your thinking and taken some calculated risks. Confidence is largely dependent on work ethic — the harder you're willing to *work* at being confident, the more likely you are to *be* confident.

Confidence ebbs and flows, but you always have control over the process for improving your confidence. Even the best athletes in the world struggle with confidence sometimes, so you're totally normal if you do the same. The key is to keep working at building your confidence. And in this section, we show you how.

The confidence that we discuss in this chapter is about how you feel about your abilities in your sport. We've worked with many athletes over the years who have a lot of confidence in their athletic abilities, but who lack confidence in the rest of their lives. Often, these athletes have tremendous ability and may be among the best in their sports, but they can't see it because of their low *overall* confidence. If you're suffering from a lack of confidence in *all* areas of your life, not just in your sport, address this issue with a sports psychologist or another mental health professional. If your overall confidence is low, it can put a limit on the specific confidence you develop in your athletic endeavors.

Focusing on day-to-day success

Building your confidence takes time, so you need to keep your focus on the small, incremental changes over time. Your confidence will grow every time you take a risk that pays off, but you have to be patient and allow that process to unfold.

Think of building your confidence as a long-term investment. Legendary investor Warren Buffett doesn't get upset when the market has a string of bad days, a bad month, or a bad year. He takes a long-term perspective right at the outset. In fact, he has said, "My favorite holding time [for stocks] is forever." Slow and steady gains win the day. If you take this same view when you're building your training around increasing your confidence, you won't fall victim to despair and frustration.

There is a real power to building your confidence one day, and one small victory, at a time. It's about progress, not perfection. You won't feel confident all the time, and not every risk you take will pay off. But focus on the success you *have* had, and you'll build confidence over time. If you give too much power and weight to the mistakes, your confidence will suffer.

Pay close attention to your small successes. Every journal entry you write after competition or practice should begin with what you did well. Even if it was a terrible game or practice overall, you did *something* well, and that's what you want to start with. Eventually, you'll see that you're doing something well every single day, and your confidence will increase.

Tracking your confidence over time

A simple method for tracking your confidence, and one that can easily be implemented into your training plan, is to use a 5-point scale, with 1 being the low end and 5 being the high end. For example:

1 No confidence

2 Minimal confidence

3 Moderate confidence

4 Good confidence

5 Supreme confidence

Using this simple scale, rate yourself at the end of every practice and competition. Track it on a daily, weekly, and monthly basis, using averages if needed. This will allow you to keep your metaphorical finger on the pulse of your confidence levels.

After you've tracked your confidence levels, you can readily adjust and modify your training plan accordingly. For example, if you notice that your confidence level for the last two weeks has been averaging a 3, and your typical monthly average is a 4, than you need to make some adjustments in order to improve your confidence in your sport. Maybe you need to modify technical aspects of your training or change your strategy. Maybe you need to have a pep talk with your coach or mentor. Or maybe you need a refresher session with a sports psychologist.

When you track your confidence, you have the peace of mind that comes from knowing that all your hard work can and will pay off.

Concentrating on process, not outcomes

A crucial step to becoming more confident is to switch your focus from what you're trying to achieve (the outcome, or increased confidence) to how you go about trying to achieve it (the process, or your training habits).

In sports psychology lingo, we call this "controlling the controllables," which simply means taking responsibility for those things that are under your direct control at all times: your thoughts, your feelings, and your behaviors. You need to think in ways that are productive and optimistic, no matter what's going on around you. When you're doing that, you'll feel in control of yourself and, ultimately, more confident.

You can't control outcomes, but you can control the process. If you allow your confidence to be dictated by outcomes, you're at the mercy of circumstances beyond your control. Think about it: You may play really well and still lose the race, game, or match — or you may play poorly and win. Winning doesn't always equate to success and losing doesn't mean failure.

Check out the following lists of things you can control and things you can't:

Controllables	Uncontrollables
Attitude	Weather
Diet	Wins
Sleep	Losses
Amount of practice	Coaches' decisions
Mental training	What other people think, say, or do

TIP A good way to measure whether you're controlling the controllables is to use feelings like frustration as alarms or red flags. You'll feel frustrated many times when you're focusing on things that are outside your control and influence.

TIP You want to have a *mastery focus* instead of an *ego focus*. Stay focused on mastering tasks in your sport — these tasks are the day-by-day building blocks that keep your confidence moving in the right direction. Your confidence may not improve every day, but you'll continue getting better. For example, when golfers make changes in their swings, they often go through periods of higher scores. So, during these times, they have to stay focused on mastering the individual changes involved in that swing. If they focus on the fact that they're taking the steps to master the swing basics that will eventually lead to lower scores, they'll be able to maintain and build their confidence. On the other hand, if they maintain an ego focus (where they're more concerned with winning or losing), their confidence will go up and down more than a roller coaster on a busy weekend. In order for confidence to grow consistently, mastery focus is the answer.

Tackling the Obstacles That Get in the Way of Confidence

Half the battle in improving your confidence is getting past the obstacles that try to sabotage the confidence you *do* have. Like all athletes, you'll come across your share of obstacles. In this section, we cover some of the most common ones and tell you how to move past them, confidence intact.

It's not what happens to you that matters — it's how you respond.

When you have a bad game

Everybody has a bad game from time to time — it's part of competing. Many competitors, however, have trouble allowing for bad games in their training. They think bad games should never happen, and that they can somehow prevent them. The problem is, bad games are inevitable, so when these athletes are faced with one, they fight themselves the entire way. They simply don't allow space in their lives for bad performances.

A better way to approach this obstacle is to actually *anticipate* occasions in which you won't be on top of your game. Assume that it *will* happen from time to time. We tell our athletes to rate their games on an academic scale — giving themselves an A for their best performance, a B for above-average performances, a C for average performances, and so on. Every now and then (hopefully, not too often), you'll get an F on a test. Maybe you didn't study hard enough for the test, or you were sick, or you studied the wrong material. It happens. The same is true with sports. When you're used to grading your performances, you see that you're not always failing — sometimes you actually get A's and B's. This helps you cope with the occasional lousy performance, because you know it's not the norm.

When you haven't anticipated ever having a bad game, but you find yourself in the midst of one, you can cope. Here's how:

- ✔ **Change your strategy.** For example, if you're a tennis player, and your normally killer backhand has deserted you, you may need to rely on your forehand or aggressiveness instead. If you're a basketball player and your jumper isn't falling, you may need to go in for the layup or pass to your teammates.

- ✔ **Focus on the one or two things you *are* still doing well.** This will allow you to at least salvage something from the game and build on it for next time.

- ✔ **Change your mindset.** If you reframe the situation (which is that you're having an F game), you can allow yourself to take more risks, try new things, change up your pace, and so on. The usual way isn't getting the job done, so why not try a new mindset and approach? It's not like it can make things much worse!

Sports are about consistency, not perfection. You're going to fail, but that's part of being human! You may feel disappointed or angry after a poor performance, but you don't have to let that feeling reduce your confidence. Confidence is like the foundation of a home: When it's solid, it doesn't crumble and waver when a storm blows through. Windows may break, shingles may be torn off the roof, and trees may be knocked over, but the foundation remains. In the same way, if you have a solid core of skills and strong preparation habits, your occasional losses or poor performances won't affect your confidence.

When you're not getting playing time

When your coach isn't putting you in the game, it's easy for your confidence to take a hit. You can't control whether your coach plays you. But you can control your attitude and perspective. You can look at not getting playing time as a sign that you need to work harder or work smarter.

Coaches are notorious for changing their minds. The player who's starting today may not be starting tomorrow. What this means is, you have an opportunity. Make sure your mind and body are ready to go if that opportunity arises.

If you focus on your lack of playing time (an outcome over which you have no control), you're allowing your confidence to be dictated by another person's opinion. Your coach may have a very good reason for starting someone else instead of you, and she may be justified in her decision, but you have to keep your focus on getting better and improving.

No one can take away your confidence without your permission.

When you aren't getting playing time, talk with your coach. Tell him, "I want more playing time. In your eyes, what do I need to do better in order to give myself more opportunities to compete?" This way, you're taking ownership of something over which you have control — your performance and preparation. By keeping your focus on building your skills and getting better, you're automatically going to raise your confidence level. We can't guarantee that that will translate into more playing time, but your confidence *will* grow, which ultimately will translate into better performance — whether you play or not.

When you're sick or injured

Get used to playing sick. The sports world doesn't stop for sick athletes. Colds, the flu, aches, muscle strains — you name it, they happen, and usually at the worst possible time. In cases like this, your best bet is to start by gauging how sick or injured you are.

You should sit it out if:

- ✔ You're putting yourself at risk of further injury by competing.
- ✔ You'll be a detriment to your team by competing.

When you're sick, you need to pay special attention to energy management (see Chapter 12) and be sure to pace yourself. When your body is fighting off illness, it has less energy available to help you fight your opponent, so you won't be able to go as long at your usual pace. You may need to change your strategy — for example, letting your opponent do more of the work or tire himself out. Accommodate your reduced level of energy if you want to stay competitive while sick.

When you're working through an injury, especially one that doesn't allow you to participate in practice or training, it's easy to suffer a loss in confidence. But you can maintain your confidence, regardless of your ability to compete. Here's how:

- ✔ **Develop an imagery plan.** Even though you may not be able to execute certain physical parts of the game because of your injury, you can still see the images of yourself performing in your mind. Imagery can help maintain your confidence as you recover. (See Chapter 7 for the complete lowdown on imagery.)
- ✔ **Study the game.** Anytime you can't compete, you can still learn more about the game by reading, studying, and/or watching film. Use your downtime in the most effective way possible. Ask questions, talk to coaches, and study the game from different views and angles. These activities will help you maintain your confidence level, because you're improving, just in a different way than usual.

When you aren't as prepared as you could be

Lack of preparation usually has a detrimental impact upon confidence. The less prepared you are, the less confidence you'll have. Preparation strongly builds confidence, and the good news is, it's something completely under your control. If you aren't prepared and your confidence level is low as a result, you know you didn't do your job and you have only yourself to blame.

Sure, coaches sometimes share in the responsibility for how well their players are prepared, but your performance and your skills are your responsibility to develop, and that development comes through hard work and discipline. These factors are under your control — always.

Some of the common reasons for lack of preparation include

- ✔ Laziness
- ✔ Lack of discipline
- ✔ Lack of motivation
- ✔ Not knowing how to prepare
- ✔ Poor task management (see Chapter 9)
- ✔ Poor lifestyle decisions (for example, not getting enough sleep or proper nutrition)
- ✔ Resentment or anger toward other players or coaches

No matter what the reason for your lack of preparation, your choices are what make the difference in your athletic life. If you want to be great, solid preparation is essential.

Preparation takes place in five different areas:

- ✔ **Physical:** You must prepare your body by eating right, getting enough sleep, hydrating yourself, and making sure you're as fit as possible.
- ✔ **Skills:** You need to prepare from a skills standpoint, executing and practicing your athletic skills over and over.
- ✔ **Strategy:** You must know the game plan so that all you have to do is execute your skills. This comes from working with the coach, watching films, studying plays, and listening or paying attention.
- ✔ **Mental:** You must get yourself in the right mindset to compete to the best of your ability. This means getting focused on executing your game plan, making sure you review your strategies and routines (see Chapter 10), and managing your self-talk (see Chapter 8).
- ✔ **Balance:** You have to prepare by getting all the other things in your life in balance, so that they don't interfere with your athletic performance. For example, if you have a test the day after a practice or game and you're worried because you haven't studied, then you didn't prepare for the game or practice as well as you could have.

Preparation isn't just about your sport — it's about taking care of all your responsibilities so you can focus on your sport in practices and games.

The more prepared you are in *all* these areas, the more confident you'll be.

Part II
Your Mental Toolkit for Success

In this part . . .

Successful athletic performance has less to do with physical talent and more to do with what happens between your ears. Your skill level plays a part in whether you can execute a certain athletic movement, but your mental skills determine whether you can do so when it truly counts. The higher you climb up the ladder of success, the more critical your mind becomes in determining what you can achieve.

In this part, we tell you how to use and apply some of the most important mental skills for success in your sport. Focus is a major part of success, and in this part we show you ways to improve your abilities in this area. When your focus is where it needs to be, your odds of athletic success will improve.

The art of imagery is another important skill used by the best athletes in the world. In this part, we explain how to begin, develop, and evaluate your own personal imagery plan.

One of the greatest tools for athletes — and one that's difficult to master — is positive self-talk. When your self-talk is filled with anger and criticism, you decrease both short- and long-term athletic success. The good news is, you can change your self-talk so you're consistently effective and productive, creating a more positive and relaxed mindset from which to play your sport.

Finally, because athletic success requires great amounts of commitment and dedication, you have to be sure to manage your time and tasks in the same way that the best athletes in the world do it. One of the most challenging and important habits for athletes to develop is the ability to manage all the various components of sport and non-sport life. After reading this part, you'll be able to do just that.

Chapter 6

Mastering the Art of Focus

The ability to focus is among the most important traits you can have as an athlete. The best athletes in the world are masters of focus — they can tune out everything that doesn't matter, focus only on what does, and perform well under pressure. Focus is a skill like any other, which means you can learn it and get better at it with practice. In this chapter, we explain what focus is and how it affects your athletic performance. We explain the different zones of focus — you can't maintain intense focus for an entire game, but you can move between the zones of focus and use them to your advantage. We show you how you can reduce or eliminate the pressure you feel in competition and be in the moment when you're on the field. Finally, we explain some of the roadblocks to focus and tell you how you can take your own focus to the next level.

Sports psychologists make a distinction between focus and concentration. You can think of concentration as being broad in nature, whereas focus is narrow. Concentration has a longer duration, while focus has a much shorter duration. Concentration is the target, and focus is the bull's-eye. For the purposes of this book, the distinction between concentration and focus isn't necessary, so we opt to use the term *focus*.

What Focus Is and Why It Matters

Focus is the ability to devote your full attention to the task at hand, tuning out distractions. This ability is, in many ways, one of the single most critical factors determining your athletic success.

Successful athletes (and successful people in general) are able to optimize their focus. Whether it's focusing on a big-picture level (such as improving their fitness or defensive skills over the duration of a season or off-season) or focusing on the immediate details (like improving footwork during practice) their level of focus is high.

In fact, one of the characteristics of successful athletes is their ability to focus intently during practice and competition. Top athletes in every sport pay attention to what matters (the task at hand) and ignore what doesn't (everything else). In fact, what you focus on when you're practicing and competing has a great deal to do with how successful you are. If you're focused on the task at hand (watching the baseball), then your performance (swinging the bat and connecting with the ball) will improve. If you're focused on other things (such as what you did your last time at bat, how good the pitcher's fastball is, the fight you had with your girlfriend last night, or the grade you got on today's math test), your chances for success decrease.

Distractions can be internal (negative or off-task thoughts) or external (like the noise of fans in the stands).

Your focus is also directly related to your arousal level, which affects your muscle control and, consequently, your performance. For example, if your mind is centered on your fears of striking out, you'll probably feel nervous and worried. These thoughts create muscle tightness and a rapid heart rate — neither of which is helpful to your performance.

On the other hand, if you're focused on what's necessary and relevant, your body will respond accordingly. For example, if you're a quarterback and your internal focus point is "Relax and release," your body stays calm and relaxed and you're able to execute the skill of throwing an accurate pass. That doesn't mean the receiver will catch it, but it does mean that you're more likely to execute a good pass. On the other hand, if your focus point is in the future or past (such as worrying about the outcome of the game or remembering an interception you threw last quarter), your likelihood of executing in the moment decreases. Figure 6-1 illustrates this relationship.

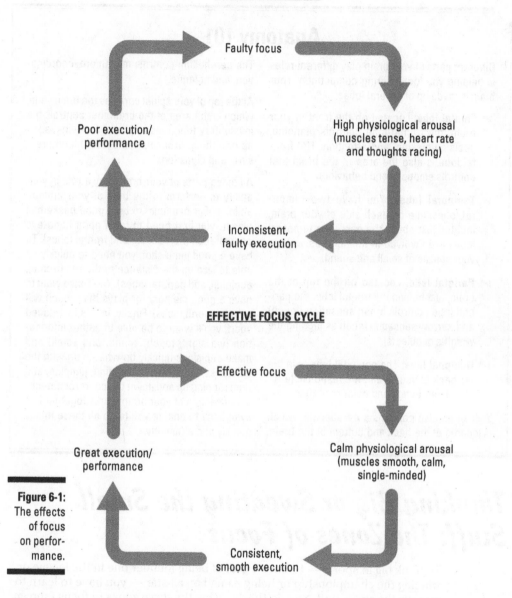

FAULTY FOCUS CYCLE

Faulty focus

High physiological arousal
(muscles tense, heart rate
and thoughts racing)

Inconsistent,
faulty execution

Poor execution/
performance

EFFECTIVE FOCUS CYCLE

Effective focus

Calm physiological arousal
(muscles smooth, calm,
single-minded)

Consistent,
smooth execution

Great execution/
performance

Figure 6-1:
The effects
of focus
on perfor-
mance.

Anatomy 101

Different parts of your brain play different roles in helping you focus during competition. Your brain is made up of several lobes:

- **Frontal lobe:** Located on the front of your brain, the frontal lobe controls planning, decision making, and attention. The frontal lobe is also the area of the brain that controls emotions and behaviors.

- **Temporal lobes:** You have two temporal lobes, one on each side of your brain, located just above the ears. The temporal lobes are involved in memory, as well as your senses of smell and sound.

- **Parietal lobe:** Located on the top of the brain, just behind the frontal lobe, the parietal lobe controls broad sensation (touch) and narrow sensation (such as judging the weights of objects).

- **Occipital lobe:** The occipital lobe is in the far back of your brain. It's responsible for visual perception and color recognition.

Your brain also contains a cerebellum, which is located at the back and bottom of the brain.

The cerebellum controls movement, coordination, and balance.

At the top of your spinal cord lies the brain stem, which is the area of the brain that controls the involuntary functions essential for living, such as breathing, arousal, heart rate, blood pressure, and digestion.

All these parts of your brain play a role in your ability to perform to the best of your athletic abilities. For example, to be a good basketball player, you first need to have good hand-eye coordination (cerebellum and frontal lobes). To have a good jump shot, you need to quickly be able to size up the distance to the rim (frontal, occipital, and parietal lobes). You'll also want to have a good memory for plays that coach will call (temporal lobes). Finally, in this fast-paced sport, you'll want to be able to gather information (via sight, touch, sound, and smell) and make decisions quickly on what to do with the ball (pass, shoot) while stopping, jumping, and then running up and down the court repeatedly. Every section of your brain works together in a symphony to enable you to do all these things quickly and efficiently.

Thinking Big or Sweating the Small Stuff: The Zones of Focus

To think big in sports — to have a goal of being number one in the league or winning the championship or being named an all-star — you have to learn to manage the small stuff. You do this by using the three zones of focus (shown in Figure 6-2) to your advantage:

Zones of Focus

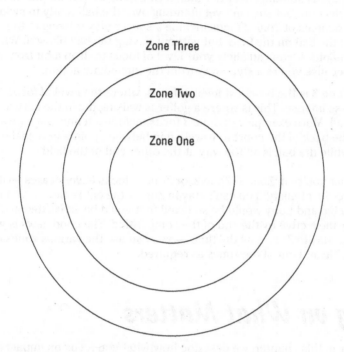

Zone Three

Zone Two

Zone One

Zone One
Highest level of focus, most intense
Examples: Golfer standing over ball, tennis player right before serve,
quarterback over center

Zone Two
Slightly less intense focus
Examples: Golfer sizing up shot, looking at distance, wind, club selection,
quarterback and wide receiver in huddle

Figure 6-2:
The zones of
focus.
Zone Three
Still focused, but less
Examples: Football offense on bench, golfer walking in between shots,
tennis player in between games

✔ **Zone 1** is where you have your highest level of focus on the immediate
task at hand. This is where your focus is laser-like. For example, a golfer
teeing off or standing over a putt would need her focus to be Zone 1.
More examples of Zone 1 focus include a quarterback or wide receiver
ready to start the play, a tennis player ready to return serve, or a shortstop awaiting the swing of the bat.

✔ **Zone 2** is a slightly lower degree of focus than Zone 1. This is where a golfer is standing near her ball, trying to figure out the wind and club selection, but she isn't yet standing over the ball ready to swing. More examples of Zone 2 focus include a soccer player being in the vicinity of the ball on the field, but without having the ball himself. When you're in Zone 2, you can allow your level of focus to drop a bit from Zone 1 because you're a step away from the immediate action.

✔ **Zone 3** is the broadest level of focus, where the level of focus is even less intense. This is where a golfer is walking down the fairway to her ball. More examples of Zone 3 focus include a tennis player walking to the back of the court to towel off in between points or a goalie in his box while the ball is all the way at the other end of the field.

Whether you're in Zone 1, Zone 2, or Zone 3, focus never ceases — it just changes in intensity. You can't stay in Zone 1 the entire time. If you tried to, your mind and body would be so taxed that you'd be exhausted and completely ineffective by the end of the competition. The good news is you don't *have* to stay in Zone 1 all the time — you can use the various zones of focus, moving in and out of the zones as required.

Focusing on What Matters

Earlier in this chapter, we describe how what you focus on impacts your performance (see "What Focus Is and Why It Matters"). When your mind is focused on the right things, your body responds by performing in the ways it knows how — the way you practiced over and over. But when your focus is on the wrong things, your body responds with tightness and anxiety, which increases your chances for mistakes.

So, the key is knowing what to focus on. All the various things you could focus on can be divided into two categories: relevant and irrelevant.

Relevant points of focus

Relevant points of focus are ones that actually have a direct relationship to and impact on your performance. For example, a relevant point of focus for a softball pitcher might be pitch selection, relaxing the arm, or cue words. All these things are relevant because they influence the success of the pitch. Points of focus are relevant because you have control over them and because they impact your performance.

Here are some more relevant points of focus:

- ✔ Your attitude
- ✔ Your practice goals
- ✔ Your fitness levels
- ✔ Your rest and diet
- ✔ Your mental preparation
- ✔ Your knowledge of your sport
- ✔ Your specific game plan
- ✔ Your quality and amount of practice
- ✔ Your study of game film

Irrelevant points of focus

Irrelevant points of focus are ones over which you have no control and that do not have any direct relationship to performance. For example, an irrelevant factor for a tennis player would be how many people are watching him, the location of the tournament, or what the other coaches or media might think about him. These factors are irrelevant factors because they have nothing to do with performance. The tennis player will still have to execute the same technical skills whether he's in Europe or the United States. A serve is a serve and a forehand is a forehand, regardless of how many people are in the stands.

Here are some other irrelevant points of focus:

- ✔ Your opponents' actions
- ✔ Your teammates' actions
- ✔ The venue
- ✔ Your coach's decisions
- ✔ The fans
- ✔ The opinions of others

If you don't have control over a factor, it is irrelevant, and you don't need to waste energy on it. You don't have any control over whether you win. You do have control over how you perform.

Broad or narrow, external or internal: Types of focus that matter

Relevant points of focus can be broken down into four main areas, as outlined by Robert M. Nideffer in *The Inner Athlete*:

✔ **Broad and external:** Broad and external points of focus are all about assessing a situation. An example is a quarterback dropping back to pass and scanning the field. This is both broad (he's looking at the whole field) and external (he's looking outside of himself at what's happening around him). Other examples: a golfer scanning the fairway off the tee, a volleyball player looking at the opposing team's setup, or a batter looking at the positions of the fielders.

✔ **Broad and internal:** Broad and internal focus is about coming up with all the pieces for a solid game plan. Having a broad and internal focus means you think about certain areas you need to improve in order to reach top athletic performance, such as your fitness, skill, or mental training. An example is a diver assessing her mental skills in competition. This is both broad (all her mental abilities when it comes to diving) and internal (they're things going on within herself). Other examples: a baseball pitcher formulating his game plan, a runner planning how she'll attack the course, or a lacrosse goalie assessing and evaluating his levels of focus in competition.

✔ **Narrow and external:** Narrow and external points of focus are outside of yourself, but smaller in size. An example is a softball player tracking the ball coming toward the plate. This is both narrow (the ball is a small object) and external (it's coming toward her from the mound). Other examples: a lacrosse goalie tracking the ball, a golfer addressing the ball, or a rifle shooter zeroing in on the target.

✔ **Narrow and internal:** Narrow and internal points of focus are small, minute details within yourself. An example is a runner focusing on her breathing tempo. This is both narrow (she's focusing on her breathing, which is a small part of her overall performance) and internal (she's looking at herself, not at anything around her). Other examples: a skeet shooter focusing on his neck and shoulder tension, a soccer player taking a deep breath before a penalty shot to relax his legs, or a tennis player relaxing her arm before a serve.

The points of focus vary from one sport to another, but these four elements of focus are a part of all sports. Break down your sport into these four areas so that you know exactly what's relevant to great execution in *your* sport. The better you know these focus points, the better you can be at focusing on them, and the better your performance will be. You can practice zeroing in on these points of focus using imagery or journaling.

Zeroing in on the present

The present moment is the single most important moment you have as a competitor. Research shows that when athletes are having a great performance, they're focused solely on the present moment. They aren't thinking about the past or the future. If you're thinking about the past or the future as you compete, you're wasting mental energy on details that are irrelevant to your performance. What you did last week or last game — good or bad — doesn't matter. If you focus on the past or the future, you're distracting yourself from the present moment and decreasing your focus, opening the door for potential mistakes. By not being in the moment, you automatically increase the chance for errors and decrease your chance for success.

So, how do you stay in the present moment? Here are some helpful tips:

✔ **Practice staying in the present moment every day.** Set a goal to focus on the present moment in every practice. Listen to what your coach is saying and the words that she's choosing to express her point. Focus only on the immediate execution of a technical skill for your sport, such as shooting a perfect free throw. Make sure you evaluate your ability in this area after practice. The more you make staying in the present moment a conscious practice, the better you'll get at doing it during competition.

✔ **Choose an object — a candle, a point on the wall, or even a piece of sports equipment like a ball — and stare at it for 30 seconds, without looking away or thinking of anything else.** Try to add more time to this practice each week, up to a minute. By just staring at an object and thinking only about only that object, you're in the present moment — you aren't thinking about what you did earlier in the day or about what you need to do later in the evening. This drill sounds simple, but many athletes find it difficult. Stick with it, and your ability to focus will improve.

✔ **Bring awareness to your internal state through a technique known as *centering*.** Pay attention to your breathing, your muscle tension, and how clear your head feels. Bring these physical and mental sensations to a balanced state — center yourself. You can also ground your feet so that your entire body feels centered and balanced.

✔ **Practice yoga.** Many athletes and teams practice yoga, not only for greater flexibility but also to train themselves to be more in the moment. The more you practice yoga, the better you get. Take a class at a gym or studio in your area. Suggest to your coach that he bring a yoga instructor into practice once a week. Or, to work on yoga on your own, check out *Yoga For Dummies*, 2nd Edition, by Georg Feuerstein, PhD, and Larry Payne, PhD (Wiley).

✔ **Keep a present moment log.** You can practice being present off the field and, as a result, get better at this skill in your on-the-field performance. Simply make a commitment to trying to be more present in all your daily activities. At the end of the day, write in your present moment log about the various times during the day when you were successful at being more present.

Using Focus to Reduce or Eliminate Pressure

You probably feel pressure in most practices and every competition. You may even assume that pressure is just part of playing sports. We have news for you: Pressure is a figment of your imagination. Yep, you read that right — pressure exists only in your mind.

Think about it: Situations are not pressure-filled in and of themselves. How you view those situations are what does or doesn't result in a feeling of pressure. And whether you feel pressure is directly related to what you focus on. For example, say it's the bottom of the ninth inning and you have the chance to hit a game-tying RBI. You may or may not feel pressure in this situation, depending on what you're thinking about. If you're focusing on possible outcomes — such as "What if I strike out?" — you'll probably feel pressure, have tightened muscles, and decrease your chances of getting that RBI, because tight muscles can't swing a bat as freely as loose muscles can. On the other hand, if you're thinking about the process of putting the ball in play — "Relax and hit it solid" — you won't feel pressure, your muscles will be looser, and you'll have a better chance of success. This is why some athletes excel in situations that others feel are "packed with pressure" — the ones who feel all kinds of pressure aren't viewing the situation in the same way as the ones who don't.

If you've ever felt an increased heart rate, tightened muscles, or knots in your stomach before a competition, you can bet you were focusing on irrelevant details that had nothing to do with performance. So which came first — the thoughts or the physical reaction? The negative thoughts actually *caused* the negative physical response — it's just easier to recognize a knot in your stomach than it is to monitor your thoughts. But here's the real kicker: When you start to have negative physical responses (like the rapid heart rate and the knot in your stomach), you'll be more likely to focus on those physical sensations even more, making the situation even worse.

The good news is, you can train your brain to focus on things that are effective and help you relax your body and improve performance. Here are some specific tips for keeping your focus where it needs to be during competitions (see Chapters 11 and 12 for even more suggestions):

  ✔ **Focus on the process rather than the outcome.** For example, a golfer needs to focus on swinging smoothly (process), not on the fact that he has to make a birdie to win (outcome). When you focus on process, you create a more positive, effective mindset and state of readiness for competition. Make sure you focus on how you're going to execute athletic tasks — and set aside everything else.

✔ **Practice deep breathing.** You can never go wrong with taking some deep breaths as a way to relax and get your focus back to where it needs to be. If you focus on managing your breathing, you'll relax your muscles and help to neutralize the physical effects of any negative thoughts.

✔ **Focus on what you can control.** Focusing on controllable factors reduces the amount of pressure you'll feel during competition. For example, you have direct control over your fitness level, your diet, how much you practice, and how hard. If you think about the things that are uncontrollable, however — such as winning, whether your coach pulls you from the game after a mistake, or how your teammates will view your performance — you'll create a negative and nervous state of mind, which will manifest itself in physical symptoms.

Overcoming the Obstacles to Focus

If focusing were easy, we wouldn't need to devote an entire chapter to it. And the reason it isn't easy is because all kinds of things get in the way of focus. In this section, we fill you in on the biggest obstacles to focus, so that you can work to overcome them.

Thinking about outcomes

Thinking about outcomes is probably the greatest obstacle to focus in all of sports. You play sports because you want to win, but this focus point is one of the greatest causes of loss and poor performance.

At first glance, focusing on outcomes makes sense because it's how athletic success is typically measured — one team wins, one team loses. When you check out the box scores in your local paper, you see outcomes such as wins and losses. Box scores don't provide information on effort, strategy, or mental toughness. So, when you're bombarded by the relentless focus on outcomes in sport every day, it's no wonder that you would do the same when competing.

You have to train yourself to focus on the process — the specific skills you're performing. When you focus on the process and not the outcome, you dramatically increase your chances for success. The process is what you have control over. You can play or compete your very best and still get beaten by a better opponent. You can also perform poorly and still eek out a win. If you focus on how you compete, the outcomes will take care of themselves.

Use cue words to help yourself get your focus where it needs to be. (Turn to Chapter 7 for more on cue words.)

Getting too emotional

Another frequent obstacle of focus is allowing yourself to become too emotional while competing. When your emotional arousal level gets too high, your concentration level drops. When you become too emotional, two major things occur:

- **Your body changes in a negative way.** Your muscles tighten, your heart rate increases, and you have shallow breathing.

- **Your focus becomes clouded.** You're thinking about being angry or nervous (or even excited and happy) instead of focusing on what it takes to perform well.

Here are some ways you can combat the tendency to become too emotional:

- **Become more aware of your emotional arousal levels.** You need to know the warning signs that you're becoming too emotional, such as a faster heart rate, shakiness, jittery hands or legs, a knot in your stomach, racing thoughts, or muscle tightness. The earlier you can catch yourself, the easier it'll be for you to calm down.

- **Manage your mistakes.** Write in your journal or think about how you'll handle situations in which you make a mistake. You need a strategy — if you get too emotional after making a mistake, and you don't have a strategy in place to help you when you do, you only increase the odds of making another mistake. (See Chapter 13 for more on bouncing back from adversity.)

  Your emotional reaction may be understandable, especially after a bad call or after you make a mistake, but you have to learn to stop it before it spirals out of control. You hurt your own performance as well as your team's chance for success if you don't.

- **Walk away.** You may just need to cool down and step away when there's a break in the action, such as at the end of an inning or quarter. Step away and get your focus back to where it's effective.

- **Practice relaxation.** Chapters 11, 12, and 13 address specific ways to relax. These skills are important ones to have in your mental toolbox. Sports are emotional events and experiences that require you to have not only the ability to pump yourself up but also the ability to calm yourself down.

Letting off-the-field stuff get in the way

You're more than just an athlete — you have other things besides sports to address and manage in your everyday life. You have family relationships, friends, academics, a job, financial concerns, and other stressors. Each person's combination of stressors is unique, but all athletes must learn effective strategies for dealing with them.

Here are some ways to better manage your life outside of sports:

- **Face your issues.** If you have off-the-field issues, make sure to face them and deal with them in the best way possible, as soon as possible. Dealing with stressful situations isn't easy, but if you continue to let these issues fester in your mind and body, they'll hinder your ability to focus on the field.

- **Write it and leave it.** Write down all your off-the-field concerns before going to practice or competition. Then, after you write them down, make sure to leave them in your locker, in your car, or at home. They'll be there when you get back, but they can't help you bring your focus to athletics. When you leave practice or the game, you can put your full focus back on those other issues.

- **Create consistent and solid practice and competition routines.** Routines help you to place your focus where it needs to be. They lock you in and help you focus on what's relevant at the time (your performance) and not on what's irrelevant (off-the-field stuff). (Turn to Chapter 10 for more on routines.)

  We're not saying that the off-field issues, like your family and schoolwork, aren't important — in many cases, they're far *more* important than sports. We're just saying that focusing on those other issues will only hurt your performance, which makes them irrelevant while you're on the field.

- **Seek support.** If your concerns and challenges are taking over your life and you're having a hard time managing them, don't hesitate to seek support from friends, family, teammates, coaches, or a sports psychologist. Asking for help is a sign of strength, wisdom, and courage.

Dealing with fans, officials, and coaches

How many times have you gotten upset and lost your focus after a bad call from an official? What about when a fan yells something at you? How about when your coach pulls you out of the game? All athletes experience these moments at some point in their athletic careers. Some athletes even get ejected or see a dramatic drop-off in performance because of their inability to deal with fans, officials, and coaches.

You don't have any control over fans, officials, or coaches. And anything over which you have no control is irrelevant to your athletic performance. Continue reminding yourself of this fact throughout your career, especially because fans, officials, and coaches have a way of getting inside your head.

If you're having trouble ignoring fans, officials, and coaches, keep in mind the following:

- **Identify what's relevant and what's irrelevant.** Fans, officials, and coaches are irrelevant to your athletic performance. Your athletic tasks and emotional arousal levels are relevant, and they're what you should focus on.

- **Plan and visualize.** Write in your journal about the specific situations in which you've lost your focus. Come up with a plan for how a composed athlete would handle these situations, and then use imagery (see Chapter 7) to see yourself managing them in this productive way. Planning and visualizing will help you maintain your focus when those same situations arise in the future.

The loss of focus that athletes and coaches experience after a questionable call (even if the call is questionable only in their minds) happens daily in sports. In fact, many athletes and coaches get ejected because of their own inappropriate behavior after calls they haven't liked. What does this do for athletic performance? Absolutely nothing. Not only do you lose focus in that moment, but you may also experience a drop in concentration for the next few minutes, if not the remainder of the competition. We hear athletes say that the officials' poor calls caused their anger and loss of focus. Wrong! Their loss of focus was caused by their decision to pay attention to the official's call and not their performance.

If you see opponents getting upset at a call by an official, take advantage of their lack of focus. Put the ball immediately in play when your opponents are not focused. And make sure you don't give your opponents the same advantage over you.

Improving Your Focus

You can improve your focus in a variety of ways, many of which we cover throughout this chapter. Here are some additional ways to improve your focus:

- **Prepare, prepare, prepare.** The more prepared you are for practice and games, the better you'll be at keeping your focus where it needs to be. Make sure that you know your role and game plan, and that you've prepared yourself better than your opponent to execute that role and game plan.

✔ **Know your cue words.** Have your focus cue word, phrase, or image in mind at all times. It should be something simple, like *focus, loose,* or *relax.* It can be a skill-related phrase as well, such as *hit solid, follow through,* or *quick feet.* (For more on cue words, turn to Chapter 7.)

✔ **Know the focus points for your sport.** Every sport has unique focal points — from the ball in baseball, to your breathing and stroke in swimming, to the point where you want your serve to land in tennis. The clearer you are about your sport's unique focal points, the easier it'll be for you to execute those skills when competing.

✔ **Simulate competition.** The more that you simulate competition in practice, the more opportunities you have to make sure you can handle the pressure of game day.

✔ **Relax.** You need multiple ways to relax before competition so that your mind is in the ideal zone for focus. You may want to read, listen to music, take a nap, or do some muscle relaxation exercises. (Turn to Chapter 10 for more on the routines you can use to prepare for competition.)

✔ **Use imagery.** The more time you spend with effective imagery, the better you get at paying attention to relevant details of your athletic success. In your imagery practice, see yourself focusing on relevant details so that when it comes time to compete, you've trained your brain to pay attention to those things. (See Chapter 7 for more on using imagery.)

✔ **Develop your own ideal routines.** Routines help you to stay focused on what's relevant by keeping your emotions in their ideal state and your mind centered on performance. (See Chapter 10 for more on routines.)

✔ **Have a specific goal or purpose for everything you do that is related to your sport.** The more specific your goal or purpose, the more you teach your brain to focus on that goal or purpose and move toward success.

Chapter 7

Seeing Is Believing: What You Need to Know about Imagery

Elite athletes such as Tom Brady, Serena Williams, and Kobe Bryant use imagery. You may have heard them refer to it by the more commonly used term *visualization* (see the nearby sidebar "Visualization vs. imagery: What's in a name?"), but if you're like most people, you're not quite sure what this tool is, how they use it, or how *you* can use it to improve your own athletic performance.

Imagery is a skill you can develop just like any other — in fact, we frequently teach it to some of the best athletes in the world. In this chapter, we explain what imagery is, why many elite athletes use it, and how you can begin practicing it, too.

One final point before we dive in: Imagery isn't just for touchy-feely, new-age people. Using imagery *can* involve quieting your mind and closing your eyes, but you can also practice imagery by writing in a journal, watching a film, listening to music, or watching your favorite and best athletes compete. Those are all great ways to use imagery. The key is to use what works for *you*.

Visualization vs. imagery: What's in a name?

Although the term *visualization* is more commonly used among athletes and coaches than the term *imagery* is, we use the term *imagery* throughout this book. Here's why: When you think of visualizing something, you may only think about "seeing" it in your mind. The fact is that the best form of imagery uses *all* your senses — sight, hearing, smell, touch, and taste — as well as *muscle imagery* (feeling the muscles move in a way you want them to). The term *imagery* better encompasses all of what's involved in using the power of your mind to achieve your goals.

Introducing Imagery

Imagery is using all your senses to create or re-create an experience in your mind. You can think of it as "focused daydreaming" (see the nearby sidebar "Imagery: It's not just daydreaming" for more on the distinction between the two). You may not have realized it, but you've probably already used imagery — both in your athletic training and in your everyday life.

Do you ever think about a game or competition the night before and picture how you'll perform? Do you see yourself making the winning shot in the last seconds of the game or throwing the winning touchdown pass? Can you hear and feel the soft thump of the racket as you ace your opponent with your killer serve? If so, you're using imagery.

Imagery can be broken down into two broad categories: internal and external. We cover both in the following sections.

Research in the area of internal and external imagery is mixed with regards to which form of imagery is most effective for improving athletic performance. Most studies find that elite athletes typically use a combination of both forms of visualization in their mental training. The research *does* show, however, that imagery increases motivation, improves focus, reduces anxiety, and increases self-confidence. Not a bad return on your investment!

Internal imagery: From your own point of view

The term *internal imagery* refers to the experience of imagining an athletic experience from your own point of view. It's the most common form of imagery.

For example, maybe you imagine yourself hitting a home run to deep left field in the bottom of the ninth inning of an important baseball game. In your mind, you see the pitch headed straight down the middle of the plate, belt high. You feel yourself extend your arms and turn your hips quickly as you connect solidly with the ball. You feel the sweet thud that accompanies solid contact. As you watch the ball begin its ascent into the sky deep toward left field, you can feel your excitement building. The ball gets smaller and smaller and eventually flies over the left-field wall, landing in the bleachers, among the throng of cheering fans. This experience, from your own point of view, is an example of internal imagery.

External imagery: Looking at yourself from the outside

External imagery, on the other hand, is where you look at yourself from the outside, as if you're being filmed. External imagery is less common than internal imagery.

For example, maybe you imagine the pitcher throwing the pitch, but this time, from the viewpoint of someone sitting in the stands behind home plate. You can see the ball cross the plate, and watch yourself turn on it suddenly and powerfully. You watch the trajectory of the ball and the speed with which it lofts deep toward left field. You see the left fielder turn his back to the infield and attempt to make a catch at the wall. You see the crowd rising up in their seats in anticipation of the home run, and you can hear the deafening roar as they scream in unison in delight. As the ball lands beyond the left-field wall, you can see yourself rounding the bases at a quick pace, with a smile on your face. You see yourself cross home plate and high-five your teammates. This experience, from the point of view of a bystander, is an example of external imagery.

Imagery: It's not just daydreaming

Have you ever sat in class, pretending to listen to your math teacher mumbling something about the Pythagorean theorem, while you were thinking about the big game coming up that weekend? Even though your body was physically in class, your mind was somewhere else. You were engaging in *daydreaming* — that phenomenon where you engage in fantasy thinking, usually of a happy sort, about something pleasurable in your life.

Daydreaming is one of those activities we engage in when we're bored and our minds wander. Daydreaming tends to be an unplanned, subconscious, and unfocused event. This doesn't mean that your daydreaming is irrelevant or trivial, but it lacks the purpose and intention that accompanies imagery.

When you use imagery, you're doing so purposefully, with the intent of improving some aspect of your performance. You're consciously deciding to engage in this skill. You're intentional about what you want or need to visualize about. Maybe you're preparing for an upcoming competition, trying to relax and sleep, or trying to see yourself executing a solid game plan. Whatever the reason, your decision to visualize is a conscious one, complete with intention and purpose. It's a directed effort to improve your physical skills through successful mental rehearsal of those skills.

High-achieving athletes from all sports don't simply daydream — daydreams are fantasy without direction. The best athletes in the world use imagery, and they make it part of their mental toolbox. They're driven and intentional about it, and they know how to use it to achieve success.

Determining What Type of Imager You Are

In order to get the most out of imagery, you need to understand what type of imagery works best for you. Some people are very visual — they can easily remember the visual details of situations or experiences. Others are more auditory — they remember what people said at those moments or the roar of the crowd. Still others are physically oriented — they can easily recall how the experience felt for them, down to the feel of the bat in their hands and the pounding of their hearts.

You use all three types of imagery at one time or another, but you may find yourself naturally drawn to or preferring one type. Knowing which type of imagery you prefer is important, because it allows you to create images that make the most sense to you. When we work with athletes and coaches, we try to find out what their preferred images are so that we can help them build the imagery program that's most useful to them.

Which type of imager are you? In the following sections, we show you some ways to answer that question for yourself.

Even though you may lean toward one type of imagery over another, you can and should look for ways to make your imagery as vivid as possible, and that means incorporating all the senses. Knowing what type of imagery resonates most deeply with you should help you kick your images up a notch, not limit you in any way.

Visual: Monkey see, monkey do

Many people are visual learners. They learn new concepts and retain memories best through *seeing*. If you fall into this category, you have the following characteristics:

- ✔ You learn best by reading.
- ✔ You can easily recall details, such as the color of someone's eyes or clothing.
- ✔ You give or need directions based on visual landmarks, such as "Turn right at the gas station with the green sign" or "Turn two streets past the McDonald's."
- ✔ You have an uncanny ability to recognize faces (even though you may not remember a person's name) from your past, such as a classmate from 20 years ago.

If you tend to be a visual learner, try designing and thinking about images that are more visual in nature. So, when you're thinking about how you'll perform in tomorrow's game, do so with visuals or pictures. For example, a soccer player would see what the ball looks like as it bends toward the net, a tennis player would see her serve as a "ball of fire" traveling over the net with high speed, and a golfer would picture his ball as a red laser line going straight to the hole.

Auditory: I hear you loud and clear

Auditory learners use their hearing as their most important sense when trying to remember something. You know you're an auditory learner if the following characteristics apply to you:

- ✔ You learn best by listening to your teacher or coach.
- ✔ You can easily remember the exact wording that someone used when relaying a message to you.
- ✔ When listening to music, you can identify songs quickly, sometimes after hearing only a couple of notes.

If you're an auditory learner, use sounds as part of your imagery practice. For example, a basketball player would hear the swoosh as the ball travels through the net, a gymnast would hear soft classical music in her mind as she prepares to relax for her next event, and a quarterback would hear the voice of his coach saying, "Stay calm and confident."

Physical: I feel you, man

Physical learners rely primarily on muscle movement and muscle memory. They do best when they feel their muscles execute skills. They can sit perfectly still and know what their muscles feel like when they're shooting a perfect free throw, placing a great baseline shot, or swinging the perfect drive off the tee.

Many athletes rely on physical imagery because movement and muscle memory are an important part of athletic movement.

Here are some characteristics of physical learners:

- ✔ You learn best by doing and by feeling the proper movement. It's not enough for someone to explain it to you — you have to do it.

- ✔ You feel more confident when you can practice skills repeatedly to ingrain those skills in your muscle memory.

- ✔ Images and words make you think about and feel your muscle movement. Your palms get sweaty, your muscles start firing, and your heart starts pumping.

If you're a physical learner, try to include feel and muscle movement in your imagery. For example, a rifle shooter will feel her hands soft and relaxed on the gun, a golfer will feel his shoulder turn inside his body, and a gymnast will feel the powerful push off the mat into a round-off handspring.

Considering the Key Characteristics of Ideal Images

Each athlete is unique in the images that work best for him, but every ideal image — whether it's visual, auditory, or physical — has two key characteristics:

✔ **Vividness:** When you experience your images, they should be crystal clear, like the image you see when watching an HDTV. You can hear the crowd, smell the fresh grass field, feel the cool temperature of the air, taste the sweat rolling off your upper lip, see yourself executing drills perfectly, or feel the looseness and smoothness of your muscle movements. The more vivid the image, the better.

✔ **Successful:** You should see yourself executing skills flawlessly. For example, a tennis player should see herself hitting a powerful serve and watch the ball speed by her opponent for an ace. A quarterback should see himself relaxed in the pocket as he throws a perfect, tight spiral and hits his receiver in stride. You want to control the images you experience. See only what you want: success!

We cover both of these characteristics in the following sections.

Painting images with vivid detail

How clear and vivid you make your images will determine in part how successful your performance will be. Research clearly shows that the more vivid your images, the better you'll perform as an athlete. When you first start working on using imagery, you may find that making your images vivid is difficult. But, just as with your athletic skills, the more you practice, the better your images will be.

One of the best ways to improve vividness in your imagery is to start by trying to make simple images as vivid as possible. For example, read the following narrative and then see if you can close your eyes and see the image vividly:

Picture a lemon right in front of you. Pay attention to the texture of the lemon. See the exact color of yellow. Adjust the color in your mind to create the exact color that you want to see. Are there any marks on the skin of the lemon? What's the texture of the lemon like? How large is it? Now see the lemon being cut in half. Notice the smell of the lemon. Notice the pulp and the juice dripping from the halves of the lemon. Is your mouth watering? Maybe your tongue can feel the distinctive tart flavor of the lemon. What sound is made if you squeeze the lemon? Can you feel the acidic juice and the sweet stickiness on your hands? Notice the smell wafting into your nostrils.

Try to master this image with all the details you can draw upon to make it as lifelike as possible. Now that you have a better idea of what we mean by vividness, here are some more examples that you can practice with. Start with these and then move on to more advanced images, when you get the hang of it.

✔ Visualize the place where you spend a lot of time practicing your sport, whether it be a tennis court, a football field, an ice hockey rink, a track, a swimming pool, or someplace else. See yourself right in the middle of your field of play. Notice everything around you. Are you outside? Inside? Is it sunny? Cloudy? How bright are the lights? Do you notice any smells — grass, sweat, chlorine, the distinctive odor of an old gym? What sounds do you hear? Are other players there? Practice imaging this place, and make the image as clear as possible.

✔ Visualize a piece of your sports equipment. Notice the exact color. Are there any marks on it? If so, what are they? What is the brand of this piece of equipment? What is the texture of the equipment? Is it rough or smooth? Picture and visualize everything about this piece of equipment just as if it were in your hands right now.

As you practice, try rating your vividness on a scale of 1 to 5 (with 5 being the most vivid). This evaluation is particularly important when you first start using imagery, because it'll help you track your progress. You can give yourself an overall vividness rating for the imagery, but also for the individual senses as well (sight, smell, taste, touch, hearing, and muscle movement). By rating each sense, you'll become better at using all of them.

As your simpler images become more vivid, you can begin trying more complicated images, such as seeing yourself execute your skill in actual game situations. (For more on evaluating your imagery, check out "Evaluating the Success of Your Imagery," later in this chapter.)

Picturing images of your success

In order for your images to be successful, they must be images of you experiencing success. You need to see yourself being successful in terms of both outcome and skills. Whatever the image in your mind, your brain reacts to it by getting appropriately aroused, and your muscles follow suit. So, if you see yourself screwing up or losing, you're essentially preparing your body to fail. On the other hand, if you're able to imagine things exactly as you want — with perfect execution and success — you're increasing the probability that these things will happen.

For example, if you're a golfer stepping up to the tee, and you start to worry or see your shot going into the trees, more often than not, guess what happens next? You'll find yourself in the trees!

Imagery happens intentionally *and* unintentionally. When you're sitting down with the intent of using imagery, you probably won't have trouble picturing yourself doing well. However, the imagery that creeps into your mind when you least expect it can be just as powerful, and you need to get control of that imagery as well. Part of a successful imagery program is using imagery consciously and consistently, so that you can counteract any unintentional negative imagery that might creep into your mind.

If you're having a hard time seeing yourself being successful when you use imagery, you need to try to figure out why, so that you can work to counteract that tendency. Difficulty in coming up with successful images can be due to a variety of factors, including the following:

- ✔ **You may have had a recent poor performance, or a string of recent poor performances, and you're having trouble letting go of the negative images.** If so, try to go back in time and find a better, more successful performance to use in your imagery.

- ✔ **You may have just learned a new skill or found yourself in a new game situation, and you're having trouble seeing successful performances in your mind because you haven't had any yet.** If so, try to imagine how others (maybe famous athletes you've watched over the years) have performed (or *would* perform) in those situations, and then place yourself in that situation, performing as they did.

    Videotape yourself. Then, when you do it successfully, you'll have it on tape and can view it over and over as part of your imagery program.

- ✔ **You may not have prepared enough to create successful images.** Have you practiced enough? Are you prepared well physically? Are you as fit as you can be? If not, you need to be better prepared. In the short term, copy someone else — perhaps a more successful athlete you admire. In the long term, develop better practice habits and get in the best shape you can be in.

- ✔ **You may be trying to make the image in your mind too complicated.** If that's the case, try to break down the image into smaller parts. Remove some details. (Don't worry — you can always add them back again later.) For example, if you're imagining yourself kicking a field goal from 45 yards, you can remove details (for the time being) about the crowd noise, time of day, or weather, and instead build an image around lining up your kick, the approach and hold, and connecting solidly. When you have this image down pat, you can add back those extra details to make your image even more vivid.

Getting Started with Imagery

As you begin to practice imagery, it can be helpful to start in a disciplined and structured manner. Just like any new skill, you need to get comfortable with the basics and build a strong foundation.

Designate a specific time and place in which to practice imagery. In our work with athletes, we've found that morning (just after waking) and evening (just before bed) are the best and easiest times to engage in imagery. After you've established the basic habit, you can begin to experiment with different places and times for your imagery.

You also have to take a systematic approach to learning and improving your imagery skills. You can't just practice imagery every once in a while and expect long-term results. Research shows that imagery is practiced by the best athletes in the world on a consistent, if not daily, basis. It's hard to argue with their success!

You may find yourself tempted to stop practicing because you don't think it's helping fast enough, or you may think that it takes too long, but hang in there! You didn't develop your athletic skills overnight, and the same will be true of your imagery skills. But the reward is worth the effort.

Although you can certainly master imagery on your own, you may be able to master it more quickly by working with a sports psychologist. A professional can help you build a solid understanding of imagery right from the start, which will accelerate your skills in using this tool.

What to image

The list of things you can image — things that deal with successful performances in your sport — is virtually endless. In the following sections, we offer some general categories for you to try when developing your own imagery program. See which types of images work best for you. And, down the road, remember to come back to the ones that don't work for you so well right now. As you grow as an athlete, your imagery will evolve as well.

Imagine in real time. Start in slow motion (especially when you're learning a new skill, so that you can perfect the action image in your mind) and eventually move to real time or fast-forward as your images improve. The goal is to see yourself competing at the same pace and tempo as if it were actually occurring.

Skill development and execution

One common form of imagery is imagining yourself executing a certain skill with absolute perfection. For example, a tennis player can visualize herself executing a powerful and focused backhand. A lineman in football can see himself jumping off the line quickly and pancaking the defensive lineman opposite him.

Research shows that if you're learning a new skill, you'll learn it faster if you add imagery to your regular practice schedule. Use that to your benefit by visualizing yourself executing technical aspects of your sport perfectly. The more you visualize skill execution, the more consistent your skills will become.

As you're practicing the imagery, break down the particular skill (for example, shooting a free throw) into technical steps (feet shoulder width apart, arm bent at the elbow in an *L* shape, and so on).

Mental state

Imagine the mental state you want to have when you're competing. If you want to be confident, then see yourself behaving, feeling, and talking confidently — imagine yourself holding your head high, back straight, smooth and fluid in your movements, with a pep in your step. If you want to work on being focused, see yourself acting, thinking, and feeling this way.

The more comfortable and consistent the state becomes in your mind, the more consistent it will be on the field and in real life. The mind can't differentiate between something that is vividly imagined and something that is actually experienced.

Energy level

You can imagine yourself maintaining ideal energy levels. For example, a football player may want to see himself calm an hour before the game to reserve energy, but then see his energy level explode each and every play of the game, all the way through the fourth quarter. A golfer may want to see herself remaining very calm and centered throughout an entire tournament, never getting too high or too low emotionally or mentally.

Response to mistakes

Because you *will* make some type of mistake every single practice or competition, you need to be able to anticipate mistakes and form a plan of attack for how you'll manage them. If you don't have a plan, you run the risk of compounding your mistake with another one.

For example, if you're a basketball player and you lose the ball bringing it up the court, you may find yourself getting angry and fouling the opposing player who stole the ball in retaliation. With an imagery plan, you can see yourself reacting quickly and trying to get in between the player and the basket, waiting for your team to come back for support. If you're a tennis player, imagine yourself responding like a champion after you double fault, being focused on the next shot and not getting caught up in the mistake emotionally.

When to use imagery

When you're just starting out, it's important to practice imagery at the same time and in the same place, if possible. By doing so, you put your sole focus on this skill, and your disciplined approach to its development will eventually pay off.

When you get more comfortable with imagery, you can begin to practice and use it in many different places and times. You'll also see that practice will provide you with the ability to achieve greater results in shorter periods of time, because you'll be much more effective at using it.

Imaging before, during, and after practice

If you were to practice your sport once a week (right before a game or competition), you probably wouldn't get optimal results or performance. The same applies to your mental training, including imagery. You need to be practicing your imagery as often as possible during the week. Regular and frequent practice will make you better and more efficient in practice, thereby increasing your odds of successful performance. These imagery practice sessions are meant to simulate your desired mental state prior to competition.

Before practice

In this drill, you take ten minutes before practice to write in a *performance journal* (a journal in which you track your goals and thoughts about your practice and competitions). Write down what you're trying to accomplish during practice that day. After you've done this, close your eyes and imagine yourself accomplishing your practice objectives. See yourself doing so as vividly as possible.

We've encouraged many coaches to dedicate the first ten minutes of team practice to imagery, but you can do this on your own if your coach doesn't make the time for it — just get to practice ten minutes earlier than everyone else.

Greatness takes discipline and hard work. If you can take this time to get focused and be intentional about what you're seeking to get out of practice that day, the quality of your practice and skill development will rise dramatically.

If writing doesn't come easily for you, you can use a recorder to verbalize your ideal performance before you begin practice. Some athletes find that saying it out loud is even more effective than writing about it. When you record yourself (depending on the type of recorder you use), you can save these recordings to your computer, phone, or iPod and listen to them repeatedly.

If you have a prerecorded imagery program — maybe done by a sports psychologist or motivational speaker — you can take this time before practice to listen to the audio.

During warm-up

Warm-up is an ideal time for you to be thinking about and imagining yourself being successful. You can create the ideal mental state you desire immediately prior to a competition.

You can also use this time to see yourself being successful and focused in practice. If you're successful and focused in practice, chances are much greater that you'll be able to repeat that great performance in competition.

During breaks

In practice, regardless of your sport, you usually have breaks in the action. You can use these times to practice imagery. If you're in one of those breaks, quickly imagine yourself succeeding in the next drill. This can be especially important if you're having difficulty getting a certain drill or you're having a particularly rough practice. Take some time to imagine how you want to perform, and then go do it!

After practice

Make sure to evaluate and image after practice. If the practice was successful, you can use the images that are still fresh in your mind to mentally mark what success looks like. If you didn't perform the way you hoped in practice, you can imagine yourself performing more successfully next time. Using imagery after practice leaves you in a better place mentally.

Many athletes have difficulty forcing themselves to practice imagery after practice, because they just want to get out of the locker room as soon as possible and get something to eat or move on with their day. But don't neglect this critical part of your imagery program. You just practiced for a couple hours — take another five minutes to jot down or think about what you did well and what you need to improve. Make post-practice imagery part of your daily practice routine.

Imaging before competition

One of the primary benefits of doing visualization the night before and the morning of a big game or match (if it's a late-afternoon or evening competition) is that it helps you keep your mind and body focused on those things most relevant to performing well. It's all too easy to let your mind wander to the "what ifs," such as "What if we lose?" or "What if I screw up?" or "What if we don't make the playoffs?" It also helps you to take time to quiet and clear your head from all the clutter of the past week, both on and off the field. At this point, competition is your opportunity to have fun, execute your skills as best you can, and compete fiercely.

 When it comes to imaging before competition, a common theme with most athletes is to simply see themselves putting it all together and competing well. Your physical practice sessions are now over, and the only thing remaining is to prepare your mind and body for the upcoming competition.

 One journaling technique you can try is to write a newspaper or magazine headline for the day after competition. Then write the story of what's going to happen as if it already did. For example, your headline might read "Local Pitcher Dominates in Title Game, Gets Looks from Scouts." Act as if this headline will appear in the newspaper the day after your performance and your task is to write the story that readers will see. This journaling technique is a very powerful form of imagery.

Make sure not to practice imagery if you're too tired — you don't want to fall asleep during your imagery practice, nor do you want to wear yourself out mentally trying to imagine the next day's success. If you're too tired, the imagery won't be effective. Finally, if you get pumped with too much adrenaline after imagining greatness in your sport, you may find it hard to sleep. If this sounds familiar, do your imagery earlier in the evening, not right before bed.

Many athletes train and practice extremely hard and then get extremely nervous 24 hours before competition. If this sounds familiar, keep in mind that this is the time to *enjoy* playing your sport. The hard work is over — now you can compete, which is why you play your sport to begin with. The fun comes from challenging yourself in a competitive situation. This is when your visualization can pay off — as you see yourself relaxed, enjoying competition, and putting together all the pieces of your training to go out and kick some major butt!

Where to use imagery

 When you're just getting started, you should try to practice imagery at a similar time and place every time you do it. You'll probably learn the skills best when you manage the environmental variables (noise, light, and so on), and keep as many of them the same as you can. A consistent environment will help you learn the skills without having to adapt to different times and places.

That first location for your imagery practice should be

- ✔ **Quiet and free of distractions:** Try to choose a place where you have less possibility of being interrupted or distracted by noises coming from nearby rooms or outside. Basements are good places for this.

- ✔ **Private and large enough for you to sit or lie comfortably:** If you don't have enough room, or you're worried that someone is going to walk in on you, you'll be distracted.

- ✔ **Not too warm or too cold:** If you're too hot or too cold, you'll be distracted. Look for a place that's about 70°F (21°C), or a temperature that's comfortable for you.

After you've practiced imagery for a while and you've become more comfortable with it, you'll have far fewer limits on where or when you can perform this skill. You can do it in the bus on the way to practice or a game, in the locker room, on the bench, or even on the field or court. Eventually, you'll be able to use imagery in just a couple of minutes, even with distractions. In fact, when you're able to use imagery at various times and in different places, you know that your skill level has reached great heights!

Evaluating the Success of Your Imagery

The success of your imagery depends on your systematic and consistent approach to it. If you only do it every now and then and don't evaluate your progress, your imagery won't improve and it won't help your athletic performance. On the other hand, if you regularly practice using imagery, and you evaluate yourself and learn along the way, you'll get better at using imagery — and you'll see better results in your athletic performance as well.

Think of your imagery practice the same as you do your athletic skills and physical fitness. If you practice well and practice often, you improve. If you only give it a half-hearted effort, and only when you feel like it, you won't improve. It's as simple as that.

On a basic level, you need to evaluate the vividness and success of each of the images you use. For the first 30 days that you practice imagery, evaluate yourself every time, to track your progress. After this initial evaluation period, you may feel more confident in your skills and not have to formally evaluate yourself as often, but we recommend you continue to evaluate your imagery at least once every two to four weeks, just to make sure you're keeping this skill sharp. As you know from your athletic skills, just because you get good at something or master it, doesn't mean you can slack off. You always have to continue to refine and practice the skill; otherwise, you get rusty and may even lose the skills you worked so hard to develop.

Figure 7-1 is an example of an evaluation form you can use (taken from Todd's book, *Athlete's Journal,* which you can find at `www.athleticmind institute.com`). You may want to photocopy this page, and store all your evaluations in a binder or file folder to track your progress, and see which images are particularly effective for you.

Imagery Evaluation

Date: _____   Location: _____

Images

1. _____

    Vividness   1   2   3   4   5

    Successfulness   1   2   3   4   5

2. _____

    Vividness   1   2   3   4   5

    Successfulness   1   2   3   4   5

3. _____

    Vividness   1   2   3   4   5

    Successfulness   1   2   3   4   5

Total time: _____

Ideas and lessons for future imaging practice: _____

_____

_____

_____

_____

_____

Figure 7-1:
Evaluating
your imag-
ery is a key
part of your
success.

A sample imagery script

The following imagery script is a sample for a baseball or softball player in an upcoming game. You can create your own scripts based on what you're trying to imagine — accomplishing a goal in practice, staying relaxed in pressure situations, staying focused amidst numerous distractions, keeping your energy up when you're tired and exhausted, or staying loose throughout a game.

Although this script is for a baseball or softball player, you can easily adapt it to your own sport and individual skills. The following text is meant to give you some basic idea of what imagery is when it's all put together. Notice how we've incorporated all the senses — this is the best and most effective method of imagery.

Get yourself into a comfortable position. Take a few deep cleansing breaths to bring yourself into the present moment, and begin to allow your mind to slow down as you feel your muscles relax. Feel the excitement over the upcoming game slowly rising in your chest, knowing that this is why you practice so hard and so often — so you can have fun competing and playing well! You know that this imagery exercise will allow you to see yourself compete and play exactly as you know how and exactly as you desire.

Before imagining the upcoming game, think back to a game when you played your best. Remember how well you performed, how relaxed you felt, and how excited and yet calm you were. You were at the plate, and everything was quiet in your mind. All you saw was that ball coming from the pitcher's hand and how slow it was coming, as you counted the laces on the ball, and how good it felt to make solid, strong contact as you ripped a base hit. You felt tremendous confidence at the plate, and you knew how

quick your hands were, and that you were going to hit well that day. Even though the ball was coming at a high rate of speed, it seemed to slow down. You were completely zeroed in on the ball.

You can even remember teammates and coaches cheering and jumping up and down after this great hit. You can even remember how fluid and strong and quick your body felt. The crowd and fans were cheering and rooting you on! You recall the joy and excitement and confidence you felt, and how well you performed. Remember that feeling of how effortless and automatic it was that day. No thinking, no "trying" — just letting your body do what you trained it to do. Think about the word you might've used that day as a cue word, such as "quick hands" or "hit solid." Take these feelings, thoughts, and emotions and feel them throughout your body, because you know that this is how you think, feel, and behave when you're performing well.

Now begin to think about your upcoming competition. Think about the venue — you're on your home field. Notice everything as if you're there right now. Notice the temperature, and how it feels on your cheeks and your arms. Notice all of the different people — coaches, teammates, opponents, fans, family, friends, and umpires. Feel the wind and the sun. Take in all the sounds around you as well — talking with your teammates, coaches building you up, fans cheering, music playing. Notice any smells — perhaps the freshly cut grass of the field. Feel your muscles being warmed up and ready to go. You feel light on your feet, you feel strong, your muscles are fluid and relaxed, your entire body just feels ready, confident, powerful, and strong. You can

(continued)

(continued)

even taste the salt in your sweat as you're readying yourself to compete! You feel the excitement, the calmness in your mind, the fun of finally doing what you enjoy doing most!

Now you see yourself at the plate. You're calm, yet very intense and focused at the plate, like a cat intently watching a mouse. You walk to the batter's box and stare down the pitcher. You're going to hit anything this pitcher throws your way. You're too good, too prepared, and too focused — the pitcher has no chance of getting the ball past you. You feel how relaxed your arms are, knowing that your hands can

get around on any pitch, in any location. You repeat your cue words, "quick hands," over and over again in your head quietly as you stare down the pitcher. When the pitch is thrown, you simply see it all the way in and you feel your body in motion forward, making hard and powerful contact, just as you knew you would. You start running the bases, feeling ever so confident and knowing that you can get another hit next time. You feel strong and powerful, unbeatable, and you see the disappointment in the pitcher's eyes as you stand on base, ready to do it all over again next time!

Chapter 8

Self-Talk: Making Sure You're Not Yelling in Your Own Ear

*W*hether you realize it or not, you're in a constant conversation with yourself, called *self-talk*. Sometimes that conversation is spoken out loud (for example, when you talk to yourself on the baseline before a serve, or when you psych yourself up as you approach the starting block), but more often, the conversation is in your head.

Sometimes the messages you send yourself are positive — "I know I can do this," "I'm the best hitter on the team," "Damn, I'm fast!" And sometimes the messages are negative — "I'll never win this race," "I can't catch a pass to save my life," "I suck." What you tell yourself — positive and negative — is powerful. And most important, you have control over the messages you send, which means you can harness the power of your own thoughts to improve your performance in all areas of your life, including sports.

In this chapter, we describe the consequences of positive and negative self-talk and help you use self-talk to your advantage.

Considering the Consequences of Self-Talk

Your self-talk — the messages you send yourself — directly affects how you feel and then how you behave. The good news is that you can choose which type of self-talk you engage in — minimizing the negative and maximizing the positive. In this section, we take a look at the two types of self-talk, and then explain the consequences of both.

The two types of self-talk: Positive and negative

Self-talk can be positive or negative, and both types of self-talk have a profound effect on performance.

Positive self-talk is made up of thoughts that lead to positive emotional reactions. Here are some common examples of positive self-talk in athletes, along with possible resulting emotional reactions:

Positive Self-Talk	Resulting Emotional Reaction
"I can do this!"	Excitement
"I've been here before."	Relaxation
"I'm not going to let them beat me!"	Determination
"I did it. It was all worth it."	Relief

Negative self-talk, on the other hand, leads directly to unwanted, unproductive, and harmful emotional reactions. Here are some common examples of negative self-talk in athletes, along with possible resulting emotional reactions:

Negative Self-Talk	Resulting Emotional Reaction
"I have to win!"	Anxiety
"What if I screw up?"	Worry
"I always mess things up."	Hopelessness
"I let down my team again."	Sadness

In our experience, having worked with top athletes from all over the world, we've found that people are much more conditioned (by society and western culture) to jump to *negative* thoughts. People are critical of every aspect of their lives, including their sports participation. And it's not just *athletes* being hard on *themselves* — fans cheer when athletes succeed and boo loudly when they fail. As an athlete, you can break that pattern. And when you do, you'll perform better — because you'll be more relaxed, excited, hopeful, and so on.

How self-talk affects performance

Self-talk affects performance in a very physical and measurable way. For each and every thought you have, there is a corresponding emotion and resulting physical response, all of which affects performance. Here are some examples of self-talk, the resulting emotions, and the physical consequences:

Self-Talk	Resulting Emotion	Physical Consequence
"I can do this!"	Excitement	Relaxed muscles
"What if I screw up?"	Nervousness	Muscle tightness

A story of your self-talk

It's a nice spring day. The sun is shining, a few puffy clouds are in the sky, and it's about the perfect temperature. You feel the heat from the sun, but it isn't too hot — just right. You decide to take a walk through a local park. You're simply walking along through the park, not too many people are out and about because it's a weekday afternoon. You see a young child coming toward you on her bike. She looks as happy as can be, just being a kid and enjoying riding her bike and being in the park. As she comes on the path toward you, she hits a bump, her back tire slides, and she falls off the bike. You're there to witness this fall. You know it wasn't a serious fall, but it was still scary for a kid.

What would you do in the situation? Why might you say to the child? Odds are, you'd probably help her up, make sure she was okay, and then maybe say something like, "Don't worry. Get back up there on that bike. You can do it."

Or maybe something like, "It's okay. I fell off my bike too when I was your age." In other words, you'd probably be encouraging and helpful.

Let's change the scenario in the story a bit.

What if you were riding the bike and fell off? What would you say to yourself? Think about this for a second.

You probably wouldn't be that nice. You might scream, "You're such an idiot!" — either aloud or in your mind. You may even throw in a few expletives. You probably wouldn't treat yourself the same way you would treat that little girl. And you would never dream of screaming at that little girl the way you might berate yourself.

The things we actually say to ourselves are things we would seldom say to others. Try to be aware of your self-talk, whether positive or negative. *Remember:* Either way, it comes true.

The following ABC model, developed by famous psychologist Albert Ellis, is an easy way to remember how self-talk affects performance:

- **Activating event:** The situation (for example, striking out with the bases loaded)
- **Belief:** How you think (for example, "I should never strike out")
- **Consequences:** How you feel (for example, sadness, worry, and anxiety)

The situation is the starting point — it "activates" your thinking pattern, which creates your reaction. The most important aspect of this model is that your beliefs, or your self-talk, determine your reaction to that activating event. In fact, the situation itself has *no* impact — what you say or think about the situation creates your reaction. Therefore, the responsibility lies with *you* to control your thoughts. No opponent or umpire can cause you to be angry or upset without your consent.

You don't say . . .

Sometimes, self-talk affects not only your own performance, but also that of other players. During a recent tennis match, Leif was watching a client face off in the finals of a tournament against a difficult opponent. It was a tight match. On the court behind his client, a men's semifinal match was going on. Suddenly, and very loudly, one of the players yelled, "I suck!", at the top of his lungs after he lost a big point.

Spectators started laughing, and so did my client, who was about to start her next game. She played that game very relaxed and ended up winning. What about the player who yelled at himself on the other court? Not surprisingly, he played very poorly and was defeated (rather quickly) by his more focused (and less negative) opponent.

Every thought you have — and you have many, many more than you realize — is linked to a physical consequence (such as heart rate, breathing rate, or degree of muscle tension). Your thoughts can even change the amount of stress hormones (such as cortisol and adrenaline) that your body releases into your bloodstream. So, there is a very definite reason to change the way you talk to yourself: Your health may depend on it!

Cortisol is a stress hormone that is released from the adrenal gland, along with adrenaline, during times of stress. In small doses, cortisol can help improve performance by lowering your sensitivity to pain, improving memory, and giving you a burst of energy. Chronic stress and prolonged levels of elevated cortisol in the bloodstream, however, have been shown to have negative effects on the body, such as impaired thinking, elevated blood pressure, and slower healing from injury.

As an athlete, whether your self-talk is positive or negative is very important. If your self-talk is negative, you'll feel negative emotions (such as fear, worry, and panic), you'll experience corresponding changes in your body (such as muscle tightness, shallow breathing, and rapid heart rate), and your athletic performance will decline. If your self-talk is positive, however, you'll feel positive emotions (like relaxation), you'll experience corresponding changes in your body (such as decreased muscle tension), and your performance will improve.

Want a practical example? Consider a baseball pitcher. When his self-talk is negative ("I can't believe I've walked three batters! My slider stinks!"), he'll get nervous and/or angry, resulting in tight muscles. Can a pitcher with tight muscles throw as hard and as accurately as one with relaxed muscles? No. On the other hand, if the pitcher's self-talk is positive ("One pitch at a time. Relax and throw to the mitt."), he has a much greater chance of being relaxed and composed, resulting in smoother muscle movement and better chance of executing his pitches.

In order for you to consistently be at your best, you must make sure that your self-talk is consistently positive. Even a few words of self-talk can make a huge difference in your performance, for the better or for the worse.

Don't lose sight of the *tone* of your self-talk. A harsh and critical tone, even with encouraging words, can hurt performance.

Todd was working with a college golfer who has recently had some success on one of the mini-tours. During his collegiate golf career, the player realized the importance of making his self-talk more positive, especially if he wanted to win at the national level and compete for a spot on the PGA Tour. In the beginning, he did very well practicing and changing his self-talk to be more positive. Sometimes, however, he said all the right words — such as "Relax" and "Just this shot" — but he would be screaming the words at himself in his mind, full of frustration. Even though the statements were *intended* to be positive, his tone overshadowed the content and led to poor performance. You need to pay attention not only to *what* you're saying, but to *how* you're saying it.

Changing the Channel on Negative Self-Talk

Negative self-talk has all kinds of negative repercussions (see the preceding section). Most of the time, you're probably not aware of your own self-talk because it happens so quickly. All you feel (and then notice physically) is anxiety and pressure, and you have no idea how it got there. The self-talk that you use when you feel nervous or anxious is illogical and irrational. But you need to be aware of it before you can start to change it. So, the first step is to become more aware of how your self-talk — positive or negative in nature — happens. When you recognize what you're saying to yourself and when, the next step is to stop the negative thoughts. And then, finally, you can replace those negative thoughts with positive ones.

Self-talk is how you think. It's what happens in that small gap of time between an event (the stimulus) and your response. You're responsible for what you tell yourself, and you can change the emotions you feel simply by changing what you say to yourself.

Paying attention to the messages you send yourself

Recognizing your own self-talk is challenging. Thoughts occur so quickly — and you have so many thoughts running through your mind all day — that it's difficult to become more aware of them.

Start by tracking your thought patterns. Here are some ways to do so:

- **Make the commitment every day, every practice, and every game to try to pay attention to your self-talk.** You'll get better at paying attention with time, but it starts with your commitment to doing so.

- **Think back and describe (in writing) your own successful and unsuccessful athletic performances.** Try to remember what you thought and how you felt. The goal here is to link your positive self-talk with your winning moments and your negative self-talk with your losses or failures. Don't worry if you can't remember exactly what you were thinking or feeling — just jot down whatever you remember and look for patterns.

- **Carry a small self-talk notebook with you.** You can keep this notebook in your car, locker, or gym bag. At the end of every practice or game, write in your journal. Review your practice or competition and identify both positive and negative thought patterns and how they affected the day's performance. The sooner you can write about your experience after it happens, the more likely you are to remember exactly what you were thinking or feeling.

When you've begun tracking your thought patterns, identify whether they're positive or negative. If they're negative, ask yourself which of the following categories your self-talk falls into:

- **Perfectionism:** Believing that you have to be perfect and that mistakes are unacceptable.

- **Catastrophizing:** Turning a small mistake into a major negative event; making a mountain out of a molehill.

- **All-or-nothing thinking:** Not leaving room for a middle ground. Things are either "all bad" or "all good."

- **Personalizing:** Believing that what others say and do is somehow connected to you.

- **Buying into the fairness fallacy:** Thinking that sports are supposed to be fair and equal at all times.

- **Blaming:** Holding other people responsible for your feelings; the opposite of personalizing.

- **Generalizing:** Reaching a conclusion based on a single event or outcome.

- **Fortune telling:** Believing that you know what's supposed to happen; thinking as if you're a fortune teller.

- **Results-only thinking:** Believing that your self-worth is based on your athletic achievement.

When you can identify your the two or three categories that your negative self-talk falls into, you can begin paying attention to your negative self-talk throughout your day. Journal about how you engage in this type of negative self-talk, whether at school, during practices or competitions, or in your relationships.

This heightened awareness will help you begin to change your thinking pattern. For example, you can become aware of saying "I'm just not a good hitter, and I never will be," and change it to something more positive and realistic, like "I had a bad day at the plate, but I'm a good hitter and I'll keep working at it tomorrow."

Stopping the negativity

After you've started to identify your positive and negative self-talk, the next step is to stop the negative thoughts as quickly as possible. When you notice a negative thought entering your mind, say to yourself (or even out loud if you're in a private place), "Stop!" Continue saying "Stop!" as many times as you need to in order to reduce the number of negative thoughts you have in your mind. If you tend to be a visual learner, you can visualize a bright red stop sign. The idea is to interrupt the negativity as soon as it starts.

You can also ask a coach or teammate to help you stop your negative thoughts by telling you to stop when they hear you say something negative, or when your body language looks as though you're starting to get down on yourself. All they have to do is tell you "Stop!", and you'll become aware that you had a negative thought and that you need to change it as soon as possible. If you want, you can have them replace "Stop!" with a cue word (like "Focus!") or a gesture (like a whack on the rear) that serves the same purpose.

If you want a technique that doesn't require you to actually talk to yourself out loud, you can stop negative thinking by wearing a rubber band around your wrist and simply snapping the rubber band every time you have a negative thought. This technique isn't for the faint of heart, because it actually does hurt a bit. Of course, that's the point — you want to link your physical pain to the psychological act of thinking a negative thought.

Replacing negatives with positives

It isn't enough just to stop your negative thoughts (see the preceding section). You need to replace those negative thoughts with positive alternatives. There are three simple but powerful methods to dispute and change your negative self-talk: countering, reframing, and affirming. You can use all three of these methods to replace your negative self-talk with positive self-talk.

Countering

When you find yourself saying something negative or noticing a certain thought that you have repeatedly, you need to counter it with a more rational and logical thought. This is particularly true when you find yourself engaging in one of the thought categories mentioned above. For example, your negative thought might be, "I'll never make the team." But you can counter that negative thought with the following:

What makes me think I'll never make this team? Where's the evidence that I'm not going to ever make this team, and would it hold up in a court of law?

When you catch yourself thinking negatively, you can dispute that thought by asking logical, level-headed questions. Then the negative thought becomes less powerful and loses its grip over your emotions.

Reframing

Reframing is a method of looking at a situation from a different and more positive perspective. Your parents could put one of your kindergarten finger paintings in a beautiful frame, and even if your painting doesn't suddenly look like great art, it'll look a whole lot better. The same is true in your mind — you can take a situation that may, at first, appear negative and frame it in a less dreadful or damaging manner. For example, let's say you're having trouble hitting your first serve in a tennis match. Your negative self-talk might be, "I'll never get this. I've tried and tried, but I'll never get a first serve in. I just can't do it!" You can reframe the situation like this: "I'm not hitting my serve yet, but I can get better. It's still early in the match."

Reframing is a good tool to use when you want results quickly, because you simply take your initial reaction and put a pretty frame on it, immediately improving your view of the situation.

Affirming

Affirming allows you to construct and practice positive self-talk on a habitual basis. The first step is to take some time to write out positive and affirming statements about your performance — those that make you feel better, more focused, and so on. Here are a couple examples of the kind of statement we're talking about, one from a swimmer and the other from a golfer:

- ✔ "I'm the hardest working swimmer in the 100-meter fly. Few people can match my desire. I'm successful because I out-train everyone, and when race time arrives, I feel calm because I'm prepared.

- ✔ "I stay with my process every single time I prepare to putt. I put a great stroke on the putt and then move on. I expect to make every putt. I expect myself to make long putts. My mind is clear and focused because I feel every stroke smoothly."

Make sure your statements are

- ✔ **Written in the present tense:** "I am" instead of "I will."

- ✔ **Specific:** "Make smooth strokes" instead of "play good golf."

- ✔ **Positive:** "Composed" instead of "not nervous."

After you've written your affirmations, spend a few minutes each day reading and meditating on them. You'll be surprised at the changes that occur!

Table 8-1 is an example of a self-talk log that you can adapt and/or discuss in your performance journal to become more aware of, change, and improve your own self-talk.

Table 8-1		A Self-Talk Log			
Athletic Situation	Emotions and Feelings Associated with That Athletic Situation	Your Self-Talk That Created Those Emotions	If Negative, Identify Pattern	Change Your Self-Talk to Make it More Positive Next Time	Anticipated Results and Feelings from Doing So Next Time?
Didn't start in the game	Angry, resentful, disappointed	"I got screwed!", "I'll never start!", "I should just quit."	Catastrophizing, all-or-nothing thinking	"It's just one game. Let's keep working." "When I get in, I'll make the most of it!"	Motivated, upbeat, positive, committed to success

Using Self-Talk to Improve Your Performance

When you're aware of how your thinking controls your reactions to your athletic experiences, you need to be more intentional about creating positive thought patterns over time. After all, anyone can do it for one game or one day — it takes sustained effort to create positive thought patterns over time. You'll want positive thinking and optimistic outlooks to be a part of your everyday habits.

Reducing or stopping your negative self-talk is a good first step, but it's not enough. You need to replace those negative thoughts with positive, confidence-building self-talk statements.

Just as you would when trying to get better at swinging the tennis racquet or golf club, you have to manage your self-talk more consistently in order to improve it. It takes effective practice. Establishing solid patterns and habits is very important because how you practice is how you play. In the following sections, we offer some tips for how to improve your self-talk.

Your mind is like a muscle, and just like a muscle, it has to be trained and worked out consistently. Although it may seem like a lot of work to prepare and change your negative thoughts and patterns, it takes practice to build up your endurance and ability to use these skills when needed. If you're a runner, and run only once a month to increase your endurance, you're going to be fighting an uphill battle. You need to be running at least three or four times a week if you want to build the endurance you need for races. Your mind is the same way.

Journaling before practice

Spend a couple minutes before every practice or game thinking about and writing down your commitment to positive and productive self-talk. No matter what happens in practice, make sure that you work to look on the bright side. The more you engage in positive self-talk in practice, the greater the chance it'll automatically occur in competition.

Write down three goals you have for every practice and competition you compete in. If improving your positive self-talk is one of your goals as an athlete, use this goal-setting exercise to set goals for the self-talk you use during competition. For example, one goal may be to more consistently remind yourself how hard you've worked to get to this point in your development. Or you may want to work on improving your self-talk in certain situations (for example, the last minutes of the game, or the first five minutes of the race). Or you may want to reverse your dominant negative thinking pattern. For example, if you know that you battle with perfectionism, set a goal to be more accepting of your own mistakes. Have a positive thought — such as "easy does it" — ready to go, so when you find yourself being a perfectionist, you can remind yourself to take it easy on yourself. You can even write the phrase on a piece of athletic tape wrapped around your wrist, as a constant reminder.

Write down these goals before you practice or compete, and then refer to them after you're done practicing or competing. Grade yourself on your ability to achieve your goals for that practice or competition. How well did you do? What can you do better? How will you improve next time? Evaluating your self-talk allows you to make changes quicker and develop better discipline in achieving your goals.

Coming up with cue words

Develop specific *cue words* — words that will enable you to remain focused on staying positive and optimistic, such as *focus* or *hustle*. Write down some phrases as well, to help you remain positive during practice and games. Keep them short and simple. For example, phrases like *Keep going* and *I can do it!* are great to have in your mental toolbox. Some athletes prefer *Let's go!* or *Breathe*.

Cue words can be very effective tools for improving performance because they're quick reminders that help you regain focus. They help you get right back on task after moments in which you might've lost your cool or experienced a bad break or simply lost a big point. In the heat of battle, staying mentally focused can be difficult when your emotions are surging and you feel like screaming or yelling. Cue words can help you stay calm.

Make sure to keep your cue words where you can see them. For example, write them on a piece of athletic tape wrapped around your wrist or on a piece of equipment, such as a glove, a wristband, or even your golf ball. Some athletes even write their cue words on their practice and competition clothing.

Creating a mental recovery routine

You'll make mistakes in pretty much every practice or game — that's a guarantee. So, you need to have a mental recovery routine in place so that you know what to do after you make a mistake. This routine can be as simple as using a cue word to help you bounce back from adversity (for example, you might tell yourself to relax or focus), or it can be as complicated as taking a minute between points in tennis to face the back fence, adjust your strings, and take several deep breaths. The key is to develop this routine before you need it in competition. Try using different cue words and different recovery routines in practice, and see which ones feel most comfortable (and effective) in the heat of the moment.

Journaling for performance

Performance journals can be a powerful tool in your sports psychology toolbox. As an athlete, you have so many aspects of your sport to focus on — everything from your nutrition and sleeping habits, to your training and technique. Using a journal can help you sort out the helpful from the non-helpful, and it can make a big difference in how effectively you practice and compete. Many of our clients have found that performance journals are a great way to organize their training and focus their efforts on techniques and strategies that help them compete better more consistently.

Your performance journal doesn't need to be anything fancy. A simple college-ruled spiral notebook will do. The important thing is that the journal should serve the purpose of tracking your performance statistics and observations.

After you've chosen a performance journal, be sure to use it! Here are some ways our clients have used their journals:

✔ To list daily practice goals and objectives

✔ To track opponents' strengths and weaknesses during competition

✔ To track their moods and tendencies during competition

✔ To chart strategies for an upcoming practice or competition

✔ To list positive self-talk statements to use during practice or competition

✔ To chart opponents' tendencies

✔ To note future improvements and adjustments to be made

The possibilities are endless, but the key is to use your journal in a way that helps you stay organized and on task — before, during, and after practice and competition. Start using your own version of a performance journal today, and you'll notice an improvement in your game!

Some athletes also like to have a physical action to take in combination with their cue words. For example, golfers may pick up some blades of grass and gently toss them into the wind while saying their cue words as a way to let go of the mistake. Batters may gently toss dirt after striking out, and goalies may walk away from the goal for a few seconds. Simply snapping your fingers or taking a couple of hops can help you let go. Choose an action that works for you and allows you to move on when you make a mistake.

Mental recovery routines are like parachutes — they slow things down and allow you to hit the ground gently after tough moments in competition. You need to have both a quick routine (something like a cue word) and a more comprehensive routine (taking a time out, taking a bathroom break, and so on). Your performance journal can help you track which mental recovery routines work and which ones don't, so your development in this area can be more deliberate.

Your self-talk has a direct influence on your mental performance. It can improve your confidence, focus, and composure. Here are some examples of positive self-talk statements that you can use throughout your practice and competitions as a part of your mental recovery routine:

- ✔ **When you need confidence:** "I can do it!" "I've done this hundreds of times before."

- ✔ **When you're trying to focus:** "Just this task." "Next shot." "Next play."

- ✔ **When you're trying to maintain your composure:** "Go easy." "Relax." "Deep breaths."

- ✔ **When you need to put in extra effort:** "No fear!" "Never give up!" "Keep moving!"

These aren't the only cue words or phrases. We encourage you to come up with some versions of your own.

Practicing positive imagery

Imagery (covered in greater detail in Chapter 7) can help you plan and improve on your positive thoughts. Take time to close your eyes, relax, and imagine the positive thoughts that will run through your mind while competing. Here are some good times for practicing positive imagery:

- ✔ Before practice (on your way to practice, after getting dressed in the locker room, and so on)

- ✔ After practice (while showering, getting dressed, driving home, and so on)

- ✔ Before bed (in those few moments where you're mentally winding down from your day)

- ✔ After waking (in those few moments prior to jumping into the chaos of your morning)

When you practice positive imagery to improve your self-talk, you create a template in your mind for what you want to happen in the critical moments of competition. You can practice helpful responses to emotionally challenging moments during competition. The better and more often you practice this skill, the better and more often you'll be able to use it during competition.

Chapter 9
Getting a Hold of Your Schedule

$\cdots\cdots\cdots\cdots\cdots\cdots\cdots\cdots\cdots\cdots\cdots$

In This Chapter

▶ Identifying the difference between time management and task management

▶ Clarifying your values in order to better manage your time

▶ Prioritizing your goals

▶ Making sure you're using your time effectively

▶ Holding yourself accountable

$\cdots\cdots\cdots\cdots\cdots\cdots\cdots\cdots\cdots\cdots\cdots$

Athletes aren't exactly beating down our door, dying for help with time management. We understand. At first glance, it's a dull, dry topic. After all, how many ways can you improve your time management? You just need to make a list and then start checking off the items on that list, just like your mom taught you, right?

Well, not exactly. First, managing your time isn't that easy — if it were, nobody would ever be late, miss a deadline, or feel rushed. Second, managing your time isn't as simple as making a to-do list and checking off items as you complete them. How do you know which items to put on the list? How do you know which ones need to be given top priority?

This topic may seem boring at first, but time management is actually one of the most important skills you can improve as an athlete. Many successful athletes, coaches, and business leaders use their own personal coaches to keep them on task, prioritize their endless to-do lists, and hold them accountable for accomplishing these tasks.

Accountability is key to staying on schedule. When you're accountable for how you spend your time, you'll see a dramatic improvement in reaching your goals.

In this chapter, we give you the tools you need to be in charge of your time. We start by telling you the difference between time management and task management, and explain why the latter is the way to go. Then we help you clarify your values in order to get control of your time. We outline some of the common obstacles that get in the way of task management. And we give you proven strategies for managing your time — strategies used by successful athletes, and that'll work for you, too!

Time Management versus Task Management: Recognizing the Difference

There are two schools of thought on productivity: the old-school version called *time management,* whereby you manage the hours in your day and the days in your week, using to-do lists and checklists; and the new version, popularized by people like effectiveness guru Stephen Covey, called *task management,* in which the focus is on getting the right things done, not the hours you spend engaged in doing them.

Time management: The old way

Time-management principles are based on the notion that you need to maximize how you spend your time. You have 168 hours in a week, so the key is to make sure you're spending certain amounts of time doing certain high-priority activities. So, you need to allocate hours in your week according to your priorities. If you're a student-athlete, this might mean allocating the required 20-plus hours for practice, a certain number of hours for classes and studying, and a certain number of hours for recreation on the weekends, in addition to the hours you spend sleeping and eating.

Time management is all about staying disciplined with the way you spend your time. Typical time-management schedules are made up of 15-minute, 30-minute, or 60-minute blocks of time. Days are broken up into typical eight-hour days.

The problem with a time-management approach is that you're rationing your time arbitrarily. For example, say you have a two-hour block set aside to study biology. But when you sit down to work on biology, you may end up reading only 15 pages in that two hours when, in fact, you needed to read 20 pages and answer 5 study questions. The truly important component to this objective was not the two-hour time block, but getting the 20 pages read and the 5 questions answered.

Task management: An easier way to manage your time

Task management is based on the notion that time management is inefficient and arbitrary in how time is allocated. For example, allocating two hours for practicing your putting or one hour for working out doesn't take into account how difficult or boring each activity might be for you, nor does it take into account how slowly or quickly you practice or work out.

Task management seeks to maximize output, without focusing on input. With task management, your focus is on completing important objectives rather than allocating time to complete each task. So, instead of blocking off two hours for practicing putting, you simply focus on putting until you can make seven out of ten putts from 15 feet away from the cup. If it takes only a half-hour, great! But if it takes three hours to do it correctly, that's okay, too. The goal is to get the task completed. How you do that and how long you may take to do it are irrelevant.

We think that task management is a much more effective approach than time management. When you focus on output rather than input, you won't get caught up in wasting time, because time is no longer a factor. Task management places your focus on getting things done. If you want to be a more effective athlete, we recommend you keep your focus on getting the essential tasks of high performance done — such as mastering strategy and tactics, getting in excellent physical shape, and executing sport-specific tasks to the best of your ability.

When you perform tasks is not nearly as relevant as completing your objectives is. Whether you work out at 6 a.m., 3 p.m., or 11 p.m. is irrelevant. Getting the high-priority task done is the most important thing. In the same way, hitting a more powerful serve in tennis, throwing a better slider in baseball, or feeling more confident with a wedge in your hand from 50 yards are tasks important to achieving greater skill and success. When you practice or how long you spend practicing these tasks doesn't matter — what matters is that you get them done. After you complete each task, you can move on to mastering (or simply improving) others.

Time management at work

One of Todd's clients, a first-year college student-athlete, was having trouble managing both his academics and athletics. His classes were so much more difficult than they were in high school, and the jump to collegiate athletics was challenging. He said he wasn't performing well in practice because his stress prevented him from sleeping and lowered his focus.

Todd immediately recognized that his client was more focused on his time than on his tasks. The athlete was dividing his schedule according to academics and athletics. He had his scheduled booked from 8 a.m. to 10:30 a.m. and 3:30 p.m. to 5 p.m. for athletics, with academics in between. But he hadn't put his games and travel on his schedule.

Todd helped the athlete to look at his classes from a task-management standpoint, where he needed to accomplish certain objectives each day. First, they broke down and prioritized the most important skills he needed to work on when it came to his sport. In team practices, the coaches already had established expectations, so he couldn't work on these individual skills during practice. He just knew that he needed to work on his specific skills each day to get better. So, they broke down these skills and came up with drills to practice each day.

He did some drills early in the morning before class and then stayed after practice to accomplish others.

In the classroom, he was taking two classes that required writing papers. Todd helped him break down these papers into small tasks — picking a topic, getting approval of the topic from the professor, searching the Internet for resources, going to the library to get books on the topic, making an outline, writing the introduction, writing conclusion, writing one supporting paragraph, write another supporting paragraph, and so on. *When* he accomplished these individuals tasks didn't matter — he just knew he had to get them done. He found himself accomplishing these small tasks for his papers in the oddest of times — in between classes, while eating his lunch, and while waiting for his girlfriend to come pick him up.

After setting a clear task schedule for the week, the athlete found that he was able to get the important things done. He didn't have to stay up as late at night to study, and his stress decreased. He started noticing major improvements in his performance in practices, too. His lowest grade that semester was a B, and he was seriously contending for more playing time.

Clarifying Your Values

In order for your task-management plan to be effective, you need to start by clarifying your *values*. Your values are your guiding principles in life; they determine what's important to you, what you stand for, and what you're committed to achieving. Top-level athletes are very aware of their values and what priority they hold, and you should be, too. Why? Because all your decisions — whether in sports or life — flow from them. For this reason, it's important that you understand and clarify what your own personal values are.

Here are some values that are crucial to excellence in any sport:

- ✔ Hard work
- ✔ A commitment to staying in top physical condition
- ✔ A commitment to continuous learning
- ✔ An appreciation for details
- ✔ A belief that teamwork is essential to any athlete's success
- ✔ A commitment to never giving up, no matter the situation
- ✔ A belief that talent is only one part of being a successful athlete
- ✔ A commitment to maximizing athletic strengths and minimizing athletic weaknesses
- ✔ A commitment to pursuing something you're passionate about
- ✔ A willingness to prepare and compete with integrity

If you're committed to becoming a better athlete, you can use this list of values as a good starting point. The key is to clarify your values, and to understand that they'll be your guiding principles as you seek to get the most out of your athletic talent.

Table 9-1 can help you become more aware of your values. Rate each value on a scale from 1 to 5, with 5 meaning that you hold this value as a top priority; then rate yourself in terms of how you live and behave in sports according to this value. The results will help you see what you value most and which areas of your life you may need to change in order to better live by your values. Fill in the blank lines with any values not listed here.

Table 9-1	Traditional Sport Values Inventory	
Value	*Hold This Value*	*Live This Value*
Hard work		
Continuous learning		
Fitness		
Stick-to-itiveness		
Attention to detail		
Passion		
Integrity		

Table 9-2 is about *motivational values* — values that deal with your passion, willingness, and motivation for your sport. Rate yourself again on a scale of 1 to 5. Your responses can help you identify your values — for example, maybe you're totally satisfied playing at the high school level, but you want to play a variety of sports and you don't want to compete in college. If you know that, but you see that you're still pushing yourself as if you're going for a career in the pros, you've identified a discrepancy between what you value and how you're living, and you can work to change your behavior accordingly. (Again, use the blank lines to add your own values.)

Table 9-2	Motivational Values Inventory	
Value	*Hold This Value*	*Live This Value*
Competing at the high school level		
Competing at the college level		
Competing at the professional level		
Specializing in one sport		
Competing for myself, not others		
Obtaining a college scholarship		
Training year-round for improvement		

Setting Priorities

When you're clear on your personal values (see the preceding section), you can set priorities based on those values. Why do priorities matter? Because if everything is a priority, nothing is a priority. Without ranking your priorities, you won't know which goals are more important than others, and you'll lack direction and focus.

As an athlete, there's always room for improvement. But you need to decide what specific areas you need to focus on in order to improve your athletic performance. For example, skill and fitness are both important, but you may realize at the end of the season that your less-than-ideal fitness level led to lower performance and contributed to nagging injuries. So, you might then make fitness your top priority and skill development your second priority going forward.

You'll need to be able to clarify some general categories of priorities in your life, and then rank them according to their value in your daily life. For example, here are some common categories we typically use with our athletes:

- ✔ Spirituality/religion
- ✔ Health (mental and physical)
- ✔ Family
- ✔ Friends and social life
- ✔ Money
- ✔ Career
- ✔ Athletics
- ✔ Academics

Evaluate these categories for the level of importance they play in your life. Try to rank them in order, from highest priority to lowest priority. Keep in mind, though, that the last category on your list is still important — it just isn't as important as the things that are higher up on the list.

After you rank your priorities, double-check your list for accuracy. Use simple "what if" situations. For example, say you've ranked friends above career. What if your boss asks you to work additional shifts this week, but you'd have to cancel plans with your friends to do so? Would you take on the extra shifts or not? If you'd tell your boss no, then your ranking of friends above career is accurate. But if you'd tell your boss yes and reschedule your time with your friends, then you need to put career higher up on the list than friends.

Your priorities may change at some point, which is why you need to revisit them periodically. For example, fitness may be your top priority at the beginning of the season, so that your body is ready to physically compete and withstand the beating it'll take in the months ahead. When your fitness is at a high level, you'll still maintain it, but then your priorities can shift toward skill mastery. As the season approaches, you can turn your priorities to performing as a team, executing set plays, and strategizing against certain opponents. All these areas are important, but you have to determine what your priorities are at any given point in time, and reassess them as the season progresses to make sure you're still prioritizing your goals appropriately.

Identify the one or two areas of your sport that you need to work on the most. Where will you get your greatest return on investment? For example, if you're a golfer and your wedge play really prevented you from achieving a higher level of success last season, working on your wedge play would be your top priority. Although you still have to continue working on your driver and long irons, the priority would be working on wedges. Or, let's say you're a sprinter, and you have great finishing speed, but you need to improve your starts. You'd dedicate more time and energy to your starts because you've determined it's the key to getting the greatest return on your investment.

Ask your coaches and trusted teammates to help assess your priorities. Share with them your goals and ask them where they think your priorities need to be placed to reach those goals. Getting feedback from experts is a key aspect of maximizing your training.

Adding Up the Hours You Waste

When you know what your priorities are, you need to see how your current activities match up with those priorities and how much time you waste — time you can reclaim for the things that matter to you. If you're like most people, you'll find that you're wasting time and energy pursuing activities that have little to no positive consequences on your goals.

 To get an estimate of how you're currently using your time, try this simple exercise: Start with the number 168, which is the number of hours in a week. From that number, you'll want to subtract the number of hours you spend doing the following *every week:*

- ✔ Sleeping
- ✔ Attending practice
- ✔ Attending classes or school
- ✔ Working
- ✔ Eating
- ✔ Showering and getting dressed
- ✔ Talking on the phone, texting, or e-mailing
- ✔ Watching television
- ✔ Surfing the Internet
- ✔ Playing video games
- ✔ Hanging out with friends

Add to this list anything else you can think of that you do every week. Subtract the hours you spend doing these things every week from the total number of hours in a week (168). The number you're left with is the number of hours you can't account for. Some people have 20 hours or more every week that they waste.

When you realize how much time you're wasting, you see how much more time you have to actually spend on your top priorities, so that you'll be far more effective with the time you do have.

Eliminating time wasters

Time wasters add very little value to your everyday effectiveness as an athlete. Some typical time wasters include:

- Surfing the Web
- Spending time on Facebook and other social networking sites
- Talking on the phone
- Watching TV
- Playing video games
- Hanging out with friends and family

Remember: These activities are *often* time wasters, but not always. You need balance in your life — and spending time with family and friends is part of that.

Be honest with yourself when you're trying to determine if something is a time-waster. Even though you may enjoy doing something, the extent that you do it and the degree to which it has nothing to do with your athletic goals will dictate how much of a time-waster it truly is.

Being great at something requires commitment and sacrifice. Sometimes, identifying your time-wasters is simply a matter of asking yourself how great you want to be and how important it is for you to be great.

Maintaining Accountability

A key part of task management is accountability. If you want to make sure that task management becomes a way of life, you need to set up a network of people to help support you along the way. Here's how:

- **Enlist the help of your best friends and teammates.** Tell them you're trying a new way of scheduling, and explain your new task approach. Ask them to hold you to accomplishing those daily and weekly tasks, and tell them what your self-imposed deadline is (for example, hitting 200 first serves and 200 second serves every single week). The more public you make your goals, the more likely you'll be to follow through on them.

- **Make sure you set up your schedule at the same time of day on the same day of the week.** Sundays are a natural day to do this, but you can do it whatever day works best for you. Determine which tasks you're going to do every day that week, and review them to make sure that the tasks you've set up for yourself reflect your priorities.

- **Reward yourself along the way.** If you meet three or four weekly goals in a row, go out and get that new CD you've been wanting. Don't wait until you achieve your yearly goal. Reward your efforts as you go in order to maintain momentum.

✔ **Choose a specific accountability partner to work with.** This is a dedicated person who is also trying to do that same thing you are with your task management.

✔ **Work with sports psychologist.** She can assist you in learning how to improve your process as well as hold you accountable. Sports psychologists can help you reach goals, and this is one of the ways they do so.

In order to have the best accountability, you must have clear and specific tasks. You and your accountability partners need to agree on exactly what you're going to be accountable for. A goal like "training hard" is difficult to be accountable for. Make your tasks as specific and measurable as possible so that accountability is easy. Instead of "training hard," have your task be something like "running on the treadmill four times a week at an eight-minute pace." The more specific the task, the easier it is to hold yourself accountable.

Staying on task: Why effectiveness is more important than efficiency

To understand the importance of effective task management, you need to first understand the difference between *effectiveness* and *efficiency*. *Efficiency* is the ability to get things done with the least expenditure of energy and resources. So, getting groceries, running errands, visiting the team physician, and picking up the notes from a class you missed, all in the same afternoon (instead of making four separate trips), would be efficient. You're busy and you get a lot done.

Effectiveness, on the other hand, is measured by whether you accomplish your high-priority tasks. So, a day where you had a talk with your coach about his expectations, went to class and got the review sheet for the upcoming midterm, and learned a new skill at practice would be a day in which you were effective. You may

have spent less time and effort than you did on the efficient day, but the activities you engaged in were important ones for your priorities. Contrast that with the efficient day, where you *did* many things, but some of the things you did (for example, getting groceries) weren't high-priority activities.

Being *effective* with your task management is far more important than being efficient. Make sure you don't confuse being busy with being productive. Being busy drains your energy on tasks unrelated to your goals, but being productive ensures that your energy is focused. If you follow the methods laid out in this chapter, you'll be far more effective with your task management, and, in turn, your productivity and ultimately your athletic performance will improve.

Part III
Staying Competitive: Sports Psychology in Action

The 5th Wave   By Rich Tennant

"Don't laugh — it's added 30 yards to his drive."

In this part . . .

To become a better competitor, you need to nail down a routine that leads to success — and we tell you how to do that in this part. When you develop better habits in your sport, you'll develop a reputation as an athlete who gets the job done, no matter the circumstance.

Speaking of circumstance, is any situation more stressful than the pressure-filled moments at the end of the game? This part shows you all you need to know about how to perform when the stakes are high and all eyes are on you.

In this part, we also help you master your arousal levels so that you can instantly call on your energy reserves when you need them the most.

Finally, this part addresses one of the biggest issues you'll face as an athlete: adversity. Whether the adversity you face comes in the form of an injury, a slump, or underperformance, you'll be able to bounce back — and more quickly than you've done in the past — using the strategies in this part.

Chapter 10

Winning Habits: How Routines Improve Performance in Competition

A routine is a well-planned course of thoughts and actions that enable an athlete to focus and perform better, almost automatically. When you have solid routines, you can stop thinking and just play, letting your body do what you've trained it to do. Routines eliminate distractions — whether you're an elite athlete dealing with the media or a high school athlete juggling academics.

You probably have routines that you engage in before competition, but you may never have thought about why you even have them, and you may not engage in routines before practice. In order to establish the most effective routines, you need to understand why routines are important. And you need to set routines for practices, not just games. How you practice truly is how you perform — if you don't have practice routines, you won't focus as well as you could, you won't get as much out of practice as you could, and you won't do as well in games as you could.

There is no such thing as a "good" or "bad" routine, or a "right" or "wrong" routine. Instead, some routines are simply more effective than others. In this chapter, we help you establish *effective* routines, because they help you to perform at higher levels consistently.

We start this chapter by explaining how routines improve focus and, consequently, performance. Then we outline the difference between routines and superstitions. (Here's a hint: Routines are effective, and superstitions aren't.) We give you some sample routines of elite athletes, so you can see what goes into an effective routine. Then we help you establish your own effective routines, both for practice and competition. We end the chapter by explaining when you might need to adjust your routines and tell you how to do so.

Champion habits

The greatest athletes in the world have achieved that status because of their habits. They do things differently, and more consistently, than other athletes do. Across all sports and across all levels of competition, top athletes and competitors are different. Here's how:

✔ **They're more dedicated to their sports in the off season.** Top athletes at all levels are easily distinguished by their dedication to their sports in the off season. They spend more time working out when it's not required, and they put in more time than their competitors do on skill development, regardless of their current skill level. Larry Bird used to show up at his high school gym early in the morning, hours before school started, to shoot free throws. As a star in the NBA, he also was the first one out on the court to warm up, hours before tipoff. Top athletes in every sport do the same thing. They have an insatiable need to develop their talent to the best of their abilities.

✔ **They master the fundamentals.** Even though fundamentals are typically seen as boring aspects of the sport, top athletes learn that the quickest way to success is to master the fundamentals of their sports. By mastering the basics, they improve their execution and do better statistically at the basic skills of their sports, whether it's free-throw shooting in basketball, foot spacing in basketball, or tackling form in football. The more they work on their fundamental skills, the more automatic those skills become, and the better they perform overall.

✔ **They work harder.** Supreme competitors love to work hard. Whether they're motivated by the fear of losing or the love of winning, top athletes simply put in more time and at higher levels of intensity than their competitors do.

✔ **They tolerate pain and distress better.** Working hard isn't enough for top athletes, and it frequently leads to higher levels of physical pain and discomfort. Top athletes are able to tolerate this pain and discomfort better than regular athletes. They master the art of dissociating, or focusing on external factors such as family, long-term success, or pride when things get tough.

Champions in every sport, and at every level, tolerate the pain inherent in their sport at higher levels than their competitors do. Lance Armstrong is a good example of this principle: He used his ability to push through the pain of built-up lactic acid in his legs to help him become the best and most dominating professional bicyclist of all time.

✔ **They despise losing.** An easily seen trait of champions everywhere is the obvious trait of hating to lose. Top athletes despise losing — not only at their sports, but at anything. They can't fathom that someone else can be better than they are at their sports.

✔ **They prioritize better.** Priorities make champions. Top athletes do a better job of not only setting priorities, but pursuing those priorities as well. Whereas mediocre athletes may pursue their priorities from time to time, champions show a single-mindedness that is second to none when it comes to

pursuing their priorities. Dan Gable, the greatest wrestler of all time, used to run to class in college with ankle weights on as a way of further distancing himself physically and aerobically from his opponents.

✔ **They set higher goals.** Whereas most athletes are content with being good at their sports, top athletes and world champions are not. They don't seek to win. They seek to dominate, and to do so in a fashion that leaves no doubt in anyone's mind who the better competitor is.

✔ **They pay attention to details.** Great athletes pay attention to details in many areas. They focus on diet, sleep, lifestyle, workout routines, and skill mastery. They watch film tirelessly. They spend lots of time learning about their sport, down to the minutest of details. They're always looking for any type of an edge.

Identifying How Routines Improve Focus and Performance

One of the primary roles of routines is to help you become more focused so that you can perform well in both practice and competition. Effective routines allow you to keep your mind on the tasks in front of you and not become distracted by all the irrelevant things around you.

Think of a funnel with a ball in it — the funnel represents your routines, and the ball represents your focus. At the top of the funnel is the beginning of a pre-performance routine. It includes the thoughts or behaviors you implement as you start getting ready for performance (whether that's in a practice or a game) — for example, showing up at the locker room at a certain time, beginning to listen to music on your iPod, or getting dressed in a specific manner. As the practice or competition gets closer, you engage in additional routines — for example, the way you warm up — and your focus starts to narrow. At the base of the funnel, the ball drops through the narrowest part of the funnel, and this represents practice or game time. Your focus gets narrower and narrower as practice or game time approaches. There is no veering off course. In the funnel, the ball will eventually roll into the bottom. Similarly, once you begin your routines, your focus remains where it needs to be and doesn't wander.

Here's an example: Say you're a football player, and you have two hours in the locker room before kickoff. You need to stay focused for that entire time, and your focus needs to get sharper and sharper as game time approaches. Your routines allow you to do this. The first thing you do when you arrive at the locker room is see the trainer to get taped. After taping, you take your time getting your pads on — you don't want to be rushed. Then you might put your headphones on and listen to a few songs that get you pumped up. Your team will also have a routine — such as the coach coming out about ten minutes before going on the field to go over last-minute reminders and provide a pre-game pep talk — so you need to make the team's routines part of your own. All these routines help to keep your focus where it needs to be before the game.

Without a set routine, the hours before the game would be a random series of events, and your focus would be unpredictable. You could walk into the locker room and talk with other players, hang out with trainers, or get distracted by other people in the locker room, losing sight of how close game time is. Your routines guard you against being distracted or negatively affected by distractions. Your routines prevent other things from entering your mind.

Routines don't *guarantee* that you won't get distracted, but they dramatically increase the likelihood that you'll be focused and ready for performance. At game time, your skills and fitness levels are set. The only piece of the puzzle that hasn't been determined is your mindset. Routines are the key factor in finalizing your mental readiness.

Recognizing the Difference between Routines and Superstitions

You may have heard of an athlete wearing the same socks he wore the day before if he played well, or another athlete eating the same meal before each and every meet. These behaviors may seem like routines, but they're more than likely superstitions.

So, what's the difference between routines and superstitions? Routines are consistent, not compulsive, and they're geared toward improving focus. They have nothing to do with luck. Superstitious actions are used to help athletes feel more comfortable, and they have little to do with focus. Instead, they're all about luck — a lucky pair of socks, a lucky meal.

Routines are effective and help improve focus and performance. But, if your routines start becoming *compulsive* (where you feel like you have to do everything exactly the same way, no matter what), then your center of focus is starting to shift from your athletic performance and onto your routines (see Figure 10-1). Your compulsions can become superstitions where you believe that a certain behavior must be performed in a very specific and rigid way in order for you to play well. Your focus is then entirely on the superstition, completely distracting you from mentally preparing for competition.

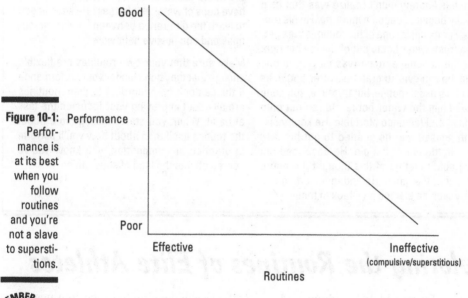

Figure 10-1: Performance is at its best when you follow routines and you're not a slave to superstitions.

Routines are helpful, flexible, and effective. Compulsions are rigid and ineffective.

Water, water everywhere, but not a drop to drink

Andrew, a professional goalie, had finally reached the top of his sport. He'd been the starter on the team for two years in a row. At the start of his third season, however, he had a few shaky games, and he knew the coaches had noticed. Andrew was determined to address all facets of his athletic performance. He came to Todd because he thought that he needed to sharpen his routines — he felt like he'd become a little lax about them lately.

But what Andrew didn't realize was that he'd actually begun to become more *rigid* in his routines. For example, one of his routines was getting a fresh water bottle out of the ice bin right after the national anthem was played. In one game, he ran over to grab his water bottle, as part of his usual routine, but this time, someone *handed* him the water bottle. He ran out onto the field and felt uncomfortable. He kept thinking to himself that he needed to get his *own* water bottle out of the bin. He described not being able to let go of this thought the entire first half of the game. He ended up letting in a goal, which he blamed on a lack of focus.

The pressure Andrew was feeling was causing him to become compulsive and superstitious and had gone beyond a routine — and it was negatively affecting his performance. Todd explained that routines are consistent. Getting fresh water before going out onto field was effective, but that routine becomes ineffective if the water has to be from the ice bin. What would he do when he was playing on the road? What if there were no ice bin? What if it wasn't the same brand of water? What if they only have cups of water, not bottles? He soon began to learn the difference between consistent routines and compulsive behaviors.

Make sure that your own routines are flexible enough that they don't hinder your performance if things don't go according to plan. Routines are all about improving your focus on the task at hand. When you start thinking more about the routine itself than about how you'll perform in practice or competition, you know you've veered off into the land of superstition.

Exploring the Routines of Elite Athletes

Every athlete is unique, and every athlete will develop her own routines. But you can learn from other athletes' routines — picking and choosing parts of those routines that you think would work for you. In this section, we give you three examples of routines from professional athletes we've worked with. Use these to get a sense of the traits of an effective routine, and feel free to modify these to make them work for you.

Example #1: First on the field

John, a professional soccer player, begins training when he leaves home in the morning. On the drive in to practice, he thinks about what he wants to accomplish during training that day. He narrows his focus to two or three key objectives so that his training is sharp and purposeful. He also arrives at least an hour before the start of training so that he has plenty of time to get taped, as well as be mentally alert.

After he's been taped and has worked with the trainer, he gets his equipment on. As he's putting on his equipment, John is thinking more about his objectives while visualizing himself accomplishing them. He spends a few minutes joking and chatting with teammates before he heads out onto the field. He goes out on the field about 15 minutes before training starts — in fact, John is usually the first player on the field. Getting out on the field early helps him to feel more relaxed and focused.

This consistent method of preparation helps him get the most out of his practices. He knows that if he practices with intensity and focus, he'll be able to perform with intensity and focus.

For games, John again arrives at the stadium early, about 90 minutes before game time. He likes to be in the locker room when there are few people there. He takes this time to start getting his equipment ready and meet with the athletic trainer.

As in practice, John is one of the first players out on the field. He likes to take his time warming up. He goes through his own personal warm-up and then has the goalie coach or backup goalie strike some balls at him from various positions and directions on the field. Then he's ready to join the rest of the team for the team warm-up.

After the team warm-up, John returns to the locker room, takes a quick shower, and gets his game uniform on. By this time, many of the other players are back in the locker room and the final team preparations are being made. John is typically one of the players who's trying to get the energy up among other players, as a way to keep his own excitement in check. He also likes to be the last one out of the locker room. He slaps the hands of every player heading out of the locker room onto the field before he leaves the locker room himself.

Example #2: Leisurely and relaxed

Lori, a professional tennis player, takes a relaxed approach to getting ready for practice. She gets up early to eat breakfast and stretch, without feeling hurried.

She likes to be mentally clear and focused on her objectives. Before she leaves for practice, she writes in her journal, addressing specific objectives she wants to accomplish in practice that day. She also make sure to discuss these objectives with her coach before training begins. Her coach discusses his own objectives, as well as the plan for how they'll accomplish these objectives. Lori is better able to relax when she and her coach are on the same page before practice.

After each practice, Lori and her coach review their objectives and evaluate their success. Lori writes in her mental training journal, highlighting and evaluating various mental strengths and weaknesses, how well she accomplished her objectives, and any other important miscellaneous notes.

Before a tournament, Lori likes to arrive at the location at least two days ahead of time, if possible. She likes to stay very close to the venue, preferably within walking distance. (She knows that she doesn't want to have to worry about traffic and getting to the venue on time.)

Lori likes to take a leisurely and relaxed approach before her first match. Two days before the first match, she does her fitness training. The day before that first match, she plays with a designated hitting partner in the morning and then does some light fitness in the afternoon. She finds out the exact time of her match and, if she can, scouts her opponent. The night before the match, she eats a healthy, nutritious dinner. She prefers to eat in her hotel and not go outside of the hotel the night before a match.

Lori gets plenty of sleep and gets up in the morning in time to eat a light breakfast and arrive at the venue well before match time. She hits with a hitting partner and then gets a stretch from her coach or massage therapist. Then she goes onto the court for her match. While waiting at the court, she has her headphones on, listening to music and blocking out all other distractions.

Example #3: Movies and meditation

A professional golfer, Kevin has been on the mini-tour for 18 months. Because he has the tendency to overthink and worry about performance, effective routines are very important. He begins his routine the day before the first day of the tournament. He gets off the golf course by 2 p.m. that day, because he knows that being relaxed is more critical than getting more practice.

The night before the tournament begins, Kevin hangs out in his hotel room. He may do a cardio workout. Then he eats dinner around 6 p.m. After dinner, he goes back to the hotel and watches a movie. This helps him relax and get his mind off of golf. Kevin is a very spiritual person, so he also spends time in prayer and meditation as part of his routine the night before the tournament begins.

On the morning of the tournament, Kevin starts with a healthy breakfast and arrives at the course at least an hour ahead of time. He doesn't want to be rushed. He has a set routine that he goes through on the range. He plays the first three holes on the course, which helps him to warm up physically as well as mentally.

Then Kevin proceeds to the short-game area to get his feel with putting and chipping from various distances. He makes sure to remain calm and centered. He goes over his mental reminders for the day and sees himself blasting his tee shot down the middle of the fairway.

Coming Up with Effective Practice and Game-Day Routines

You already have routines (whether you're aware of them or not), because you engage in certain behaviors and thoughts before practices and games. In this section, we walk you through developing effective routines. You can fine-tune your existing routines, too — you don't have to reinvent the wheel.

Routines aren't carved in stone. You'll want to evaluate your routines periodically and adjust them as you go, from one practice or competition to the next, and from one season to the next.

Practice routines

Effective practice routines can make or break your performance, no matter what your sport. But the truth is, most athletes we've worked with have no real practice routines when they first come to see us. Creating effective practice routines is something that most athletes can improve on in their performance plan. After all, how you practice is how you perform. In this section, we offer our recommendations for establishing your own practice routines.

Before practice

When it comes to establishing practice routines, there are three times you need to pay attention to: the night before, the morning of, and the hour before practice. We cover each in the following sections.

Coaches hold practices at different times of the day — morning, afternoon, evening. But regardless of what time your practice is, these time periods still apply.

The night before practice

The night before practice is when you should be focusing on

- **Technical planning:** Technical planning is all about what you'll be facing in the upcoming practice, and what you need to do to be prepared for it. For example, will you be facing a hard-hitting football practice in 85-degree heat? Or will you be facing a shorter, less-intense practice? How will you get better in the next practice? What will your mindset be?

  You don't need to call your coach to get this information — just answer the following questions:

  - Do I have all my equipment ready? Do I need to pick up, repair, or wash anything?

  - How will I get better skill-wise tomorrow? What's my purpose for practice?

  - What mindset will I have throughout practice? What can I improve on mentally?

  - Are there any potential distractions I need to address tonight?

  When you know what lies ahead, you'll have a more productive and more focused practice.

- **Nutrition:** The night before practice, you're fueling your body for the next day. As an athlete, you need a basic understanding of the necessary fuel or nutrition for your body, such as the importance of complex carbohydrates, which usually come in the form of whole-grain pastas and breads. For more information, check out *Nutrition For Dummies,* 4th Edition, by Carol Ann Rinzler.

The morning of practice

Your morning routine doesn't need to be very elaborate, but it should be consistent.

Make sure that you eat a healthy breakfast every morning. In fact, the worst thing you can do is miss breakfast, because it puts your body into starvation mode and slows your metabolism. Eating a healthy breakfast will ensure that your body has the nutrients required to meet the demands of the day, as well as the coming practice.

In addition to a healthy breakfast, your morning routine should include preparation for practice. Make sure you have all the gear you need for practice. Spend some time thinking about your objectives for practice, and write down a cue word or phrase that will remind you of them. You can also take a few minutes to visualize yourself successfully achieving your goals in practice. A little forethought goes a long way toward making sure you're ready to go come practice time.

The hour before practice

One hour before practice, hydrate your body — drink at least 8 to 16 ounces of water (more if you'll be practicing in hot weather, for a long time, or at a high level of intensity).

You may want to listen to music — either relaxing music to calm your nerves or energetic music to get you pumped up and ready to roll. Or you may want to read your performance journal (see Chapter 12) and make adjustments for the upcoming practice. If you'd rather not listen to music or review your journal, you may want to simply meditate or even hang out with your teammates. The activity you choose will depend on your personality, but the key is to choose the activity that gets you ready to perform in practice.

During practice

Just as important as pre-practice routines are those routines that you perform during practice. The purpose of in-practice routines is to help you pump yourself up, calm yourself down, or focus yourself — quickly. Here are some examples of during-practice routines:

- Practicing free throws without the basketball
- Using cue words to calm yourself during breaks in the action
- Putting from increasing lengths, starting at 2 feet and moving out to 20 feet
- Shadow wrestling
- Using mental imagery when waiting in the on-deck circle

✔ Thinking about new goals when going from drilling to playing for points

✔ Looking at cue words or objectives in your journal when there is a break in the action

✔ Pulling off to the side and taking some deep breaths when you're struggling in practice

In-practice routines need to be short and sweet — they may even be only 5 to 10 seconds in length. Just make sure that you have at least one routine to pump yourself up, one to calm yourself down, and one to get yourself focused. You should be able to use these routines at any given moment during practice to get you back into the proper emotional state to perform at your peak level.

After practice

Post-practice routines are, in our estimation, the most neglected aspect of athletic competition. Most athletes think their work is done when practice is over. But you still have some work to do, especially if you want to get a distinct edge over your competitors.

Post-practice routines have two specific purposes:

✔ To cool you down

✔ To gather and collect important information for the next practice or game

Make sure that you evaluate your objectives and your progress in accomplishing those objectives after practice. Try to do so as soon after practice as possible, when your memory is fresh. If you put it off until later, you're more likely to forget important details or skip the evaluation altogether.

Here are some things to write about in your journal after practice:

✔ Did you accomplish your objectives? Why or why not?

✔ Describe your mental game. Was it effective? Was it where you wanted to be?

✔ What are your goals for tomorrow's practice?

✔ Did you notice anything today that you need to bring up with your coach, trainer, or sports psychologist?

You may want to listen to calming music while recording your thoughts about practice in your performance journal.

Game-day routines

Establishing a game-day routine is key to performing your best. Similar to practice, there are three time periods you need to focus on: before the game, during the game, and after the game. We cover each of these in the following sections.

Routines prepare your mind and body for competition. They send a message to your brain that you've been here before and that you're comfortable and ready to go.

Before competition

Just as with your pre-practice routines, your pre-competition routines need to be set up for maximum effectiveness. Specifically, you want your routines to set your mind and body on autopilot.

Here are some common examples of what athletes may do before a game:

- ✔ Arrive at the competition site at a certain time.
- ✔ Visualize on your way to the game.
- ✔ Listen to preselected music on your iPod player in the locker room.
- ✔ Read final reminders that you've stashed in your locker or brought in your gym bag.
- ✔ Get a massage or chiropractic adjustment.
- ✔ Warm up for a set period of time in the same way before every game.
- ✔ Spend time socializing with other players.

Make a list of three to five thoughts and behaviors you believe help you get ready. There are no right or wrong answers here — your goal is to choose thoughts and behaviors that you think will be best for you. They are things you do, think, or say that help you feel ready to compete.

Your routine isn't carved in stone — you can and should adjust it over time. So don't pressure yourself to find the "perfect" routine right now. You may try some things, move on to others, and stick with still others. (For more on changing your routines, check out "Knowing When and How to Adjust Your Routines.")

During competition

You probably already use some routines during competition — maybe without even knowing it. The routines you use during competition help you focus and relax. Here are some examples of in-game routines:

- What a basketball player does before shooting a free throw
- What a soccer play does before making a free kick
- What a football player does before each and every play
- What a field-goal kicker does before going onto the field

In-game routines are habits that help you stay relaxed and focused on the task at hand.

Basketball players always have some sort of routine before shooting a free throw — taking a deep breath, dribbling a certain number of times, and then bending at the knees. A tennis player bounces the ball a certain number of times before tossing it for a serve. A baseball player may adjust his glove or take a certain number of practice swings before stepping up to the plate. Athletes have all different versions of these routines. The key is that you have a routine to help you feel focused and confident before executing a skill.

You also want to have routines when there are natural breaks in the action, such as at halftime or between quarters. You can develop certain habits to make sure that you're mentally ready when play resumes. Some athletes pull out their journals and take a quick glance to make sure they're doing what they planned. Others get a bite to eat or fuel up on sports drinks. Top athletes use this time to remind themselves to stay committed to their game plan.

After competition

If you don't have a post-game routine, you don't learn from the competition — win or lose.

You may reflect on a loss and what went wrong, but learning from wins is just as important. You need to take time to think about what made you successful so you can repeat your success the next time you compete. Plus, even if you won, you probably weren't perfect — you can still find mistakes to learn from, even in a win.

In the following sections, we give you a couple ideas for post-game routines.

Focusing on fitness

Even though athletes depend on their bodies as one of the most critical components to their success, many of them don't have a post-competition cooldown or stretching routine. You need to have some sort of a routine in which you take care of your body after a competition. After all, you've probably just pushed your body to its limits — now you need to take care of it. You can do so by stretching or getting a massage. Win or lose, treating your body right is an important post-game routine.

Journaling

After each game, write in your training journal about what you did well and what you need to improve upon based on that competition. The sooner you can do this after the game, the better, so it's fresh in your memory — shoot for journaling within one hour of the game.

Try to have some structure for your journal entries to make sure you aren't forgetting anything. Here are some questions and issues to consider:

- ✔ Make note of relevant statistics — the final score, your win/loss record, stats important to your sport.

- ✔ Did you accomplish your specific objectives? If so, what made that possible? If not, what got in the way?

- ✔ Describe your mental game. Was it effective? Was it where you wanted to be?

- ✔ Assess your mental "stats" — how relaxed you were, how focused you were, how confident you were, and so on. Determine which "stats" are most important to you and your sport, and rate them on scale of 1 to 5.

- ✔ What did you learn from today's competition?

- ✔ Did you notice anything today that you need to bring up with your coach, trainer, or sports psychologist?

- ✔ What will you do differently in the next competition?

Knowing When and How to Adjust Your Routines

In order to make your routines successful, you need to regularly measure their effectiveness. The easiest metric or method for doing that is your comfort level while competing. If you're feeling comfortable and excited to compete, your routines are serving you well. If you're feeling uncomfortable or inconsistent, then you may need to adjust your routines a bit. You also need to evaluate your routines for effectiveness. Is your performance improving? Are you competing at a higher level? If so, your routines can take some credit. If not, your routines may be one reason.

Here are some signs that you need to adjust your routines:

- You're slow to start in competitions.
- You start out too fast and tire out too quickly.
- When you make mistakes, you take a long time (or at least longer than you'd like) to recover from them.
- You feel like you're giving away points or strokes or otherwise making errors.
- You aren't happy while competing, or you're just generally dissatisfied.
- You lack motivation.

If you're having trouble telling how well you're doing, you can ask coaches, teammates, family, or friends what they're seeing. You may also want to videotape yourself and review the tapes.

If you've determined that your routines aren't as effective as they could be, you can make a change. Drastic changes to routines usually aren't necessary — they can actually do more harm than good. But simple and subtle changes can help. For example, you may want to try showing up earlier to practice or a competition to not feel so rushed, or you may want to make certain there is some structure to your time before practice or games (by journaling or listening to music, for example).

Chapter 11

Handling Pressure: Playing in the Fire without Getting Burned

In This Chapter

▶ Understanding what pressure is and where it comes from

▶ Distinguishing between pressure and arousal

▶ Exploring strategies for coping with pressure

. . . .

*Y*ou can't guarantee much when it comes to sports, but you can guarantee the presence of pressure. Whether team or individual; high school, college, or pro; sports are full of pressure, and the best athletes are the ones who perform well under it. You know the type — the quarterback who throws a game-winning touchdown with 30 seconds left in the Super Bowl; the golfer who birdies the 18th hole for a U.S. Open win; the tennis player who wins two sets in a row after being a set down to win Wimbledon. What the best athletes have in common is their ability to perform their best when the pressure is at its greatest.

Handling pressure effectively isn't something that only the pros can do. Regardless of where you are in your athletic career, you can learn to respond well under pressure, and in this chapter, we show you how. We start by explaining what pressure is and how it differs from arousal. Then we give you some simple ways to overcome pressure, regardless of the situation.

Probing into Pressure: What It Is and Why It Occurs

Pressure is simply the anxiety and nervousness you feel when faced with a certain stimulus or situation. Pressure *always* comes from within. Two people put into the same situation might respond differently — one might feel pressure where the other doesn't. That difference is what sets the great athletes apart from the good ones.

If you're experiencing and being negatively affected by pressure, *you* are the cause and *you* are the solution.

The signs of pressure

Sometimes, when you're in the thick of an experience, it can be hard to tell if you're letting the pressure of the moment get to you. Certain telltale signs indicate that you're under pressure:

- ✔ **Physical:** How your body feels. Here are some physical symptoms of pressure:

    - Shallow breathing

    - Increased heart rate

    - Increased perspiration

    - Restlessness

    - Muscle tension and tightness

    - Nausea

- ✔ **Mental:** Your thoughts. Here are some mental symptoms of pressure:

    - Inability to focus

    - Thoughts of dread, worry, and failure

    - A racing mind

    - Worrying about how others will view your performance

    - Focusing on having to perform perfectly

    - Obsessing about poor performances in the past

✔ **Emotional:** Your feelings. Here are some emotional symptoms of pressure:

- Anxiety
- Fear
- Nervousness
- Panic
- Irritation
- Stress

✔ **Behavioral:** Your actions. Here are some behavioral symptoms of pressure:

- Acting in a way that seems odd compared to your usual behavior
- Hurrying
- Fidgeting
- Having a tantrum
- Talking rapidly

The sooner you're able to recognize the signs of pressure, the sooner you can intervene and prevent them from causing problems in your performance.

If you allow the symptoms to continue, you'll need more time to get them under control. And at some point, it may be too late — you'll have made a mistake because of the pressure you were feeling.

It's a grown-up's world

Babies and children don't feel pressure. Think about a toddler learning how to walk. Her mind is focused only on the task at hand: walking. Her mind isn't clouded with fears of failure, how she compares to other toddlers, or what her parents think of her. She simply wants to walk, and she keeps trying to walk no matter how many times she falls down and no matter how long it takes.

Now, consider how an adult might learn how to do something new. The adult mind tends to overanalyze and worry about failure ("What if I can't do this?"), as well as what other people think ("What are they saying about me?"). These thoughts create pressure, which, in turn, results in physical consequences (such as muscle tension, increased heart rate, increased adrenaline release, knots in the stomach).

Next time you feel pressure, try to channel your 1-year-old self — or at least that part of yourself that didn't let pressure get in the way of accomplishment (or fun!).

What causes pressure in sports

Pressure is a part of life in general, but sports in particular can be pressure filled. You're out there, in front of a crowd, and all eyes are on you. Your coach may be yelling at you, your teammates are counting on you, and you start to feel the pressure to perform. Here are some other common causes of pressure in sports:

- Feeling overwhelmed by the demands of being the most talented player on your team
- Trying to prove yourself to a new coach or teammates
- Obsessing about whether your sports achievements will get you awards or fame
- Not wanting to let family or friends down
- Trying not to embarrass yourself in front of others, especially after a layoff from competition

Pressure can prevent you from performing at your best. Have you noticed that you perform better during practice than you do during games — scoring more goals, blocking more shots, or catching more balls? The skills you successfully use in practice are exactly the same as the ones you need to use during competition. *The only difference is in your mind.* Chances are, you don't worry about failure in practice as much as you do during a game. If those worries affect you when it comes time to perform, you're feeling the impact of pressure.

Each person experiences pressure slightly differently — not only in terms of the situations that result in pressure but also in terms of his response to it. Regardless of what causes pressure for you, one thing remains true: You have control over pressure — whether you feel it and how you manage it.

Even the world's best athletes feel pressure. Tiger Woods has said, "I always feel pressure. If you don't feel nervous, that means you don't care about how you play. I care about how I perform. I've always said the day I'm not nervous about how I'm playing is the day I quit." Hall of Fame quarterback John Elway said, "A lot of times the expectations of you are so high that no matter what you do, you are never going to live up to those expectations. So you better go out and do the best you can and enjoy it." And Olympic gymnast and gold-medal winner Shawn Johnson has said, "As for pressure, I feel it comes more from myself."

You won't feel pressure if you don't overthink the situation — though that's easier said than done. That amazing brain of yours, with all its infinite capacity to solve problems and remember events that happened decades ago, can be your biggest enemy when it comes to competing in sports. Although your brain is a handy tool in the outside world, in sports your thoughts can get in the way.

Why some athletes choke under pressure

Choking is taking a simple task and overanalyzing it to the point that your performance on that particular task suffers. It's the behavior the results from overthinking a situation. Here are some examples of choking:

- ✔ Striking out in the bottom of the ninth inning with runners on base

- ✔ Double-faulting in tennis on a crucial point

- ✔ Missing a field goal in the waning moments of a big football game

- ✔ Missing a key free throw at the end of a basketball game

- ✔ Shanking a shot off the tee in golf

Even professional athletes aren't immune to choking. History is filled with examples of athletes succumbing to pressure and choking during critical moments of competition — for example, Scott Norwood missing a 47-yard field goal in the closing second of Super Bowl XXV, Greg Normal losing a six-stroke lead during a disastrous final round in the 1996 Masters, or the New York Yankees blowing a three-game lead in the 2004 American League playoffs.

Choking is and always will be a part of athletic competition. It occurs every day in all sports and at all levels, from the professional leagues down to youth sports. If you participate in sports, you may face your own moment of choking. The better you get at dealing with pressure, however, the less likely you'll be to choke during competition.

Just about all athletes choke at some point in their athletic careers. And choking itself can lead to even more pressure. In fact, many times, managing the pressure that results from choking can be quite challenging. The next time you're on the field, your previous choke may run through your mind and lead to more pressure and another poor performance.

Understanding the Difference between Arousal and Pressure

You want to feel the heat of competition — in fact, a certain level of *arousal* (excitement) can actually improve your performance. It's only when you begin to overthink things and become too aroused (overexcited) that you start to feel *pressure,* and then your performance suffers.

Pressure negatively affects performance and is too high a state of arousal. Arousal is on a continuum — it can *positively* or *negatively* affect performance. Arousal is simply your body's physical reaction to your thoughts.

Pressure begins in the mind. It starts with a negative thought pattern about your performance and then spreads to others things — your muscles become tense, your mind races, you experience worry and fear, and so on. For example, if you think of free throws as pressure-filled situations, odds are, you're focusing your thinking on the what ifs, such as "What if I miss this shot?" and "What if I let down my team?" Some players have no difficulties making free throws, while others struggle. Basketball players who have high free-throw percentages focus on form, stroke, and body alignment. They don't think of the situations as pressure filled, so they don't experience arousal.

Arousal is the physical reaction your body experiences during competition. Various measures of arousal include breathing rate, muscle tension or tightness, heart rate, and sweat levels. Notice the difference between the starters and bench players on a basketball team — you'll see that the starters are warmed up and ready to go at the beginning of the game, whereas bench players are less pumped up. This is simply because the starters have prepared their bodies for immediate action, whereas the bench players have not.

Some physical indicators can tip you off as to whether or not you've achieved the ideal amount of arousal. Table 11-1 breaks down a number of different mental and physical states, showing how they vary depending on whether your arousal level is too low, ideal, or too high.

Being in the ideal arousal state means that you're more likely to get your best results. When you're not aroused enough, your body isn't ready to compete. An athlete in this position usually doesn't care about the upcoming competition, hasn't prepared himself well, and is generally not motivated to do well.

In the ideal arousal state, you're feeling motivated and excited, while at the same time relaxed and ready to go. You may have heard this referred to as being in "the zone."

Table 11-1	Distinguishing Low, Ideal, and High Arousal		
Physical or Mental State	*Arousal/Activation Level*		
	Too Low	*Ideal*	*Too High*
Breathing	Shallow breathing	Comfortable breathing	Hurried breathing
Muscle tension	Too relaxed	Relaxed but ready	Tight and tense
Mental state	Bored	Challenged	Fearful or scared
Motivation	Unmotivated	Motivated	Burned out
Nervousness	No butterflies in stomach	Some butterflies	Too many butterflies
Mental activity	No thoughts	Some thoughts	Racing thoughts

Too much of a good thing, and performance begins to decline. When you're too aroused, you feel too much pressure and aren't able to manage it. An athlete in this position typically feels scared, doubtful, worried, or distracted, and her muscles become tight and tense, increasing the chance of poor performance. She may sweat excessively, have a rapid heart rate and knots in her stomach, breathe shallowly and rapidly, and feel jittery, and her mind may be racing.

The arousal level that's right for you

Table 11-2 outlines the various levels of arousal, which generally apply to athletes in every sport and at all levels of competition. When you understand the principles of arousal, you can begin to learn what it feels like to be in an optimal state of arousal (as opposed to being too aroused or not enough aroused).

The ideal or optimal arousal level is slightly different for every athlete. For example, one golfer may have a very low level of optimum arousal because it helps him to stay calm and relaxed when competing in a tournament. This level of arousal works for him. But another golfer's ideal arousal level may be a bit higher, because he's a higher-energy person, is a more aggressive player, or has a more extroverted or bold personality. Both levels can be "right" for each individual — it just depends on which state is associated with more successful performance for each individual golfer.

Take another example: soccer. A defensive player may like to be really pumped up before and during the games and play a very aggressive style of defense, frequently looking for the tackle and consistently making hard, professional fouls. A guy in the midfield or on top in the striker position may play a more finesse-oriented game and appear more calm and passive when on the field. Both levels of arousal are ideal for each person in this situation. The levels of arousal are different, but they're both ideal and optimal for these athletes individually.

The key is to pay attention to your own arousal levels and how they affect your performance, and strive for the level of arousal that's ideal for *you*.

Here are some examples of athletes with varying levels of arousal:

- **Low arousal and low performance:** Dawn is an 18-year-old college soccer player who has difficulty getting excited about practice or games. She's burned out because she's played soccer for 15 years and hasn't taken many breaks from the game. She comes into practice and games most of the time feeling unmotivated and lacking the drive to be her best or to perform for her team. Her performance is usually low because her arousal level is low.

- **High arousal and low performance:** Rikard is a 12-year-old hockey goalie. He gets extremely anxious and feels tremendous pressure the night before games. He worries about letting in goals, his coach yelling at him, disappointing his teammates, and screwing up in front of others. He has difficulty sleeping, worries all day before the game, frequently has an upset stomach and shaky hands because of nerves, and even throws up once in a while before games because of the intensity of his anxiety. He plays with nervous energy, rapid heart rate, and weak leg muscles. He's exhausted at game time because of all the pressure he's been experiencing and hasn't been able to manage. His lack of focus, tight muscles, and tired body (because of pressure) cause him to let in goals that he would normally have stopped in practice. In fact, in practice, he's very talented — he just can't perform the same way in games. Pressure has created very high arousal levels for Rikard, and a resulting poor performance.

- **Ideal arousal and optimal performance:** Laura is a professional tennis player and has become aware of her ideal mental and emotional state. She describes herself as excited, positive, and focused on only the things she can control — her tennis, not her opponent's. Sometimes she gets anxious about whether she'll win, but she uses a variety of strategies to keep herself in a mental space of comfort and confidence. She believes in her ability and also is able to think about other things besides tennis. She notices that her muscles are relaxed and ready to go, her mind is clear, and she's enjoying the people around her as she gets ready to compete. She has a simple playing focus and keeps her mind and body in a place of composure, confidence, and concentration. She performs to the best of her ability and is happy with her performance. Even when she loses a match, she's thrilled that she did everything in her control — she knows her performance was great even though it didn't result in a win. She's excited about the next tournament because she's looking forward to continuing to perform well and getting better.

Handling Pressure like a Pro

In an interview, the legendary college basketball coach John Wooden was asked to describe what qualities he looked for in his players. One of the qualities he cited was poise, which he defined as the ability to "be yourself" in stressful moments during competition. What does that mean? It means being the best, most natural version of yourself, free from pressures. We couldn't agree more with Wooden's definition of *poise*. It's exactly what you need in critical or stressful moments of competition.

In this section, we give you some simple techniques that you can use to enable yourself to be more at ease during stressful competition.

Focusing on the task at hand

When you're about to compete, you can easily get caught up in the emotions of the moment. The problem is, if you let yourself get carried away by those emotions, your performance will suffer. Instead of focusing on your emotions, concentrate on the task at hand — the actual chore of your sport, such as hitting the forehand down the line in tennis or hitting the cutoff man in softball. If you think about it, you realize that there's nothing emotional about these tasks themselves, and that's why you want to keep your focus on what you need to get done.

The more you can focus on doing your job, the better your chance of succeeding. Say you have to make the last-second field goal in a football game. Instead of focusing on how happy and excited you'll be if you make the kick (or how upset you'll be if you miss), try focusing on the simple act of kicking the field goal. Focus on your steps, your breathing, your pre-kick preparation and targeting, and your follow-through.

Being prepared, in every way

The more prepared you are, the less likely you are to feel pressure. You can get prepared mentally, technically, and physically — and help keep pressure at bay.

Mental preparation

Have a mental game plan for every practice and competition. A *game plan* is simply a strategy for playing your best mentally. Write your plan in a note-book, and track your game plan over time. Understand your strengths as a competitor, and plan to use those strengths during the competition. (For more information on how to identify your strengths and put them to good use, check out Chapter 3.)

Practice using imagery (see Chapter 7) to reduce the feeling of pressure. Finally, work on improving your goal setting (see Chapter 3).

Technical preparation

A great way to reduce pressure is to ensure that your skills are sharp. The more confident you are in your skills, the less pressure you'll feel. Confident athletes simply perform better. By putting more time into your skill development, you'll increase your ability to perform that skill successfully when it matters most.

Physical preparation

Keep yourself in top physical shape, so that you don't need to worry about your body letting you down. The more you can trust your body to perform as needed in competition, the more confident you'll be during competition.

Being physically fit — with a combination of cardio and strength training — is important for all sports, but the balance of these two types of fitness depends on your sport. If you're involved in a sport that requires a lot of running (such as track, cross country, soccer, or basketball), you'll want to put more emphasis on cardio training. If you compete in a power sport (such as football, rugby, lacrosse, or weight lifting), then more lifting and strength training is necessary. Work with a physical trainer or coach who knows your sport so you can maximize your physical fitness for the task at hand.

Nontraditional physical training approaches — including yoga, Pilates, and spinning — have been found to improve fitness as well, because they work to increase your flexibility and strengthen your core muscles (midsection) and stabilizer muscles (the little muscles that help out the bigger ones).

It's not all in your head

Todd worked with a talented high school quarterback who wanted to increase his confidence and leadership on the field. At the time, he was a freshman and he wanted to play quarterback at the college level. He came to Todd because he thought working with a sports psychologist would help him build confidence. But during the initial consultation, he expressed self-doubts about his physical stature, arm strength, speed, and even a slight twinge of pain in his throwing shoulder.

Todd recognized right away that the athlete needed to believe in his physical body before he could do anything with mental training. Todd could've taught him mental skills to help improve confidence, but as long as the athlete didn't trust and believe in his body, he would still fold under the weight of pressure. Todd told the young quarterback that he would need to work with a strength and conditioning coach for a minimum of three months, as well

as seek medical attention regarding his shoulder, before Todd could work with him. This increased physical training would increase the athlete's confidence and, as a result, his ability to manage pressure.

The athlete did what Todd suggested and came back after four months. The difference was amazing — he felt confident and strong, and he believed in his body. He told Todd how he also tended to his shoulder and found out it was only a minor injury. He described how much confidence he had gained in the past four months — all without any help from Todd! His attitude was exhilarating and he was excited about the next season — he knew he would make an impact because of his increased confidence. He had taken a huge step in managing pressure — believing in his body. He went on to have the best summer conditioning and preseason of his life and he's on track to play at the college level.

Don't forget about nutrition and sleep — they're key to maintaining good fitness. If your body isn't fueled correctly or properly rested, your concentration and ability to manage pressure drops, because you won't have the energy to meet the demands of competition. Even if you know the latest mental-training techniques, if you don't have the actual physical and mental stamina, these techniques won't matter much.

When the body tires, the mind follows. Being confident is difficult when your body is tired or worn down, or when your physical energy is low. When you believe in and know that your body can endure all the physical pain and stamina that competition requires, you'll be more confident and less affected by pressure.

Make sure to take care of injuries immediately. Small muscle pulls can lead to larger long-term injuries if not treated.

ANECDOTE

Failure is unavoidable

Sometimes gaining perspective and understanding that failure is part of the game will enable you to perform better. Ben, a lacrosse goalie at a major Division I school, was hobbled by a fear of failure. He obsessed over being scored on in practice and in games, worrying that the goals he let through would cause his team to lose. Ben's constant focus on failure meant that he was always under pressure — and as a result, his muscles were tight and he performed at a much lower level than he was capable of.

Ben needed perspective: The best lacrosse goalies fail 40 percent of the time. Perfection doesn't exist for a lacrosse goalie. After he gained perspective and realized that failure is unavoidable — not only in lacrosse but in life — he was able to let go of his fear. He became more relaxed between the pipes, more focused, and he eventually went on to become an all-American, improving his save percentage by almost 10 percent!

Getting perspective

REMEMBER

Sport supports life — not the other way around. If you can remember that, you'll be able to deal with setbacks, successes, and failures, and you'll improve your ability to relax and enjoy each moment. Even though, in the moment, sports can mean everything to you, it's only *part* of your life — and it's never life and death. As Irv Blitzer from the Jamaican bobsled team said, "A gold medal is a wonderful thing, but if you're not enough without it, you'll never be enough with it."

If you're experiencing too much pressure prior to competition, ask yourself, "What's the worst-case scenario, and can I deal with it?" Usually the worst-case scenario is a loss or a failure, and you've dealt with both many times before in your life, which means you can deal with them again.

Changing your self-talk

Most of the time, when you experience pressure, it'll be due, at least in part, to poor self-talk. You may notice yourself saying things like "I'd better not screw up" or "What if I fail?" or "What if I let down my team?" or "What if I don't get a college scholarship?" This type of self-talk creates pressure and anxiety.

The first step to changing your self-talk is to become aware of what you're saying to yourself. Most of the time, you aren't even aware of your self-talk because it happens so quickly. All you feel is the anxiety and pressure and have no idea how it got there.

Here are some examples of negative self-talk and the resulting emotions:

Negative Self-Talk	*Result*
"I have to win!"	Anxiety
"What if I screw up?"	Worry

Productive self-talk, on the other hand, results in positive emotions — emotions that help you to perform better, such as excitement or relaxation. Here are some examples of productive self-talk:

Productive Self-Talk	*Result*
"I'm going to give it my best."	Poise, relaxation
"I can do this."	Focus, composure

Make sure you understand how your self-talk creates your emotional state. When it's negative, it creates a negative emotional state. When it's productive, it creates a positive emotional state. When your self-talk is productive, you can stay in your ideal arousal zone, which is where your best performances occur.

For much more on self-talk and ways to improve yours, turn to Chapter 8.

Understanding what you have control over

One of the causes of pressure is thinking about things over which you have no control. When you put your focus on uncontrollable factors, you experience pressure and, in turn, poor performance. Here are just some of the things over which you have no control:

- ✔ What others will think about your performance
- ✔ How much game time you'll get
- ✔ Whether you'll win
- ✔ How the fans or your parents will react
- ✔ Whether you'll make the team
- ✔ Whether you'll get a scholarship

Winning and losing are out of your control, but your individual performance isn't.

When you focus on the things you can control, you'll be poised and relaxed. Here are some of the things you have control over:

- ✔ How much you prepare
- ✔ How much you practice
- ✔ How much sleep you get
- ✔ Your diet
- ✔ How you warm up
- ✔ Your attitude
- ✔ Your mental preparation

Before competitions, make a list of the things you have control over and then focus only on these things.

Just because you can't worry about winning doesn't mean that you can't set a goal of winning. You just have to remember that you'll have the greatest chance of winning when you focus on the things you can control instead.

Journaling

Another great way to manage pressure is to write in a journal about your thoughts and feelings. Whenever you feel pressure, acknowledge and address it. You need to figure out where the pressure came from, and in what situations you feel it most intensely. Sometimes, journaling is all it takes to reduce pressure during competition.

Many athletes feel that talking or writing about their fears and anxieties is a sign of weakness. Nothing could not be further from the truth. Don't believe us? Try bottling up your thoughts and feelings for a while, and see how well you perform.

When you're feeling pressure, write all your thoughts and feelings down on paper. A good time to do this is just before competition and immediately after competition. Writing things down helps you in two ways:

- ✔ It gets the thoughts out of your head.
- ✔ It helps you analyze pressure more objectively after the fact.

The night before you compete, write down anything and everything on your mind that has nothing to do with your upcoming competition. You may have negative thoughts and worries, or you may be thinking about other things outside of your sport. Write them down, and then take a minute to rip up that piece of paper and throw the scraps in the recycling bin. This is a nice way to empty your mind of distracting or unhelpful thoughts as you're preparing for competition.

If writing is hard for you, try calling a friend, family member, coach, teammate, or someone you trust and talk to that person about your thoughts and feelings. This conversation can help you see the flaws in your thinking and help get you back to competing well.

Breathing and stretching

You can tell that you're succumbing to pressure by paying attention to your body and the signals it sends you. Earlier in this chapter, we list the signs of pressure. If you spot any of those signals, you can employ some simple breathing and stretching techniques to regain control and composure, which we cover in the following sections.

Hook me up!

Neurofeedback or biofeedback instruments use electrodes (placed on the head and chest) to monitor things like heart rate, respiration, and sweat levels on the surface of your skin. This area of sports psychology is becoming more popular when it comes to performance measurement. These instruments help athletes see and hear their own bodies and how they're reacting at any given moment, as well as learn to control their bodies.

For example, an athlete might wear a heart rate monitor and see his heart rate on the computer. He can then learn to control his heart rate — breathe heavier to increase heart rate and breathe slower to slow his heart rate. If you're interested in how these tools can help you, consult a sports psychologist.

Breathing

If your breathing is shallow or too fast, simply stop and take a deep, slow, cleansing breath. Take deep breaths throughout competition, not just when you're feeling pressure. Deep, cleansing breaths prevent the buildup of pressure. They help you get into your ideal mental state.

Pay attention to successful pitchers before they throw — you'll see them take a deep breath. Watch basketball players before they take free throws — yep, they take a deep breath. Golfers take a deep breath as part of their pre-shot routine. Coincidence? Not at all.

Brandon is a golfer on the Nationwide Tour who has made breathing a part of his pre-shot routine. When he's behind the ball picking out his target, he takes a deep breath to relax his body. He does this on every shot. When the pressure builds, such as when he has to make a birdie or is in a position to win, Brandon not only continues his deep breathing as part of his pre-shot routine, but he also breathes more deeply when he's walking between his shots.

Stretching

If your muscles are tighter than usual because of pressure, try stretching. When you stretch your muscles, you're automatically helping them relax by expending nervous physical energy. Your muscles need to be relaxed in order for you to perform your best. All athletes experience muscle tension and tightness, but you can reduce and/or eliminate it by stretching.

Golfers take practice swings to stretch their muscles and loosen tension. Baseball or softball hitters take practice swings and move around in the batter's box to eliminate jitters. Volleyball players stretch their arms and roll their shoulders before they serve.

Chapter 12

Staying Strong: The Importance of Managing Energy Levels

. . . .

In This Chapter

▶ Avoiding drains on energy

▶ Keeping track of your energy levels

▶ Using your energy levels to your advantage

. . . .

*I*f you want to reach your athletic potential, you have to learn what all professional athletes already know: how to manage your physical and mental energy levels during competition. You have only a finite amount of energy, so you need to know when to conserve it and when to expend it.

Managing the link between your mind and your physical body is the key to consistently competing at a high level. You won't always be on top of your game in every competition: Some days you won't feel your best, and your available energy will be lower than usual. On these days, you have to manage your physical output more carefully than you would normally. Other days you'll feel terrific, and your available energy will be high. You'll have more wiggle room when it comes to your energy output (but you'll still want to maximize your use of energy).

The key to learning how to manage your energy levels is to eliminate guesswork. The better able you are to quantify your energy levels and the amount of physical and mental energy you're using during competition, the more likely you'll be to track and adjust your energy output to your advantage.

We start this chapter by giving you a road map of all the pitfalls you want to avoid — all the things that drain your energy. When you eliminate the negative, you can focus on the positive — the ways to maximize your energy during competition so you get the results you want.

After we outline common drains on energy, we show you how to track your energy levels and explain why tracking is important. Then we fill you in on how to manage your energy levels during competition.

We end this chapter by telling you how to pump yourself up and, at the same time, stay relaxed during competition. Energy management isn't about bouncing off the walls like a kid who's had too much candy — it's about using energy effectively, which includes staying relaxed so that your energy isn't being wasted.

Hook me up!

A more recent advancement in sports psychology has been in the fields of biofeedback and neurofeedback. Even though biofeedback and neurofeedback tools and approaches have been used for many years, their popularity started growing back in the 1960s. Biofeedback focuses more on bodily responses, such as heart rate and breathing patterns, and neurofeedback places its attention more on brainwave patterns. These tools are often used together and have the same ultimate goal: to help people be able to be more aware of and control their mental, physical, and emotional internal responses.

The use of biofeedback and neurofeedback has grown in the last couple of decades in many areas, especially with athletes trying to find their "zone" and other ideal states of arousal. These approaches have also been helpful in treating various medical conditions, such as Attention-Deficit Hyperactivity Disorder (ADHD), reducing blood pressure, treating migraine headaches, and improving recovery time from injury. In the most recent winter Olympics, Canada's "Own the Podium" rallying cry and program including using both biofeedback and neurofeedback technology to help their athletes mentally prepare for competition. The professional soccer team A.C. Milan considered biofeedback- and neurofeedback-type technologies a secret weapon that helped them defeat Manchester United 3-0 and win the Champions League Football final in May 2007 in Athens, Greece. Numerous professional and Olympic athletes are using this technology, including Major League Baseball players, professional golfers, professional tennis players, and professional soccer players.

The basic goal of biofeedback and neurofeedback training is to help athletes achieve their optimum level of arousal for the wide variety of situations they'll encounter during athletic competition — in other words, to achieve peak performance states and gain more frequent control of and access to the "zone." Biofeedback and neurofeedback are also measurable means of helping athletes keep their physical energy levels where they want them to be. They're excellent tools for athletes to become more aware of and control their own stress responses to pressure-filled situations. Athletes can use these tools to help remain more centered and calm when the pressure is on, such as when a soccer player has to make a free kick in the penalty box to win the game or when a relief pitcher comes in in the later innings with the bases loaded trying to end the inning.

Here's how it works: Athletes have electrodes attached to their heads to measure and monitor their brain-wave activity. This information is fed to a computer for tracking. As this is taking place, the athlete begins to learn to control her brain activity, focus, concentration, and physiological responses to what she's seeing (say, for example, on a video game in front of her). In order for the athlete to "win" the video game, she has to learn to control her breathing and heart rate, and remain calmly focused on the objective of the game. Another example involves having electrodes attached that measure skin temperature and heart rate while the athlete is watching the monitor in front of him. The athlete learns to slow his heart rate down and see the visual graph and audible sounds slow down before his eyes. As he practices this type of training, he becomes measurably better at being more aware of his physical and emotional responses and then being able to keep them where he wants them to be, regardless of the external circumstances in which he finds himself.

More and more sports psychologists are seeking training in this emerging field. Keep in mind that biofeedback and neurofeedback, like other techniques, are not a quick fix or a one-time-visit sort of solution. Depending on your current abilities to manage your energy and arousal levels, they may require many sessions to help. But they're a great resource for athletes wanting to learn to control their anxiety and energy levels and try to achieve their ideal mental and emotional states more consistently.

Eliminating Energy Wasters

When you're driving, your car gets better gas mileage when your tires are properly filled with air and you drive on a smooth, freshly paved highway (rather than a pothole-filled one). The same basic principle applies to energy management: If you take care of yourself and avoid the potholes (or pitfalls) on the road of competition, you won't use as much energy, and you can devote that energy to your athletic performance.

At an athletic event, you have to regulate your energy levels and make sure you always have a maximum amount of energy available. You never know when the weather conditions are going to drain your energy. Maybe the match will be delayed and you'll have to wait to get back on the court. Or maybe the game will go into overtime. You need to make sure you're storing up your energy so it's available when you need it.

In this section, we outline three key ways that athletes waste energy, so you can avoid doing these things yourself.

Negative self-talk

Negative self-talk is one of the more common ways that competitive athletes waste energy. Too often, fleeting moments of negativity turn into longer periods of negativity. Left unchecked, negative thinking can extend throughout an entire competition. Think about that: In a tennis match, that could mean well over *two hours* of relentless negativity!

You may be calm on the outside, but if you're thinking negatively on the inside, your energy is being depleted. Negative thoughts result in negative feelings and emotions, which drain your energy. So a thought such as "I'll never win today" causes you to feel hopeless, and "What if I let down my coach?" creates anxiety and worry. These negative emotions are a tremendous drain on your physical energy.

If you notice that you're starting to engage in negative self-talk, work to turn that around — immediately! Turn to Chapter 8 for specific strategies for reversing negative self-talk.

Emotional excess

The problem with getting too emotional is that it affects your behavior. The more emotional you get, the more energy you'll expend, and the more quickly you'll tire out, which will affect your performance.

Anytime you get too emotional (even if the emotions are positive), you drain energy. The goal is to keep your emotions in check and within an effective range. You need to be emotional enough, but not too emotional.

You really can have too much of a good thing. Some athletes get so excited the night before a competition that they don't sleep well and deplete energy because of their amped-up anticipation.

If you're overly emotional and those emotions are positive ones, you can calm yourself in different ways. For example, you can use self-talk (see Chapter 8) or try some strategies for managing pressure (see Chapter 11). You can use a journal to record your thoughts, or you can spend some time meditating quietly. Simple breathing and stretching are also effective ways to calm yourself.

Most of the time, getting too emotional involves negative emotions, such as anger, frustration, fear, worry, or resentment. Every time you let your negative emotions go too far, you're draining energy — energy that you may need later in the game or even the next day.

Even the best athletes in the world make mistakes, every single time they step out on the field, court, or track. The mistakes you make as an athlete are not nearly as relevant as what you *do* with your mistakes. (If you feel you're always having trouble bouncing back from mistakes, turn to Chapter 13 for a more thorough discussion on the topic.)

Allowing your emotions to get out of control will ultimately destroy you — it will hurt your own performance and may even cause you to let down your team.

We always teach our athletes to embrace and accept feelings — even negative ones such as worry or fear. When you can accept that you're worried or scared, you won't experience the tension that comes from trying to fight off those emotions. You simply experience them, and move on.

Todd has worked with a top Major League Soccer goalie for the past seven years. We'll call him Sam. In one of the games at Sam's former team's stadium, he was amped and ready to go — too amped! Not only did Sam expend a ton of energy worrying about beating his old team (instead of just focusing on his job), but he also let in two goals and then became extremely emotional and angry. Todd could see how out of control Sam's emotions were after the goals were scored. Sam yelled at himself, yelled at his defenders, and stomped around in the goal. Sam's team did come back and score two goals to tie the game, but he was fortunate that he didn't let in another goal. Sam needed to manage his emotions — they had hurt his focus and drained his energy.

Lack of preparation

If you aren't prepared for competition, you'll find that you expend far more energy than you would've otherwise. Lack of preparation drains more energy than you may think. When you're fully and completely prepared, you feel confident, excited, and ready to go. On the other hand, when you haven't prepared adequately, there is a subtle yet constant energy drain that results from a nagging worry about how you'll perform. Your confidence is lower and your worry and anxiety are higher.

Worry is like a dripping faucet — it may not feel like much but, over time, it adds up. Instead of worrying about your lack of preparation, spend more of your energy just preparing. You'll build up the energy reserves you need to succeed.

To be prepared, you have to recognize your strengths and weaknesses. You can maximize your preparation by assessing and evaluating yourself in the following areas at least once a week. If you're preparing well in all these realms, you'll be ready to perform.

- ✔ **Physical:** Physical preparation includes being fit, getting enough sleep, eating a healthy diet, getting enough water, and being properly conditioned.

- ✔ **Skill:** Skill preparation includes paying attention to technique and your execution of the athletic skills needed in your sport.

- ✔ **Strategy:** Preparing strategically includes planning, having a game plan, and knowing your role on the team.

- ✔ **Mental:** Mental preparation includes using imagery (see Chapter 7) and positive affirmations (see Chapter 8).

- ✔ **Personal:** Personal preparation is everything outside of your sport — making sure you've done your schoolwork, met your work obligations, addressed any issues in your personal relationships, and so on.

Tracking Your Energy Levels

The first step to using energy effectively is to track your energy levels over time. Then you can make any necessary changes in diet, training, strategy, and tactics as you go, and you'll have a way to measure how effective those changes have been. This, in turn, will improve your ability to compete at a higher level.

After you make changes in your behaviors — like getting more sleep or changing your diet — allow your body at least a month before you see significant changes in your energy levels.

Tracking your energy levels doesn't need to be a scientific process. In fact, the simpler the better — that way, you won't have an excuse not to do it. A simple way to track your energy levels is to rate them on a scale from 1 to 5, with 1 being the low end of energy output available and 5 being the high end. A typical scale looks something like this:

1	Exhausted; unable to compete
2	Tired
3	Somewhat tired
4	Energized
5	Brimming with energy; ready to go

You can adjust this scale as you like. The important thing is to assign numbers to your energy levels, using the same scale every time.

In the following sections, we cover the key times when you should track your energy levels.

During practice

If your energy levels are low in practice, they aren't likely to be much different during competition. Make sure you're tracking your energy levels throughout the week so that you're tuned in to your body.

You don't want to peak too early, with too much energy during practice. Many great athletes say that they "chill and keep it real" during the week so that they're ready to go when it comes to game time.

Before competition

Prior to competing, rate your energy levels in a journal. Note your energy levels on a scale from 1 to 5, and include any notes you want to make about diet, preparation, health, and so on.

Managing energy levels in the hours before a competition is important. Many athletes get too excited and drain their energy levels needlessly just before they compete. You want to peak on the field, not in the locker room.

You can improve your pre-competition energy management with proper and effective routines (see Chapter 10).

During competition

During most competitions, you won't be able to pull out your journal and note your energy levels — at least not without getting a penalty or odd stares from your opponents and spectators! But you can make a mental note of where your energy levels are at breaks in the competition. Then, as soon as the competition is over, write down your assessments in your journal.

Monitoring your energy levels during competition is critical. Many athletes aren't aware of what's happening with their energy until after the competition is over. But if you monitor your energy during the game, you can modify your behavior to your advantage.

For example, Leif was working with a tennis player who lost a difficult first set with a higher-ranked opponent. On the change-over, she was feeling frustrated and a bit tired from overexertion. She decided to take a bathroom break, and during that break she checked her energy levels and realized that she was expending far too much energy at this point in the match. To refresh herself, she changed clothes and decided to change her mental focus as well. She had been viewing the match as a sprint, but she changed her outlook and started viewing the match as a marathon. She went back out for the second set and played in a more relaxed and controlled manner, conserving valuable energy and eventually winning the match in three sets.

Here are some signs that your energy levels may not be at their best:

- ✔ You're not performing particularly well.

- ✔ You get a penalty or foul and become too emotional.

- ✔ You make a mistake and can't let it go.

- ✔ You get angry (for any reason) and the anger lasts more than a few seconds.

- ✔ You aren't into the game.

When you track your energy level during competitions, make a note of your performance as well. For example, if you're a basketball player, you might note an energy level of 3 and then note that you had six points, three rebounds, and three turnovers. Over time, you'll be able to see how your performance is affected by your energy.

Managing Your Energy Levels

With the information you gain in tracking your energy levels (see the previous section), you can start managing your energy. That puts you in control of the energy reserve you draw upon in practice and competition — which is key to your success.

In this section, we fill you in on specific strategies for managing your energy, starting with identifying your ideal competitive state.

Identifying your ideal competitive state

An important part of managing your energy level is knowing how much energy you need to compete at your best. To improve your awareness of your ideal competitive state, use as many of the following methods as possible:

- ✓ **Written journals:** Many top athletes use journals in competition to note important details that they want to track, and energy is one of those. You can do the same, and it doesn't have to be scientific. Simply write down how you felt during competition. You can answer questions such as, "How prepared did I feel physically?" or "How did my body feel?"

- ✓ **Written charting:** Written charting is simply using number scales to track your energy level. You can create a simple chart and use that as your daily assessment tool, adjusting it as needed.

- ✓ **Video tracking:** Video doesn't lie. You can use videos of yourself competing to analyze how strong you looked physically, how tired you looked during crucial moments, and so on.

One way to get more in tune with your ideal energy level is to think back to times when your energy was at its best. Take some time to write in your journal about three to five competitions where your energy levels were where you'd like them to be. Be as specific as possible. Think and write about what made these energy levels possible: Your sleep habits? Your diet? Your mental preparation? Solid routines? You can use these experiences as a baseline for what you're trying to achieve.

If you want to learn about ideal energy levels, study great athletes. Many athletes have blogs and Web sites where they talk about how they train and perform. Take advantage of this information and apply it to your own life. You don't have to emulate a high-profile athlete — you can learn from any great high school or college athlete. Find out what successful athletes are doing to achieve optimal energy levels, and bring what you learn into your own training and performances.

Pumping yourself up

Energy management has two important aspects: the ability to pump yourself up, and the ability to relax. When you know how to do both, you'll be able to adjust to any situation, with the energy you need. In this section, we give you strategies for pumping yourself up.

Listening to music to get psyched

Almost every athlete has, at some time, used music as a way to get ready for a big game or competition. Music is a powerful tool to enhance emotions, and you can use it to your advantage.

Here are some tips for using music to get pumped for competition:

- **Personalize your music choices.** What motivates others may not motivate you. So, make sure you pick music that gets you going and gets your heart rate up.

- **Keep in mind that music doesn't have to be loud and obnoxious to motivate.** We've worked with top athletes who get pumped up to country music or The Beach Boys. The key is to know what motivates *you*.

- **Keep a library of potentially motivating music choices on hand so that you can pick and choose on any given day.** Having a diverse collection of songs that motivate you will allow you greater flexibility in your pregame routine.

Getting your heart rate up

The most important indicators of being pumped up and ready to do battle in the athletic arena are heart rate and sweat levels. Some people naturally sweat more than others, so the easier of the two to gauge is heart rate. Increased heart rate means that you're pumping blood through your body faster, and your muscles have more oxygen available to them, thus increasing their responsiveness. Your body is ready to go — ready to do what it's been trained to do.

There are numerous ways to get your heart rate up. Here are a few:

- **Breathing:** Pick up the tempo of your breathing, and your heart rate will increase. Be sure to keep your breathing in control — you don't want to hyperventilate — but get it going and see how your energy rises as well.

- **Using high-energy images and verbal cues.** Certain images and verbal cues can help to raise intensity and energy. For example, think of a speeding train, a jaguar stalking and pouncing on its prey, the best athlete in your sport performing, or one of your own best performances from the past. Phrases such as "Get it done!", "Just do it!", or "No pain, no gain!" can do the same. Find the words and images that work for *you*. There are no right or wrong images or cues — just effective and ineffective ones.

✔ **Using the environment around you:** Many athletes feed off the excitement of the crowd and the fact that they're being observed by others. If you've ever had the opportunity to play in front of a large audience of cheering fans, you know that it's a serious rush and can get your energy up. If you're having difficulty energizing yourself, go out onto the field in front of fans and spectators — they can help you get your mojo back.

✔ **Picking up the tempo:** Pick up the pace of your pre-competition warm-up. Run a couple extra sprints or treat your warm-up more like circuit training and move quickly from one activity to another. Sprint to the locker room to get your heart rate up.

✔ **Watching motivational movies:** Numerous sport- and non-sport-related movies can get you pumped up. The day or night before a competition, watch a movie that gets you amped up to compete.

Competitive relaxation: Relaxing while kicking butt

In addition to knowing how to pump yourself up (see the previous section), you need to learn the art of relaxation. Just as you need to know how to amp yourself up for the rigors of competition, you also need to know how to calm yourself down in the heat of the battle. In this section, we offer several methods for relaxation. Use whichever approaches work best for you and your situation.

Breathing deeply

Breathing is the gateway to relaxation. It also can enhance performance by increasing oxygen levels in your blood, thereby making more energy available in your muscles.

When you start feeling stressed out as an athlete, your breathing becomes more shallow and rapid. Some athletes even hold their breath for long periods. Shallow breathing and holding your breath cause increased muscle tension, and increased muscle tension decreases performance. So, learning the art of deep breathing is critical.

Breathing deeply, in a controlled manner, is a central aspect to all physical relaxation exercises. The key is to make it deliberate. Take 30 seconds during a game or competition to take three slow, deep breaths. You'll know you're breathing correctly if you feel your lower abdomen fill first (like a balloon filling with air), and then your chest. Take at least twice as long to expel the air as you did to inhale it. Make an audible exhalation sound, which can serve as a signal for tension leaving the body. These three breaths will relax you physically, as well as focus your mind for competition.

Make deliberate breathing a part of your everyday performance and routine. Successful athletes make deep breathing as automatic as taking a shower and eating — they don't even think about it. Baseball and softball pitchers regularly take deep, cleansing breaths before each pitch. They do this automatically because it helps them relax their muscles, calm themselves, and be able to maximize their athletic movement. Golfers take deep breaths as part of their pre-shot routines, and tennis players do so before serving. In the short term, these breaths relax the muscles and allow for optimal muscle movement; in the long term, they allow athletes to conserve energy for the entire competition.

Reducing muscle tension

Reducing muscle tension improves performance, no matter what sport you're participating in. A nervous mind can't reside within a physically relaxed body, and one of the most effective ways to make sure you have a physically relaxed body is to use a technique called *progressive muscle relaxation*.

Engaging in a progressive, deliberate series of contractions and then relaxations of the major muscle groups of the body will reduce the amount of muscle tension present. These exercises teach you how to better recognize the levels of tension that are present in your body at any given moment. If you can recognize tension in your muscles before the tension builds up to harmful levels, you'll improve your ability to compete to the best of your natural ability. It's that simple.

To engage in progressive muscle relaxation, you need to set aside five to ten minutes. You can do it seated or lying down. The technique is very simple: Start at the head, and successively contract each major muscle group at three levels, for approximately 5 seconds each:

- **100 percent contraction:** At 100 percent, contract the muscle groups as hard and as tightly as possible. A good way to evaluate if you're doing so is to notice if your muscles are shaking. If they are, you're at 100 percent contraction.

- **50 percent contraction:** The 50 percent level is a bit harder to recognize, but you want to cut your muscle tension level in half.

- **0 percent contraction:** Breathe out loudly when you reach the 0 percent level, and imagine that all the tension is leaving your body at that moment.

Here are some suggestions for how to contract each of the muscles:

- **Trapezius, or traps (the muscles that make your shoulders shrug):** Try to touch your shoulders to your ears, and hold them there in the contracted position.

- **Biceps:** Pretend that you're flexing for a magazine picture, or that you're showing off for your girlfriend or boyfriend.

- **Triceps:** Straighten your arms out in front of you, turning the outside of your hands inward, toward each other.

- **Pectorals (chest muscles):** Imagine yourself flexing for a magazine picture, and cross one arm over the other in front of you, forming an X.

- **Abdominals (stomach muscles):** Imagine flexing your stomach as if a friend were about to playfully punch you in the stomach.

- **Glutes (butt muscles):** Imaging trying to hold a quarter between your butt cheeks.

- **Quadriceps (the muscles at the front of your thighs):** Straighten your legs and squeeze.

- **Hamstrings (the muscles at the back of your thighs):** When seated, dig your heels into the ground and hold it.

- **Calves:** When seated, get on your tippy-toes, and hold that position. When lying down, point your toes forward, away from you or directly up toward your head.

- **Fists:** Imagine trying to crack a walnut in your palm.

Progressive muscle relaxation is one of the best ways to treat a clinical condition called panic disorder, which is a disorder in which an individual suffers debilitating panic attacks. If it can help reduce panic attacks, it can definitely help you relax and perform better as an athlete.

In addition to using progressive muscle relaxation, you can use the following to relax your muscles:

- **Imagery:** Athletes can reduce muscle tension and enter a more relaxed state through imagery. Athletes can visualize warm water running over muscles to see them relaxed or see their muscles looking like cooked spaghetti noodles or limp rubber bands.

- **Music:** Some types of music are used to get athletes pumped for competition, but other types of music — like soft jazz or classical — can relax you.

- **Cue words:** Make sure you have certain cue words available for when you find yourself in a state of tension. Repeat words or phrases such as *relax* or *slow and easy.*

Quieting your mind

We live in a day and age where information is constantly bombarding us. It's difficult to quiet the mind at any time during the day or night, not just during competition. In fact, one of the greatest problems in the United States today is the loss of sleep due to anxiety caused by a racing mind, a mind full of worry and negative thoughts. Sleep challenges can lead to physical problems, decreased concentration, increased anxiety and depression, as well as lowered performance in athletics, school, work, or relationships.

A good technique for quieting your mind, and for getting off the emotional roller coaster, is to use a cue word, such as *relax* or *breathe.* You'll be able to use this technique during breaks in the action of at least three to five minutes or more. Slowly repeat the cue word while exhaling. You can do it as many times as necessary, but the key is to focus only on the cue word. When you feel centered, you can return to competition, ready to battle anew.

Quieting your mind is simply stated, but not simply lived. It takes practice just like any other skill, but it's worth doing not only for your sport performance, but for life.

In addition to using a cue word during competition, you can quiet your mind by meditating off the playing field. Meditation has been used to train and calm the mind for over 3,000 years. It's been proven to be helpful in increasing alertness, increasing energy and productivity, decreasing self-criticism, and improving self-esteem.

Meditation is useful for athletes because, when your mind is quiet and centered, you can focus only on the task in front of you. Too many athletes make mistakes because they aren't focused on one thing — they're not in the present moment. If you think about your best athletic moments, they were probably ones in which you were focused on the task in front of you and you were in the present. Improved focus is one of the primary benefits of meditation — and more and more high-level athletes are making it part of their normal practice and training routines for this very reason.

Here are some important tips for using meditation:

- ✔ **Go into it with the right attitude.** You have to be open to the idea of meditation in order for it to work. If you see meditation as a waste of your time, there's no point in doing it.

- ✔ **Recognize that meditation requires commitment and self-discipline.** Learning to keep your mind free of extraneous thoughts is a skill like any other. If you want to improve your endurance, running once a month isn't going to do it. In the same way, you need to practice meditation regularly, making it part of your routine.

- ✔ **Set up the right environment.** Look for someplace quiet, where you won't be interrupted. Set aside 15 to 20 minutes per session.

- ✔ **Stick with it.** At first, you may find it difficult and want to give up, thinking that it isn't working. But meditation takes time, and the more you practice it, the better you'll get.

Meditation is a huge subject — one we can't possibly cover completely in this book. For much more information on meditation, check out *Meditation For Dummies,* 2nd Edition, by Stephan Bodian, which includes a CD with more than 70 minutes of guided meditations.

Relaxing in a hurry

Sometimes during competition, you need quicker ways to calm yourself down. A good way to do this is to use humor. Why humor? Because humor helps change your emotional state from angry or frustrated to happy, in an instant. Here are some ways to use humor to change your mood (and relax in a hurry):

- ✔ **Talk to yourself in a ridiculous voice.** For example, say "You can do this!" in high-pitched voice.

- ✔ **Use a gesture to break the tension.** Leif once taught a high-level tennis athlete to stop, drop, and roll when she found herself getting angry on the tennis court. She used this technique during a particularly intense match and was laughing at herself before she got up off the ground.

- ✔ **Sing the lyrics to funny songs.** For example, sing something like "I'm a little teapot, short and stout. . . ." This will distract you from your frustration.

- ✔ **Joke around with teammates.** Just joking with teammates puts things in perspective.

The key is to personalize it — but the funnier, the better!

You can't experience two emotions simultaneously. You can't be angry and happy at the same time. You can't feel frustrated and happy at the same time, either. This is why using humor is such a powerful (and quick) tool for changing your mood.

Here are some more ways to relax in a hurry:

- **Stop and slow down.** When you're able, simply stop and take a deep breath to gain perspective. It takes only a few seconds to stop the world from spinning — you just have to remember to do it. *Remember:* You have the ability to stop the racing in your body and mind.

- **Stop it before it gets going.** If you notice that you've become too excited, intervene immediately. Don't wait. The higher the energy level goes, the longer it takes to calm down. Think of a speeding car — it takes a car a lot longer to slow down when it's going 120 mph than it does when it's going 60 mph.

- **Use imagery.** Create a picture in your mind with a vertical line going from 1 to 10. At 10, your energy level is very high; at 1, it's very low. Picture where you want your energy level to be. If you need to calm down in a hurry, simply see the bar falling down quickly to the level you want. If you prefer, you can think about the mercury rising and falling in a thermometer.

Chapter 13

Handling Adversity: The Psychological Art of Bouncing Back

....

....

In sports, just as in life, you'll face obstacles and pitfalls that will test you, no matter how patient and optimistic you are. No athlete is exempt from adversity — what separates the best athletes from the rest is their ability to bounce back.

In this chapter, we explain the difference between loss and failure — outlining a simple shift in mindset that can help you deal with loss. We give you proven strategies for pulling yourself out of a slump — and tell you what *not* to do when you're in a slump. Most people, athletes included, are their own worst critics, so we tell you how to forgive yourself for mistakes, instead of letting mistakes control you. Finally, we cover injuries — how to recover from them, and how to prevent them from happening in the first place.

Looking at Loss Differently

Sports are unique. Why? Because, in sports, the bottom line is that one team or individual wins, and one team or individual loses — and just about nothing else in life is this clear-cut. Think about it: How many things in life come down to winning and losing? How can you win or lose with friendships? With love? With your career? With school? Life just isn't that simple.

When you recognize that winning and losing are inherent in sports, you can deal with wins and losses differently. You won't be so devastated when you lose, and you won't get a big head when you win.

Recognizing that loss isn't necessarily failure

The key to dealing with loss is to differentiate it from failure. Losing and failing are two separate things. Losing means that your opponent had the better score or time at the end of the competition. You can fail in your game execution or fail in your match goals but still win the competition. Failure is about whether you reached your goals; losing is only about whether your opponent bettered your score or time.

Losing does not equal failure. You might lose a game or certain competition, but not fail because it was one of your personal best performances. In the same way, you may win, but still fail because you didn't do your best.

Todd worked with a very passionate college golfer who's a great example of someone who lost in competition, but certainly didn't fail. Kate had played consistently all season but hadn't won a tournament. Although, in some ways, she was disappointed, she was also happy with her consistency. Toward the end of the season, at the conference championship, Kate was focused and motivated to win. She was in an excellent place after the first two rounds and knew she could take the lead and win on the last day: She was in third place, with the leader two shots ahead of her and the second-place player only one shot ahead of her. There were three other ties one stroke behind her. Kate began the day very well, starting with two birdies in the first five holes. She had a small slip midway through, but she was still in good shape. In the end, she shot a career low of 68. Still, Kate didn't win the tournament. Sure, she was disappointed at the loss, but she hadn't failed. She played her best golf ever and she competed well under a lot of pressure.

Next time you lose a competition, remind yourself that losing isn't necessarily failing. Focus on your performance, not on the final score.

Seeing the difference between getting beat and losing

There is a big difference between getting beat and losing. Getting beat means that your opponent outplayed you — they executed better, worked harder, stayed in the moment better, and focused and concentrated better during crucial moments. They utilized their skills better than you did. Getting beat simply means that, on that day, your opponent deserved the win more than you did. They earned it.

Losing, on the other hand, can happen in multiple ways. You can be more talented than your opponent, but if you're lazy, or if your strategy isn't up to par, or if you simply make too many errors or mistakes, you'll lose to your opponent. Losing is a reactive, passive way to describe the outcome of a competition. Your opponent didn't necessarily *earn* the win as much as you *lost*.

As an athlete, if you have to make a choice between losing and getting beat, choose to get beat every time. You want to force your opponents to play their best. If you remain on top of your game, and use the principles in this book, you can bring out the best of your athletic abilities. At that point, your opponents will need to exert a tremendous effort to beat you — but if and when it does happen (and it does, even to the best athletes), you won't have any regrets. You'll know you gave it your all.

When you get beat, you don't have regrets. When you lose, you'll have numerous regrets because you didn't do everything in your power to succeed.

Pulling Yourself Out of Slumps

Everyone who has ever participated in competitive sports for a while has experienced being in a slump. A *slump* is simply an extended period of time during which you perform worse than you normally do. Slumps are characterized by increased frustration, overexertion, and a dramatic and noticeable loss of confidence. They can last for short or long periods of time, depending on both the sport and the athlete. The key to getting out of slumps is to understand their causes. Then you can learn how to work through slumps, and minimize the damage they do to both your long-term performance and your confidence.

Poor performance doesn't necessarily equate to a slump. You'll make mistakes and have less-than-ideal performances at times, but that doesn't mean you're in a slump. You need to acknowledge performance decrements and mistakes, but it can help to think of those mistakes as a series of separate incidents as opposed to a slump, which tends to have a more long-term and negative connotation.

Understanding why slumps happen

Slumps are the result of a perfect storm — a variety of events happening all at once. The first ingredient is a statistical downturn — your shooting percentage decreases, your times are slower, and so on. But a performance decrease alone does not a slump make. Slumps happen when that performance decrease is combined with the mental aspect of trying too hard, putting constant pressure on yourself to succeed, exerting extreme effort without any results, or overtraining mentally and physically. So, failure begets more failure, particularly when you don't attend to the mental aspects of staying strong and optimistic. And the downward spiral begins.

Slumps are a normal occurrence in sports. Everybody goes through them. You *will* experience slumps — your goal is to manage their length and the damage they can do to your confidence.

Focusing on fundamentals

In order to beat a slump, you need to get back to the basics of your sport. That means focusing your efforts on improving your basic skill set. For example, if you're a baseball or softball player, that means spending time working on the basics of your swing. If you're a basketball player, it means breaking down your jump shot form. For golf, it means mastering simple, individual components of your swing and game and then letting it all come together.

You need to analyze the technical aspects of your sport. To do this, you can use tools such as video and digital cameras. You can also enlist the help of coaches or teammates, or even other technical experts in your sport. By doing so, you allow yourself to get objective, unbiased feedback.

The goal here is to get back to the basics. Focus on and execute just the fundamentals of your sport skills. Often, focusing on the simplicity of the technical aspects of your sport will allow you to recover from a slump or poor performance more quickly.

Being mindful

Besides the technical aspect of getting back to basics (see the preceding section), you must get back to the mental fundamentals. One way to do this is to practice mindfulness. *Mindfulness* is a Buddhist practice that means the art of living in the moment. Mindfulness is about being fully engrossed in the moment, without judging the moment positively or negatively. It's the ability to be in the now.

To better understand the art of being mindful, compare it with the everyday mindset that you usually experience:

Everyday Thinking	*Mindful Thinking*
Analytical	Descriptive
Judgmental	Exploratory
Past and future oriented	Present oriented
Juggles multiple thoughts	Manages one thought only at a time
Distracted	Focused

There is a distinct difference between everyday thinking and mindful thinking. One is distracted, focusing on multiple issues past and present, and the other is simply focusing on what's happening and present oriented.

In sports, being mindful is extremely helpful, because it allows you to focus on the moment. In that moment, you focus on only your task as a competitor, whether it's hitting a tennis ball, catching a football, sinking a putt, or pacing yourself on a run.

Here are some additional mental fundamentals that you can use to pull yourself out of a slump:

- ✔ **Muscle relaxation:** When you're in a slump or you're struggling with performance, your muscles will likely tighten up, inhibiting performance by making your movements more jerky and rigid. Relax your muscles through stretching, practicing progressive muscle relaxation (see Chapter 12), or even taking a simple jog.

- ✔ **Breathing:** One of the physical reactions your body has when you're nervous is shallow breathing. Take deep, controlled breaths as a way to slow your heart rate, calm your thought process, and relax your muscles.

- ✔ **Pursue simple tasks.** Often, when you're in a slump, many thoughts are running through your mind, including doubts about your skills, memories of previous poor performances, and thoughts about what you're doing wrong. Break down your tasks to the basics. For example, if you're a golfer struggling with putting, simply focus on the idea of a smooth stroke and nothing more.

✔ **Focus on the process.** Keep your mind on the tasks before you to get better. Focus on *how* you do things rather than the outcome of what you're doing. The outcomes will eventually turn around if you focus on the process of getting better.

✔ **Set small daily achievable goals.** Write down and track your practice goals daily. By accomplishing small goals each day, your confidence will build and your belief in yourself will rise prior to your next competition.

✔ **Execute skills without thinking.** Often, you can practice some of the basic skills without any thinking. For example, golfers can just relax and swing the club without worrying about where it's going to go. Tennis players can serve the ball as hard as they usually do just to relax muscles and let go. Baseball players can swing the bat multiple times as hard as they can to just relax. Soccer players can make crosses without thinking. Go on autopilot on purpose.

Athletes in slumps tend to overthink everything related to their performance. Not only will overthinking do nothing to help your performance, but it'll only serve to extend the length of your slump. You may think that you have to work harder or practice longer or perform drills until your hands bleed in order to get out of a slump, but that isn't the answer. You want to keep things quiet and simple to return to your normal level of play.

A two-week turnaround

Todd was working with a professional tennis player who, for several months, had been having problems with her game. Shannon wasn't playing how she knew she could play, and she was feeling extremely frustrated. She even thought about giving up the game because she wasn't winning or even qualifying for main draws in the tournaments she entered. One of the specific areas hurting Shannon was her second serve. She lost nearly all confidence in her second serve and consistently double-faulted.

Todd had Shannon hit 50 second serves as fast as she could, without caring whether they were in or not. She began to loosen up and allow her natural skill and form to come back. After these 50 balls, Todd had Shannon focus on a basic serve thought — "ball toss" — and had her begin to try for more accuracy. She immediately started getting more serves in because she was focused on her ball toss (the process) and not on the outcome (whether ball was in or not). When the process became more smooth and automatic, Shannon's confidence grew. Todd then had her pick a very specific focal point (a cone) in the service box. She was to try to hit this cone as many times as possible. She was amazed at how many times she came close to hitting it. Shannon practiced this way for almost two weeks and then had the chance to try it out in tournament play, where she reduced her number of double faults by 80 percent!

Sometimes all it takes to pull yourself out of a slump is to focus on the basic skills of your sport and give your mind something specific to think about.

Bouncing Back after Mistakes in Competition

Newsflash: No matter how good you get at your sport, you're going to make mistakes. You'll drop the big pass, miss a blocking assignment, miss the forehand down the line wide on a big point, or strike out with the bases loaded in the bottom of the ninth. Making mistakes is a natural part of sports. Even the best athletes in the world regularly make mistakes. But top athletes also bounce back, usually in a big way.

Everyone, from the top athletes in the world down to weekend warriors, makes mistakes. Nobody is immune from screwing up.

Knowing what happens mentally after a mistake

Most athletes, after they make a mistake, blame themselves, put themselves down, and generally make things worse. They blame their team's loss on their own mistakes, and minimize the consequences of their positive actions. This reaction is normal but counterproductive.

In the moments immediately after you make a mistake, you have two choices for interpreting what just happened. You can

- See it as an excuse to attack yourself and your abilities as an athlete
- See it as a neutral or even positive event

If you choose the former, you enter into a spiral of negativity. If you choose the latter, you can see your mistake for what it was: a mistake. You can even see it as evidence that you're at least in the game, trying to make something happen.

Which do you prefer: attacking yourself and your abilities every time something goes wrong, or making the best of the situations you find yourself in, knowing that mistakes are part of sports? If you want to be a high-level athlete, you need to learn how to make the best of bad situations, and quickly. Doing so will enable you to deal with the many adverse situations that you find yourself in as an athlete.

The more emotion you give to an experience or event, the longer it'll stay in your mind. You can probably recall the exact day, time, and place when you last made a major mistake in competition. Why? Because that mistake has strong emotional connections. You need to learn to attach strong emotions to your *positive* moments during competition and spend less mental energy on the negative ones.

If you don't bounce back from mistakes quickly, you automatically increase your risk of making more mistakes. Check out Figure 13-1 for an illustration of the two main paths after you make a mistake. Which path looks better to you?

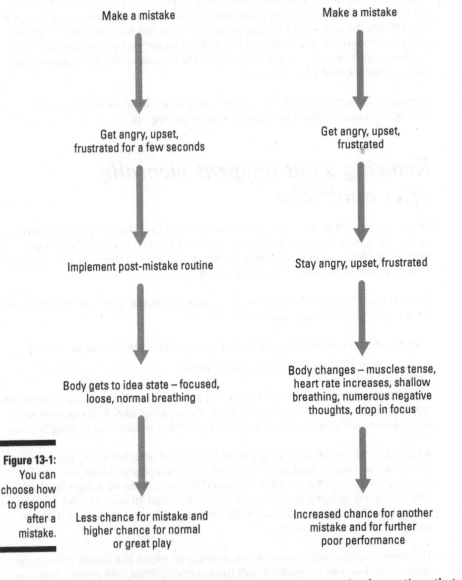

Figure 13-1: You can choose how to respond after a mistake.

Make a mistake

Make a mistake

Get angry, upset, frustrated for a few seconds

Get angry, upset, frustrated

Implement post-mistake routine

Stay angry, upset, frustrated

Body gets to idea state – focused, loose, normal breathing

Body changes – muscles tense, heart rate increases, shallow breathing, numerous negative thoughts, drop in focus

Less chance for mistake and higher chance for normal or great play

Increased chance for another mistake and for further poor performance

Read on for information on establishing the post-mistake routines that allow you to choose the more effective path.

Establishing a post-mistake routine

Whether you realize it or not, you already have what we call a *post-mistake routine,* which is simply the behaviors you engage in immediately after you make a mistake. You've probably seen examples of less-than-helpful post-mistake routines, where athletes explode in anger, lose their concentration, or blame the referees or their opponents. You've probably also seen more positive post-mistake routines, where athletes laugh it off or take a moment to gather themselves before jumping back into competition.

The way you respond to a mistake needs to be automatic. And in order to make your automatic response a positive one, you need to determine how you'll respond before the competition starts, and work on that response in practice.

Here are some examples of helpful post-mistake routines:

- **Use humor.** You can't change what just happened, so why not laugh at how silly it must seem? If you can't find anything funny about it, even faking a smile can work to help change your mood for the better. Plus, smiling confuses your opponent.

- **Find a place to go where you can gather yourself.** In tennis, this might mean heading to the fence behind the baseline. In other sports, it might be simply turning your back and closing your eyes for a couple of seconds to regroup.

- **Practice focused breathing.** Take three deep, slow breaths to clear your head.

- **Come up with a physical way of letting go of mistakes.** For example, golfers sometimes pick up grass and let it fly away, allowing them to clear their heads and execute the correct swing.

Make sure you have a simple and relevant thought that brings you back to what you need to be focusing on. If you're focusing on this thought, you can't be thinking about your mistake. For example, you may say to yourself "Next point," "Next shot," or "Let's go."

Table 13-1 is an exercise that that forces you to think about what champions do after mistakes. It makes you look at your ability to respond to mistakes. Your job in filling out this table is to think about how champions respond to mistakes, how "mentally soft" athletes respond to mistakes, and how *you'll* respond to mistakes.

Table 13-1   **How Athletes Respond to Mistakes**

Mistake	How Champion Athletes Respond	How "Mentally Soft" Athletes Respond	How I Respond
Striking out	Hustle back to the dugout, hustle back to the field, commit to be better the next time at bat	Scream at umpire, throw bat, complain and feel sorry for himself	

Once you've established a post-mistake routine, you'll have an easy and effective method for getting your focus and concentration back in competition. And when you have your focus and concentration back, you'll put yourself in a position to perform better and avoid making future mistakes. One of the hallmarks of high-achieving athletes is that they seldom make the same mistake twice, because they learn from every mistake they make. Their post-mistake routines enable them to learn these lessons on the go during competition.

Whatever routine you choose, keep in mind the following points:

- ✔ **You need to use the routine _immediately_ after making the mistake.** The longer you wait to begin your routine, the lower your chance of being able to get yourself through the difficult situation.

- ✔ **Your routine needs to be easy to use and portable.** You should be able to use it anywhere, anytime.

- ✔ **What works for other athletes may not work for you.** Just because your teammate can use humor to laugh off her mistakes doesn't mean you'll be able to — and that's okay. The key is to find the routine that works for _you._

- ✔ **The more you use your routine, the better you'll be at it, and the more automatic the routine will become.** You won't have to think about using it — it'll just happen.

Preparation is the key. You _will_ make mistakes — what you do after your mistakes and how you manage them is what matters.

Dealing with Injuries

Injuries are the ultimate and worst type of adversity that every serious athlete faces. Unfortunately, they happen too often, and they tend to happen at exactly the wrong times in your competitive career.

In this section, we start by telling you how you can prevent injuries from happening. Then, because you can't always prevent injuries from occurring, we show you some ways to cope with them so that you can get back into competition as soon as possible.

Preventing injuries

Injuries are the enemy of all athletes — the last thing you want is to be side-lined by an injury. But the good news is, you can work to prevent injuries, or at least reduce the odds that they'll occur.

Managing stress

One the biggest factors in most health-related issues — and not just for athletes — is stress. As an athlete, you're under even more pressure than most people. Pressure from coaches, teammates, and yourself can compro-mise your immune system, which can make you more vulnerable to common colds and viruses. This can, in turn, reduce your effectiveness and even put you on the bench.

Plus, stress places tension in your muscles and decreases your focus. As an athlete, you're at greater risk for a physical injury when you're competing with tight muscles.

When you're stressed, you also tend to focus on the wrong things. You may be worrying about outcomes (like getting taken out of game), making mis-takes, or something completely unrelated to your sport. When this occurs, your mind isn't focused on what you're doing, and you place yourself at greater risk for physical injury.

Research indicates that there is a positive relationship between stress and injury. Thirty of 35 studies on the topic have demonstrated this relationship. Being under stress and/or not successfully managing stress places you at much greater risk for injury.

As an athlete, you already understand how hard it is to earn playing time. You don't want to give it up to someone else because you're sick or you've suffered a stress-related injury.

Here are some things you can do to better manage your stress and stay on the field:

- ✔ **Stay on top of your schedule.** Don't let tasks and to-do lists pile up.

- ✔ **Hang out with people who are happy and well adjusted, and who make you laugh.** Avoid toxic, negative-minded people. Research clearly shows that athletes without social support and with poor coping skills are at much higher risk for sustaining injury.

- ✔ **Laugh!** Laughing is one of the healthiest things you can do to boost your immune system.

✔ **Eat sensibly, especially around special events and holiday events.** You'll avoid the guilt that usually accompanies overeating, and you'll ensure that you aren't dumping excessive sugars and fats into your body.

✔ **Get an hour more of sleep every night.** If you go to bed an hour earlier than usual and maintain this habit for one full year, you'll have added 45 more full nights of sleep (at 8 hours each) to your annual schedule! Your body can benefit from more sleep.

✔ **Improve your self-talk.** This is such an important concept that we devote an entire chapter to it (see Chapter 8). Events and situations are not, in and of themselves, stressful — it's how you perceive those events that makes them stressful or not. Work on changing your thoughts so that you see every event as a learning opportunity rather than doomsday.

Mental skills training can improve your performance and help you manage stress. Many athletes learn these skills through work with sports psychologists and coaches, and by reading (which you're doing right now!) and educating themselves in their free time. They learn to manage pressure, optimize focus, set effective goals, use imagery to manage emotions, and manage energy levels for major competitions. These skills can also be used to help you manage stressful and challenging times in your life off the playing field.

Recognizing fatigue

The more fatigued your body is, the greater the chance that you'll get injured. So, it's important that you recognize fatigue as soon as it begins to set in. Too often, people ignore the telltale signs of fatigue, only to be faced with an illness or injury shortly thereafter.

Everybody gets tired, but chronic fatigue takes tiredness to another level. Tiredness is a short-term physical state, whereas fatigue is a prolonged physical state that puts you at increased risk for disease and injury. Here are some differences between being tired and suffering chronic fatigue.

Tiredness	*Chronic Fatigue*
Increased need for sleep	Constant feeling of being sleep deprived
Difficulty focusing at times	Inability to focus for long periods of time
Sore muscles	Pinched nerves and strained muscles, particularly in the neck and back
Normal appetite	Decreased appetite for most foods or increased appetite for unhealthy foods, such as those high in simple sugars
Normal motivation levels	Decreased motivation levels

When you're tired, or certainly when you're suffering from chronic fatigue, both your mind and your body are low on energy. You tend to lose your focus or try to do things your body can't do because of this tiredness. Injuries are common in these situations. So, make sure that you recognize this tired or fatigued state and handle it by getting sleep, being conscious of maintaining higher levels of focus, or simply not trying anything risky when your body is so tired.

Make sure to recognize periods of time during the season or year when fatigue has a greater chance of occurring. For example, if you're a student, finals week is a time when fatigue occurs, putting you at greater risk for injury. Anticipate times when you'll be fatigued, and then plan to manage your time accordingly. Make sure to stick to a routine of healthy eating and sleeping, as well as taking more time to warm up before and after training. Take special care of your body during these stressful periods.

Maintaining sharp focus

When you're not focused, injuries can occur. Make sure that your focus is sharp and ready every time your enter practice or competition. We've seen athletes who've been working out in the weight room and injured themselves because they were distracted or weren't paying attention. We've also seen athletes who've been preoccupied with other thoughts and have gotten injured in competition because they weren't focused.

Before every practice and competition, make sure you're focused. Being focused will not only improve your overall athletic performance, but it'll also reduce the chances that you'll be injured.

For more on focus, turn to Chapter 6.

Coping with injuries

Injuries affect you physically and psychologically, and it's important that, when you're injured, you recuperate both ways. We show you how in the following sections.

The physical aspect of injuries

When you've been injured, several different medical personnel will probably be involved in your treatment. Your athletic trainer (if you're part of a team) will be a central part of your rehabilitation. Your team doctor and/or personal doctor will also help coordinate your care. You'll probably also work with a physical therapist, who will take you through rehab exercises.

Be in charge of your own medical care. Don't leave everything up to the staff around you. Only you know how your body responds, and only you can tell your healthcare team what's working and what isn't.

Your medical team is working with dozens or hundreds of different athletes at any one time, so you need to take responsibility for your own health and make sure you get what you need to heal.

Pain is an expected but unfortunate aspect of injury rehabilitation. You need to manage your pain and your expectations from the outset. Too often, athletes set themselves up for failure by setting unrealistic expectations for their rehabilitation. Then, when their bodies don't progress as quickly as they expected, they get even more frustrated, sad, or angry, which can set them back in the healing process.

Balance your hopes for a speedy recovery with realistic but achievable goals. You can do this by listening to your medical staff, offering your input on how your body is reacting to treatment, and doing everything you can to make sure you're allowing your body the time and resources it needs to heal properly.

The psychological side of injuries

The way you cope with your injury psychologically will go a long way toward how well (and how quickly) your body will recover. In this section, we give you some powerful ways to mentally work through and adjust to any injury.

Focusing on daily goals

When you're injured, it can be difficult to stay inspired throughout the long and often isolating rehabilitation process. One way to increase your motivation is to break down your overall rehabilitation goals into daily goals. These daily goals will help to keep you motivated and focused, and will help to fight off any feelings of hopelessness that creep into your mind.

Focus your competitive nature on your rehabilitation just as fiercely as you typically do on the court or field. This allows you to get your juices flowing in a fun and hopeful way, while allowing you to feel better about your rehabilitation process.

Your goals should be *your* goals. Even if your doctor or trainer sets some simple daily rehabilitation goals for you, you should still set your own.

Building your support team

Ask any athlete who has ever been injured, and he'll tell you that his support network played an enormous part in his return from that injury. Some athletes are naturally blessed with a built-in support network in the form of family and friends who cheer them on, but many athletes don't enjoy that luxury. If you don't have a built-in support network, you need to put a little more time and effort into building your rehabilitation support team.

Who you choose to be on your support team is entirely personal, but you may want to start with a family member you're close to, as well as some friends who understand how important your sport is to you. You can expand your support team to include your professional contacts (medical doctor, chiropractor, psychologist, athletic trainer, and/or physical therapist).

Choose your team wisely — they'll be your safety net when the process gets you down and feels never-ending. Here are some characteristics of people want on your team:

- **Sense of humor:** You want to surround yourself with people who can make you laugh.

- **Personal history and trust:** The more people you can have on your team who've known you for a long time and whom you trust, the better.

- **Empathy for the role that your sport plays in your life:** If they don't get how much your sport means to you, they're off the team.

- **History of athletic participation themselves:** Former athletes tend to understand and empathize with current athletes, regardless of which sport they played.

- **The ability to give you a pep talk:** From time to time, you'll need a kick in the pants, and you want people on your team who aren't afraid to deliver one.

- **Accountability and responsibility:** You need people who can help keep you focused on your goals and on returning from your injury as quickly as possible. They can't flake out on you after a few weeks — they need to be in it for the long haul.

Maintaining perspective

Perspective is a wonderful tonic to soothe you during your most difficult moments as an athlete. When you get injured, you tend to lose perspective about the big picture in life. You may become sad, confused, and angry at your circumstances. This is especially true when you've been injured more than once in your career, or when the same injury recurs.

Perspective allows you to move past the injury and to see the positive consequences that usually follow. These positive consequences include an eventual renewed passion for your sport, increased muscle strength, and improved relationships with your support team and network.

Here are some ways to maintain your perspective following an injury:

- **Engage in activities that have nothing to do with your sport.** Doing something else will allow you to relax a bit.

- **Stay involved in team activities as much as you're comfortable doing.** This will allow you to feel like you're still an important part of the team.

✔ **Take up a hobby.** You'll have more downtime than you're used to, so you may as well help fill that time with an activity that provides you relaxation and pleasure.

✔ **Reach out to old friends and friends you may have grown apart from.** When you connect with others, this helps you to not focus on your injury all the time. Friends can keep you distracted, help you maintain perspective, and ask you to do things socially — all good things when working through the injury process.

✔ **Hone your mental skills.** This is also a great time to practice your mental skills. Just as all the mental skills — focus, mental imagery, goal setting, and so on — can help your athletic performance, they're critical to helping your through the injury rehabilitation process. Research shows that athletes who use mental skills during recovery handle the process much better and return to their sport sooner.

Using imagery

Imagery, or focused daydreaming, is a great way to speed up the healing process. You can use healing imagery during the rehabilitation process to aid your recovery. Imagery can also calm the body, increase serotonin levels, and block the "pain gate" to the brain.

Here's how to use imagery to help yourself heal:

✔ **Use creative imagery to enhance your healing.** You can imagine that your injury is a foreign invader in your body, and that your white blood cells are the special-forces soldiers assigned to eliminate the invader. Picture these "soldiers" arming themselves and going on missions to attack the invader.

✔ **Use colors to help speed the healing process.** In particular, you may imagine injuries in red and healing in blue. When you visualize, try to imagine making the red injury smaller and more pink in color. Eventually, you can imagine it turning from pink to white, and then to a light blue, and then dark blue, which is cool and soothing, relaxed and healed.

You'll be better at using imagery in rehabilitation if you've been using it all along as part of your training. All the more reason to get started using imagery right away. For the complete lowdown on imagery, see Chapter 7.

Part IV
Improving Team Performance with Sports Psychology

The 5th Wave   By Rich Tennant

"Sure, you see a bunch of kids scraping and painting my house for free. I see the first steps in building a strong sense of team unity."

In this part . . .

Improving *individual* athletic performance is challenging enough, let alone trying to improve the performance of an entire team. In this part, we address the numerous aspects of getting a sports team to pursue the same goal, work together toward that goal, stick together despite multiple distractions and personality types, and strive for championships.

Here we focus on three important areas that dictate how well a team performs: communication, leadership, and chemistry. Like all relationships, effective communication is vital. Even with the best of athletic talent, if the communication breaks down, the team's success will break down, too. Leadership is critical to a team's success, and both athletes and coaches need to develop and maintain it. Finally, getting individual athletes and players to work together as a team has its own challenges, so we offer insight on how to foster the chemistry your team needs to function at the highest levels.

Chapter 14

Communicating as a Team

- -

In This Chapter

▶ Debunking myths about communication

▶ Using body language and tone of voice

▶ Setting the stage for good communication

▶ Communicating better with your teammates

- -

Teams can win with different strategies, different strengths, different players, different coaches, different playoff positions . . . the list goes on and on. But one thing all teams have in common is strong communication. Teams, athletes, and coaches who communicate well have fewer self-made obstacles to overcome than those who communicate poorly. They aren't trying to overcome their opposition *and* themselves at the same time. Teams, coaches, and athletes who communicate well operate with greater clarity of purpose — they know exactly why they're playing and what they're playing for.

Many teams, coaches, and athletes could have been much more successful had they learned and practiced better communication skills. We've both been part of a variety of teams over the past ten years, and we've witnessed great talent and coaching that didn't go anywhere because of poor communication. Never underestimate the power of effective communication. Many of the problems the teams we work with face have nothing to do with the talent of the athletes, the abilities of the coaches, or a lack of resources available to both. Instead, their problems are rooted in poor communication. When we show them how to communicate more effectively, their seasons turn around, sometimes dramatically.

Great communication doesn't just happen, and most people don't really know what constitutes great communication. So, we start this chapter by explaining what communication *isn't* — debunking some common myths about communication. Then we show you the ways you communicate without talking — through body language and tone of voice — so you can make sure that your body is communicating the same message that your mouth is. We move on to environment — there's a right time and place for the message you want to convey, and we show you how to find that time and place so that your message has the greatest chance of being heard. Finally, we give you specific strategies for communicating effectively with your teammates, athletes, and coaches.

Share this chapter with your team. You can go a long way toward improving communication on your own, but communication is a two-way street, and your team's performance will improve if everyone is reading from the same playbook.

Dispelling Common Misconceptions about Communication

Most people talk a good game about the importance of communication: "Yeah, communication is key. Everyone knows that." But when you ask them what makes communication successful, they don't have a clue. Worse, they may blurt out something about communication that's just plain wrong. In this section, we set the record straight on what communication is and isn't.

Communication is all about the words you say

Communication isn't just about talking. In fact, it's made up of several components — and the words you speak are just one of those components. Communication starts with what you *intend* to say — the message you're trying to convey. But before you even open your mouth, that message is influenced by what we call *mental interference* — everything from your values and your education background, to your life experiences, beliefs, and expectations. All these factors influence your message and the way you convey it.

You can reduce mental interference in your communication in several ways:

> ✔ **Be aware of that everyone has mental interference they can bring to a conversation.** We're all human, and each of us has a unique personality and background. Accept this fact and be aware of how it could affect your communication.

- ✔ **If you must assume something about the person you're communicating with, assume that the other person is intelligent and fully able to understand what you're trying to say.** Assume also that the other person will question you if he has any difficulties understanding the content of your message.

- ✔ **Work to constantly improve your self-awareness in social situations.** For example, try to become more aware of your body language when you're talking. Pay attention to your tone of voice and your word choice, too.

- ✔ **State opinions as opinions, which are subject to change at your discretion.** Too often, people state opinions as facts.

- ✔ **Before conveying a message, ask yourself what your intent is.** Are you trying to add to the discussion, or get a point across? Are you trying to be right instead of trying to be helpful? By clarifying your message in this way — prior to communicating it — you'll communicate better and more clearly with others.

Many coaches make the mistake of thinking that good communication with their teams is all about talking. Leif worked with one coach who had problems conveying to his team that he wanted them to relax and have fun while playing. His own mental interference was getting in the way of his message. For example, he was seen by his coaches and team as a micromanager, needing to have his hands in every detail concerning the team. He was also seen as a worrier — he seldom seemed relaxed and as though he was enjoying himself. What this coach didn't understand was that his message to "relax and have fun" was being interfered with by his *own* inability to relax and have fun. The result was that his team underachieved and played tight, and many players experienced burnout halfway through the season. The coach's mental interference got in the way of the message he was trying to convey to his team.

Be aware of your own mental interference when you're trying to communicate, and make sure that it doesn't prevent you from conveying the message you intend to communicate.

As long as you say it, they'll hear it

Communication doesn't stop when you finish talking. From there, your message is heard and interpreted — and it may not be heard or interpreted the way you intend.

Confrontation can do a body good

Most people think of *confrontation* as a negative, but it doesn't need to be. Confrontation can even solve a problem early in the communication sequence. For example, if you approach your coach half an hour before a game to talk to him about playing time, he may confront you by saying, "This isn't a good time to talk. Let's talk tomorrow at practice." If that happens, your coach is heading off a conversation that shouldn't happen at that moment because of environmental interference. He's preventing himself from hearing something you didn't intend to communicate, and he's giving you the opportunity to talk later, when your message is more likely to be heard correctly.

You can also use confrontation to check the message you're hearing. If you aren't sure about the intent of the message, you can stop the message in its tracks via confrontation: "Is this what you're trying to say?" or "It sounds like you're saying *x*. Is that correct?"

Remember: Confrontation doesn't have to be a bad thing. Think of confrontation as sharing your immediate thoughts, feeling, and concerns about an event, situation or person.

Fear is the greatest obstacle to confrontation. Maybe you feel like you're going to get yelled at, get in trouble, disappoint someone, or make someone angry. These fears are common, but successful athletes move forward despite their fear, and you can do the same. Never allow fear to get in the way of communicating something important.

Your message has to make it across the physical gap between you and your audience. In that gap, the environment — the physical space and context in which you're conveying your message — can interfere with the message. For example, if you need to talk to your coach about wanting more playing time, but you try to do it a half-hour before a big game, your message probably won't be heard as clearly as you'd like, because your coach will be distracted by the approaching game. In fact, if your coach *does* listen to what you're saying, he may think you're more interested in your own stats than you are in the performance of the team as a whole. On the other hand, if you wait to have this conversation until the day *after* the big game, after you've already given your all for the benefit of the team, your coach is more likely to hear you — and he may even credit you with being selfless in waiting.

Environmental interference — the timing, context, and environment in which you're sharing information — can be a major obstacle to effective communication.

Understanding How You Communicate: What You Say without Words

Just as important as *what* you say is *how* you say it: your tone of voice and your body language. How many times have you *said* you weren't angry, but your body language communicated something completely different? Your fists were clenched, your jaw was tight, your smile was faked, you used a harsh or edgy tone of voice — you were angry. Even though you *said* you weren't upset, your body language told a completely different story. Your body language and tone of voice communicate as much as the words you speak.

In this section, we explain the impact that body language and tone of voice have on your message, so that you can better manage them and communicate what you intend to communicate.

Body language

Your body language sets the tone for your entire conversation — before you say even one word. Part of communication is observing (and, if necessary, modifying) your body language. You need to pay attention to things like how you're standing or sitting and whether and how you make eye contact.

In the following sections, we introduce you to a variety of ways your body "talks."

Eye contact

Proper eye contact shows that you're serious about what you're saying. The key with eye contact is balance. You want to make eye contact with the person you're communicating with, but you don't want that eye contact to be too intense.

Especially when you're having a difficult discussion, make sure to make proper eye contact. When you avoid making eye contact, you're showing deference to the other person. He may feel he can overpower you because you're unable to look him in the eye.

Facial expression

Make sure that your facial expression is consistent with your message and shows that you're interested and engaged. Raise your eyebrows to convey interest from time to time. Smile and nod your head to convey your understanding. By showing interest with your facial expression, you indicate that you're committed — no matter how difficult and challenging the situation may be.

If you demonstrate a lack of interest, such as feeling bored, the person you're talking to may not hear your message. If she sees that you aren't smiling and you're staring off into space, she may assume that you're not interested.

Posture

If you're sitting or standing up straight, you demonstrate confidence in yourself and your message. If you slump in a chair or slouch when you stand, no matter what you say, the receiver of the message may not take you seriously. Stand upright or sit up straight, hold your head up high, and communicate your message more clearly.

Gestures

Gestures are various subtle behaviors that indicate how you feel. They include things like hanging your head, biting your fingernails, twirling your hair, folding your arms across your chest, looking away, or rolling your eyes. These gestures won't help you get your point across. Gestures like these can distract listeners from your message.

On the other hand, you can use other gestures, such as the following, to communicate your message and your interest more clearly:

- ✔ **Lean forward with your chin on your hands, making good eye contact.**

- ✔ **Touch the other person.** Touching someone's arm or hand when talking to them conveys interest quickly and in a warm and nonthreatening manner.

- ✔ **Match the other person's body language.** If he has his legs crossed, you can do the same. If he leans forward, do the same. When you match the other person's body language, you build rapport by making the other person feel more comfortable.

Physical behaviors

Physical behaviors are automatic — you likely do these things without even being aware of it. Included in this category are behaviors such as sweating, breathing heavily, swallowing, or shaking. All these behaviors may signal that you're nervous and may distract your audience from your message.

If you need help with these behaviors, you can practice things like progressive muscle relaxation (see Chapter 12) or meditation to reduce their negative impact on your communication.

Space

How close you stand to the person you're talking to communicates a lot. If you get in the other person's face by standing too close to her, you may communicate anger and intimidation. On the other hand, if you try to talk to her from across the room, or if you walk away from her as you're talking, you communicate a lack of interest in the conversation.

Make sure to maintain adequate, but professional, space. If the other person steps away from you, respect that distance and don't step toward him.

Physical space varies across cultures. In some cultures, people feel more comfortable talking in closer proximity to each other, and people in other cultures require more space. The next time you're at a coffee shop, notice the distance people keep from each other when standing in line, simply as a matter of habit.

Tone of voice

Tone of voice is just as important as body language in conveying a message. Your goal should be for your tone of voice to match the words you're saying. For example, if you're a coach trying to convey to a player that he needs to step up his effort on the playing field, you want your tone of voice to be firm and louder than normal conversation, but not aggressive or screaming and not too quiet or wishy-washy.

You may have gotten in trouble with your teachers or parents in the past for your tone of voice. You were *saying* all the right things, but the way you were saying it said something else. How many times have you been asked by your parents to clean your room, and how many times have you said, "Fine," in response. How did you say that one little word, *fine?* Was your tone of voice chipper and helpful, matching the word itself? Or did the way you said "Fine" communicate something more like "Are you kidding me? I have to clean my room *now?* You're so unfair!" Your tone of voice is often a dead giveaway for how you truly feel. If you can make your tone of voice match your message, you'll be communicating clearly.

Setting Up the Conditions for Ideal Communication

A big part of communication is choosing the right time and place to try to do it. You need to reduce environmental barriers to getting your point across. And you also have to pay attention to timing — you don't want to start a conversation with someone when one of you is distracted by something else.

In this section, we cover these two keys to setting the stage for communication.

The right time

Your conversation can get off to the wrong start if you try to have it at the wrong time. Try to choose a time to talk with your coach or teammate when you're both at ease and relaxed. Depending on the conversation, a good time might be before or after practice, on bus rides for away competitions, or during team meals.

Each person is comfortable in different situations, so try to get a feel for when the person you want to talk to is most comfortable before you try to start an important conversation.

Even if you think you've chosen the right time, you can start things off by saying, "Hey, I wanted to talk to you about something important. Is this an okay time?" This way, you give the other person the chance to tell you that, actually, another time might be better.

Follow the 24-hour rule and wait a full 24 hours after a particular difficult or emotional situation before trying to have a conversation about it. For example, if you're upset because you got benched in today's game, wait 24 hours before talking to the coach about your concerns. That 24-hour waiting period allows you time to cool down. If you ignore the rule and try to talk when emotions are high and stress is increasing, you probably won't communicate very effectively — and you may even make the situation worse.

The right place

Timing is critical, but so is location. If you want to have an important conversation with someone, you probably want to look for a place with privacy. You may not need to be in an empty room, with complete silence, but you at least need to feel like the person you're talking to can focus on a two-person conversation, instead of being pulled in a million different directions by other people who want a piece of him.

If you can't get a room to yourselves (like an office or an empty classroom) to talk in, you can tell the other person from the start that you want to talk about something important. That way, if someone else comes up and wants to join in, the two of you can make it clear that you're in the middle of something important.

Try choosing a spot to communicate that isn't threatening to the other person. Sometimes getting away from the athletic field can help both of you feel a bit less defensive and more at ease in important conversations.

You may want to consider e-mailing or leaving a voicemail for the person you want to talk to ahead of time. You can tell her that you want to talk and what you want to talk about. This way, the two of you can choose a good place to meet, and she won't feel blindsided by your conversation.

Following up on important issues

Communication doesn't stop and start, like a car headed down Main Street during rush hour. Good communication should be fluid, open, and back and forth, much like merging onto the highway at a high speed. You can ease up on the gas pedal, but you shouldn't need to hit your brakes very often if you do it correctly.

After you have your conversation, follow up with the other person to make sure he understands what you said. You can send a quick e-mail and just say something like, "Hey, coach.

I just wanted to make sure we were on the same page after our conversation today. We talked about how I felt about being benched last week, and you gave me a list of things I could do to get more playing time in the future."

By following up, not only are you able to confirm that your message was heard, but you show the other person how important the issue is to you. You also show that you pay attention to details, a key trait of successful athletes and coaches.

Improving Your Communication Skills

You're clear on what communication is and isn't. You know how your body language and tone of voice affect your message. You've found the right time and place to talk. You're ready to have that important conversation. Before you jump in, review this section to make sure your communication skills are top-notch.

Don't take things personally

You're you, so it's only natural for you to see things from your perspective, and when you get a little too hung up on seeing things from your perspective, it's easy to think everything is *about* you. The thing is, not everything *is* about you. So, start every conversation reminding yourself that whatever the other person says is more about him and what he's feeling than it is about you.

Often, the other person's mood is more a result of the kind of day he's had, and you just happen to be the next person he's come across. If you assume that his bad mood is your fault, or that his inability to focus is due to something you did, you'll likely be wrong. When you overestimate your influence on people, you overestimate your role in their lives, and you miss the mark.

Remember what they say about assuming

When you assume, you make an ass out of, well, you know the rest. People are great at making quick assessments of other people and situations. This trait is usually helpful — it allows you to make judgments about personal safety, when time is of the essence. Unfortunately, this same trait can also get you into trouble. How many times have you misjudged someone you've just met? Maybe you didn't give a new coach or teammate much of a chance. Or maybe you assumed something about a competitor that turned out not to be the case.

Most people tend to make assumptions, and you probably won't do away with that trait completely. So, keep your assumptions simple, and assume the best instead of the worst. Sure, sometimes you'll be proven wrong. But if you can go into every conversation assuming the following, your chances of good communication will improve:

- ✔ Most people are doing the best they can to make themselves happy.
- ✔ Most people don't walk around trying to ruin other people's days.
- ✔ People are genuinely good natured and well intentioned.

If you start with good assumptions, you'll be more patient, a better listener, more empathic, and a better overall communicator, teammate, and athlete. Not a bad result for such a simple strategy.

Focus on the present, not the past

In driver's ed. classes, they teach you the importance of knowing what to focus on while you're driving. Sure, you need to keep your eyes looking ahead of you. But you also need to check your rearview mirror every 5 to 10 seconds to see what lies behind you, where you've come from. To keep safe when changing lanes, you have to learn to use your side-view mirrors and check over your shoulder, to be sure that you don't cause a crash by sideswiping someone in the other lane. This combination of looking forward, glancing back and to the side, and staying focused on the present enables you to avoid getting into any danger while driving.

The same is true of communication. If you focus too much on the future, you'll miss the conversation you're having in the present. If you focus too much on what the other person just said (or what she said an hour, a day, or a week ago), you'll also miss the current conversation. Only when you keep yourself focused on the current moment — on what you're saying and what she's saying, and how those things are being said — can you communicate effectively.

The effects of resentment

Anger is inevitable — everyone gets angry now and then. But resentment is anger that you hold onto for lengthy periods of times. You choose whether to feel resentment or not. Odds are, you'll get angry with your teammates and coaches. If you choose to hold onto that anger, it turns into resentment and affects how you communicate.

Resentment doesn't hurt the other person — it's toxic only to the person feeling it. When you hold onto resentments, you're living in the past. And those resentments will affect your athletic performance today and in the future.

Remember: Think of each conversation as an isolated event. Don't drag baggage into your conversations from past conversations or life experiences. Focus on the current conversation and message being conveyed.

Never say "always" or "never"

Communication goes downhill fast when someone says, "You *always* . . ." or "You *never*. . . ." The problem with *always* and *never* is that they're generalizations that make no sense. Very few things *always* or *never* happen, particularly when it comes to human behavior.

Another problem with making generalizations is that you set up the other person to fail. After all, if you truly believe that he behaves this way *all* the time, how can he recover from that sort of sweeping generalization? He'll feel defensive and, most likely, spend more energy defending himself against your generalization, which will cause communication to slow or shut down.

Chapter 15

Leading Your Team to Victory: Athletes as Leaders

In This Chapter

▶ Knowing what leadership looks like

▶ Looking at your personal leadership style

▶ Identifying the moments when you need to lead

▶ Being a better leader

Great teams require great leadership. The history of sports is littered with examples of talented teams that failed in their pursuit of championships because they lacked leadership. Most people assume that leadership is the responsibility of the head coach. The coach is, without a doubt, a leader, but leadership doesn't stop with the coach. Athletes themselves play a big part in leading a team.

In order for your team to be consistently successful, the team needs great leadership not only from the coaches but from the players. Leadership is one of the most important components to athletic success.

In this chapter, we fill you in on the qualities of a strong leader. We help you analyze your own natural leadership tendencies, guide you in maximizing your leadership skills, and point out the moments when you can step up as a real team leader so you can be ready.

Knowing What Leadership Is (And What It Isn't)

The first step to being a better leader is to know what leadership looks like. Leadership is all about:

✔ **Earning respect:** You can only influence your teammates when you've earned their respect and established credibility. That begins with taking your sport seriously and being committed to becoming the best athlete you can be. When you've developed a solid reputation as a committed athlete, your teammates will feel that you understand them and what they're going through.

You don't have to be the best athlete on the team to be a team leader. You only have to prove to your teammates that you're working hard to be the best you can be. Not every great athlete will be a great leader. And the best leaders aren't necessarily the best athletes on the team.

✔ **Modeling desired behaviors:** You may not realize it, but your behavior has a big impact on your teammates. What you do, more than what you say, teaches your teammates the standard for behavior on the team.

✔ **Doing what's best for the team:** As a leader, you'll be faced with numerous situations in which you need to make important choices. On occasion, your own needs or wants may directly contrast with your team's. In these situations, it's important that you put your team's needs first.

✔ **Following through:** Leaders are people who do what needs to be done and make sure that they see tasks through to completion. Many of these tasks — such as holding teammates accountable, doing community service, or taking issues to coaches — can be uncomfortable or time-consuming, but leaders see them through to completion.

Leadership is not about:

✔ **Coercion:** True leadership isn't about forcing people to do things they wouldn't normally do. When you lead people effectively, they follow your lead of their own free will.

✔ **Short-term team gains:** Effective leaders don't focus on wins, goals, or points.

✔ **Fear:** Strong leaders don't have to use fear to motivate other people. They motivate others through appealing to their self-interests. Good leaders know that, although fear may be a motivator for some people, in the long run, it results in a loss of cohesion and trust among teammates.

✔ **Personal gain:** To be a great leader, you need to put your team ahead of yourself.

Investigating Your Style of Leadership

Leadership isn't one-style-fits-all. Different people have different styles of leadership, and one style isn't necessarily better than another. The key is to identify your natural style of leadership, and then use your natural tendencies to your advantage, to become the best leader you can be. In this section, we introduce you to the three main styles of leadership.

The dictator

The dictator is a powerful leader. Athletes who are very strong willed and outspoken tend to become dictators when put in leadership or captain positions. This type of leadership style is characterized by the following:

- A desire to be out in front of the pack, for all to see
- A loud and outspoken personality
- Stubbornness, hard-headedness, and a determined nature
- Actions that are quick, bold, and decisive
- Unquestioning loyalty

The dictator is easily identified as a leader. Dictators gravitate toward the big moments, and enjoy the limelight more than other types of leaders do. They think of themselves as "little coaches" and enjoy the social aspects of getting others to follow them into battle, because they have unusually high social confidence.

Dictators can create friction with some athletes. They can be seen as arrogant, domineering, cocky, and lacking respect. Because of this, dictators should make sure that everything they do is done with the best interest of the team in mind. Even though they may rub some athletes the wrong way, if dictators hold a team-first mentality, they can be extremely effective leaders, and they may also go on to lead in other areas of life.

The people's champion

The people's champion is a fun and easy-to-talk-to type of leader. People's champions are easy-going and make friends easily. In fact, it's hard *not* to like a people's champion type of leader — they're the most popular type of leaders in sports. The people's champion is characterized by the following:

- Leadership by example
- Doing things instead of asking others to get things done
- Getting along well with teammates
- High levels of confidence
- Decisions that are well thought out decisions and that consider what's best for all involved
- High credibility with coaches

The people's champion is usually the most likeable person on the team. People's champions make others feel good about themselves and are great listeners. They have a lot of credibility with both coaches and teammates because of their social, balanced, and likeable nature.

People's champions lead by example, getting others pumped up before a game or helping them hang in there during challenging times. But the people's champion may lack the verbally motivating and inspirational side of leadership. They also may have difficulty holding teammates accountable or responsible for their behavior, whether on the field or off.

The hands-off leader

Hands-off leaders are the Lone Rangers of the bunch. They lead, but not necessarily by choice or desire. Hands-off leaders can be mysterious and hard to figure out. Hands-off leaders

- Are loners by nature (at least more so than the other leadership types)
- Are less concerned with how others perceive them or their actions than other people are
- Can be more decisive than other types of leaders
- Can cause controversy because of their solitary nature and tendency to make decisions without consulting teammates
- Prefer to stay in the background unless forced to do otherwise

The hands-off leader can be effective, but it takes a little more effort on their part to induce people to follow them. They're the least social and most introverted of the three types of leaders. They also tend to be the least popular with coaches because of their tendency to do things their own way. They're usually very driven, want to be the best, and expect that everyone else should feel and act as they do. They believe that everyone should be just as driven as they are and can have a difficult time understanding when their teammates aren't. Instead of talking with their teammates about their frustration, they may get angry and keep to themselves, increasing their own level of social isolation, which can create turmoil on the team.

Being the Leader in the Big Moments

Sports are made up of what we call "big moments" — moments that can affect the outcome of the competition or season in a positive or negative way. These big moments are when your leadership can really shine and make an impact on those around you. Great leaders recognize these moments when they're happening, and step up to assume responsibility. In the following sections, we fill you in on these moments and give you strategies for being ready to lead when they occur.

Visualize and journal about how you're going to handle these situations so that you're prepared to lead effectively when they come up.

Before competition

Before competition is when you and your teammates need to establish focus and get ready to execute your game plan. Sometimes the level of focus decreases before competition because of distractions. So, this is where you need to set the tone for the upcoming competition. Set an example for your teammates by following effective routines (see Chapter 10). You can demonstrate a positive and energetic focus and attitude and help to make sure your teammates in the locker room are ready to go into battle.

Good leaders understand that playing on a team is about staying connected, so bring the focus in the locker room to the goals of the team. You can do this by giving a pre-competition speech, developing team rituals, or talking to individuals one-on-one to inspire them before competition.

During competition

Competition is a time of extreme emotion — everything from frustration and anxiety to joy and elation. Your job as a leader is to step up and make sure that your teammates are focused on executing the game plan.

You do this first by recognizing the importance of the situation (for example, the other team scores four straight goals in succession) and then making sure you communicate with your team so that they understand that the situation is an important one. Many leaders do this by calling their teammates together (in a huddle, for example) and helping calm them down by verbalizing what needs to be done ("Okay guys, let's just calm down and start running the offense again"). They encourage teammates when they've made mistakes, to make sure they get their heads back into the game. They're also "field generals," making sure that everyone is working together by communicating to teammates during competition.

Great leaders recognize the importance of continuous improvement, regardless of the score. Each competition is an opportunity to improve on the last.

When your team is getting beaten, it's easy for players to get down, feel frustrated and angry, lose motivation, and even give up. Effective leaders make sure that their teams never give up and keep fighting all the way to the end. They bring the team's focus back to doing their best, regardless of the score. They remind their teammates of the importance of self-respect, determination, and perseverance. They do this on the field as well as off, when there are breaks in the action, such as at half-time or during a timeout.

Todd was working with a professional soccer team that was down 2-0 at the half in a playoff game. They had an uphill struggle ahead of them, and the players were frustrated and stunned. The team had three elected captains, none of whom was very verbal or a strong leader. One of the captains, the quietest of them all, knew he needed to step up, and for him that meant he needed to come out of his shell. He raised his voice a bit and appealed to the players' hearts, challenging them to continue fighting. He told them that they had to come together as a team if they were to have any chance of winning. The team walked out of the locker room feeling that something special was about to happen. This leader, a quiet guy who led mostly by example, recognized what he needed to do in that moment, stepped out of his comfort zone, and got the team in the right frame of mind. They went on to score three goals in the second half, win the game, and move on to the next stage of the playoffs. The quiet captain's leadership made the difference.

After competition

Great leaders know that their post-competition role is to push their teammates to improve, regardless of whether they won or lost. When your team plays well and you still get beaten, it can be tough on everyone, and you need to be there to inspire them and remind them of what they did right. When your team loses because of poor preparation or lack of effort or focus, you need to hold the entire team (including yourself) accountable by addressing what went wrong, starting with an example of how you failed in your execution. Discuss the team's failures, and have them talk about ways to avoid these failures next time. *Remember:* Start with your own example.

We also encourage leaders to hold their athletes accountable after competition with mental training, making sure their teammates take a few minutes to write in their performance journals about what went well, what they learned, and what to improve upon next time.

Timing is key when you're delivering important messages. Sometimes these messages involve a hug, and sometimes they're about delivering a swift kick in the pants. In general, the best time to do either is immediately after the important event occurs. If it involves a hug, feel free to do it publicly. If it involves a kick in the posterior, do so privately in order to avoid embarrassing or shaming your teammate.

Monitor your own emotions and make sure you're in the right frame of mind when speaking with your teammates. If you're frustrated about your own poor performance or the performance of the team as a whole, you may be better off waiting 24 hours to talk to the team. Not everything needs to be said immediately. You're better off waiting and delivering a powerful and effective message when you're ready.

In the off-season

Because it takes much more work and effort to remain competitive in sports today, off-season training has become the norm. A leader's role becomes magnified then, because it's all too easy to let off-season conditioning and training fall by the wayside.

As a leader, you have two roles in off-season training. You have to

- ✔ **Walk the walk.** In other words, you have to be in the weight room and on the field, doing whatever it takes to physically and mentally improve as an athlete. Champions are made in the off-season, and you need to prove that you believe that by giving your off-season as much attention as you do the season itself.

- ✔ **Organize off-season training and motivate your teammates to attend.** Coaches are restricted in the amount of contact they can have with athletes in the off-season, which puts more responsibility on team leaders. Many off-season conditioning programs are optional, though strongly encouraged, and sometimes players need a little help staying motivated to train throughout the off-season.

During practice

How you practice is how you perform. So, if your team practices with 80 percent focus or intensity, that's exactly how you'll perform — and 80 percent is not good enough to get the results you want (even if 80 percent is enough to get you the win).

Staying focused and motivated during practice is much harder than it is during competition. In competition, the atmosphere and the fans help to focus your attention, and you're doing exactly what you *want* to be doing — competing. During practice and training — the long, thankless hours when no one's cheering you on — leadership is critical. As a leader, you have to push your teammates to their limits during practice, help them stay focused, encourage them to battle through the long hours in the weight room when there is no immediate gain and the season seems so far away, and keep them zeroed in on why they're training in the first place.

Here are some ways you can motivate your teammates:

- ✓ **Make sure you check in often during practice with your teammates.** You don't have to call a formal team meeting or anything. Just make sure you're keeping communication lines open.

- ✓ **Be out in front at practice.** Be where the action is. Lead by example. Make things happen.

- ✓ **Praise your teammates' efforts publicly, as often as you can.** Your teammates will feel better and will stay motivated when they realize that someone is noticing all their hard work.

- ✓ **E-mail your teammates inspirational words, quotes, or stories about great athletes.** Give them the continuous boosts of motivation we all need. Remind them of the long-term purpose and why you're doing what you're doing as a team.

You need to act as a leader in practice so that you can lead effectively in competition. If your teammates don't respect you as the leader in practice, you won't have any influence during games.

Off the field

Charles Barkley, the former NBA star, said years ago that he didn't want to be a role model for young kids. Well, he may not have *wanted* that job, but because of his position as a pro athlete, he *was* a role model, whether he liked it or not. Being a role model came with the territory.

Leaders face the same issue, whether they're playing in the pros or they're in high school. When you're a team leader, you're responsible for acting like one, on and off the field. No matter how great you are in training and competition, if you engage in questionable behaviors off the field, you lose your positive influence on your team. When leaders don't take care of their bodies — using or abusing alcohol or drugs, carousing at all hours of the night, treating their girlfriends or boyfriends poorly — they lose respect and credibility among their coaches, teammates, and fans.

If you accept a leadership position on your team — whether you're named a captain or you're a leader in a more informal capacity — you have to accept the fact that your responsibilities extend beyond the playing field. If you aren't okay with being a leader 24/7/365, then you need to give up that leadership role and let someone else who *is* willing to handle the responsibility do the job.

Sports psychology as a career

As sports psychologists, we're often asked by younger athletes how they, too, can get involved in the world of sports psychology. We're often approached by clinicians and therapists who are former athletes and want to get involved in working clinically with athletes, too. Here are our recommendations for exploring and carving out your own career in the exciting world of sports psychology:

✔ **Understand why you want to work with athletes.** Before you embark on a career as a sports psychologist, you need to know why you want to do this type of work. Many sports psychologists grew up participating in multiple sports, at different competitive levels. Continuing to work in the field of athletics is a natural extension of their interest in sports and competition — and that's a great reason to pursue a career in this field. On the other hand, if you just want to be a part of big-time athletics or hang around with top athletes, choose another profession — athletes will quickly learn to distrust your motives if you're in it for the access to celebrities.

✔ **Check your ego at the door.** Like other professions that are associated with elite athletes, the field of sports psychology seems to attract its share of big egos. One thing you'll learn quickly in this field is that sports psychology is a very "behind-the-scenes" and occasionally thankless profession. If you can understand that from the beginning, and simply enjoy being one small piece of the performance puzzle in your work with athletes, you'll do a better job and enjoy your work even more.

✔ **Start with the end in mind.** Think first about what your ideal job would be in the world of sports psychology. Do you want to have your own business? Do you want to be a part of a university or medical center? What level of athletes do you want to work with? Jobs with professional teams and professional athletes are few and far between. Know what you want prior to embarking on your career path, and you'll save yourself a lot of time and energy.

✔ **Interview people in the field who are already doing what you want to do.** This step is an important one. By interviewing professionals who are already in the trenches doing sports psychology work, you can avoid making common blunders (such as focusing only on sports psychology training) that will make you less marketable as a

(continued)

(continued)

professional later on. You'll also get a feel for styles of working and be better able to tailor your own style accordingly.

- ✔ **Know that there are numerous areas in the field of sports psychology, not just performance improvement.** Sports psychologists work with clinical issues, such as drug abuse, depression, eating disorders, and stress. They can work with all different levels of athletes, including youth and high school athletes. (Actually, because there are more youth and high school athletes than there are professional athletes, the market in working with student-athletes is enormous.) They work with coaches and coaching education, parents and youth programs. Sports psychologists also work with exercise adherence and weight management programs, even in medical settings with physical therapists and physicians. There are all kinds of exciting possibilities in the field of sports psychology.

- ✔ **Get solid and comprehensive training.** This step is critical to becoming a well-trained sports psychology professional. There is considerable debate within the field about which credentials are important for practitioners of sports psychology. We believe that comprehensive training — a doctorate in clinical or counseling psychology, plus extensive training in applied sports psychology theory and principles — is the best way to go because of the complexity of issues that can affect performance. Without clinical training, you'll find that you need to refer athletes out to other professionals for issues such as depression or anxiety, further narrowing the scope of your practice as a professional to only

performance issues. By getting both performance *and* clinical training, you open the door to many more career opportunities.

- ✔ **Buy every book you can that discusses sports psychology principles.** If you want to be in this field, you need to stay on top of the latest research and theories related to performance and sports psychology. Read everything you can, starting with this book, of course!

- ✔ **Be realistic.** Not everyone is cut out for a career as a sports psychologist. Jobs are few and far between. You need creativity and persistence. You'll need a thick skin and a determined nature to succeed, so stay realistic (even while being optimistic) along the way to your goal. There are few jobs in sports psychology — you can't simply look on craigslist or post your resume on Monster.com and expect calls. It doesn't happen. Most people in the field are doing sports psychology work part-time; they might have a part-time academic position, too. Even sports psychologists who own their own practices or businesses are usually doing a number of different things in order to make their practices financially successful.

- ✔ **Be persistent.** A career in sports psychology can be extremely satisfying, exciting, and rewarding. However, you'll need a stubborn personality and persistence to get to the top in this field. You'll need to log many long hours of hard work to achieve your dreams. Don't give up on your dream if you truly desire it!

Enhancing Your Leadership Skills

Whether you were a born leader or you have to work to assume a leadership role, you need to constantly work to improve your leadership skills. In this section, we tell you what you can do to enhance your leadership skills.

Building trust and respect

The first step toward being a great leader is to earn the trust and respect of your teammates. They won't follow you if they don't trust and respect you. Here are some ways you can work to build trust with your teammates:

- ✔ **Follow through on your promises.** Nothing destroys trust more quickly than a broken promise.

- ✔ **Be patient.** Trust can take time. Don't force it or demand it. Let it develop at its own pace.

- ✔ **Remember that your teammates are watching what you say and how you behave.** Talk and behave in a way that you can be proud of, regardless of who is (or isn't) around.

- ✔ **Listen more than you speak.** Listening helps to build trust quickly. It also shows your teammates that you value them and what they have to say.

If you want to build respect and trust, start within yourself. Respect yourself, and model that respect for those around you. If you can incorporate these suggestions into your developing relationships with your teammates, you'll find that people will be more likely to follow you into battle. If you want people to go through walls for you, they have to trust that you'll do it first — and that you'll be on the other side waiting for them when they follow your lead.

Walking the walk

As a leader, you have to not only talk the talk, but walk the talk. If you're always talking about how important hard work is and how important winning a championship is, but you aren't taking care of your body off the field or you're always late for practice, you aren't walking the talk. A true, credible, and long-term leader is one who is a good example of what she demands from others.

Holding your teammates accountable

As a leader, you have to accept responsibility for your own behaviors both on and off the field (see the preceding section), but you also have to accept the responsibility for holding your teammates accountable. Setting high standards for yourself and living up to those standards is hard enough, but holding your teammates to the same standard, and sometimes having to call them out for their failings, can be stressful.

Sometimes, you'll need to deal with a teammate who isn't living up to team standards. When this happens, you need to address it directly with that teammate, but in a private setting, which shows your teammate that you respect him. Tell the teammate that you've noticed a drop-off in his behavior lately (for example, "I've noticed that you seem to be less fiery out their on the field lately than you usually are") and that you're concerned about it. Phrase your concerns as questions, so that you allow your teammate to explain without feeling defensive. Ask him if he needs help from you or the coach to get back to playing the way he usually plays. Approaching the situation with a "we" mindset is critical to helping your teammate work through whatever caused the problem in the first place.

Holding teammates accountable is very difficult, and it can provoke fear and anxiety. Feeling worried about holding your teammates accountable doesn't mean you're a poor leader. The best leaders in the world feel fear at times — they just walk toward and through the fear instead of running from it. *Remember:* Courage is simply the willingness to face the fears you're feeling and take a step forward.

You don't have to go it alone — you can turn to your coaches, teammates, and trusted adults for help in holding your teammates accountable. If you end up needing some help, don't see this as some kind of reflection of your leadership ability. Improving leadership skills is a life-long process, and you won't always have the experience, courage, or knowledge to handle certain situations — and that's okay.

Great leaders are willing to seek counsel from others in making the best decisions for their teams. Being a great leader doesn't mean you know everything. It just means that you try to find the information you need, and make the kinds of decisions that are best for your team.

ANECDOTE

Authenticity: It's the real deal

In recent years, there has been an increased focus on leaders being more authentic, genuine, and real. Their authenticity makes them more effective in their leadership role. A soccer coach in a large Division I college decided to put this to the test. She had received feedback that she was hard to get to know, didn't show her emotions, and was rather unapproachable. Although she was hesitant about being real and authentic with her players, she decided to give it a go. After all, she had to do *something* — her team wasn't succeeding, in her eyes or in the eyes of the university.

The coach read all kinds of books about being real and authentic as a leader and in life, hired an outside consultant to help her change her behaviors, and discussed openly with her team what she was trying to do — a very big step, and a powerful way to show authenticity. Being real and authentic can seem to go against great leadership — athletes and coaches are supposed to be tough, show no emotion, and just get the job done. This was what she had always done, both in her career as an athlete and in her career as a coach. But as she practiced being more real with her players — expressing her true emotions — the players started responding to her. They saw her as human, with human emotions, a person who also makes mistakes occasionally, and someone who has difficult times like everyone else. As the players began to see this side of her more often, they felt more comfortable approaching her, talking with her, and even making their own mistakes. They didn't feel like they had to be perfect. With authenticity, the coach is much happier, the team is much happier, and lo and behold, they're winning many more games!

Whether you're a coach or team captain, being authentic and not being afraid to show weakness can win you all kinds of support from your team. Let down your guard a little, and you may be surprised at how much your players or teammates will give in return.

Modeling effective leadership

One of the best gifts you can give your team is the modeling of effective leadership. If you act as a great leader, players on your team will pick up on that. They'll have a real-life example of what a great leader looks like, and they'll be able to step in and serve as leaders themselves after you've graduated or retired.

Here are some ways you can model effective leadership:

- ✔ **Lead with integrity.** Being an effective leader requires integrity in words and action. Say what you mean and mean what you say. Leaders fall from grace immediately, when their integrity is compromised.

- ✔ **Keep lines of communication open.** Always talk with your coaches and teammates, whether one-on-one or in group settings. Many problems can be averted with open and honest communication. (See Chapter 14 for more on communication.)

- ✔ **Listen.** Being a leader doesn't always mean opening your mouth. The best leaders know when to keep their mouths shut and listen. They realize that the more they empower their teammates, the more loyalty and work they get in return from the team.

- ✔ **Put your team first.** Every decision you make needs to be done with the best interest of the team first.

- ✔ **Be a role model.** Know that eyes are on you, even when you don't expect them to be.

- ✔ **Display openness.** It isn't enough to be competent — you need to allow others to feel comfortable in your presence. People need to feel comfortable giving you both positive and negative feedback. They should feel that you're open to hearing what they have to say. You're one of the gang — you don't see yourself as removed from the team. Open leaders can quickly put others at ease and earn their trust.

Conflict and competition

Competition, by its very nature, breeds conflict, even among teammates. Athletes are in competition with others for playing time, prestige, and awards. On teams where the talent levels are deep and where there is a healthy competition for spots on the team or squad, conflict comes into play. Typical conflicts erupt over issues such as playing time, reputation on the team, playing style, off-field activities, and perceived relationships with coaches and other players.

Conflict doesn't necessarily have to be a negative and adversarial thing. Conflict can be a healthy part of any relationship, including those that you have with your teammates and coaches. It arises when there's a difference in opinions on how things should be done or where the team is headed.

Here are some examples of two different types of conflict, productive (good) and destructive (bad):

Productive Conflict	Destructive Conflict
Sharing of opinions	Battle of opinions
Expression of feelings	Invalidation of other's feelings
No right or wrong answers	Right or wrong answers
Room to disagree	No room for disagreement
Upon resolution, no hard feelings	Upon resolution, feelings of hurt and resentment
Stays in the present	Brings in past or future conflicts
Seeking to understand the other party	Blaming and accusing the other party
Not taking things personally	Taking things personally

(continued)

(continued)

As you can see, there is a distinct difference between productive conflict and destructive conflict. The bottom line is that, with productive conflict, relationships can be improved and maintained. There is no threat to the relationship that results from the conflict. However, with destructive conflict, the relationship and self-esteem of the two people involved are harmed. When destructive conflict occurs on a team, the results are disastrous, because team cohesion is directly related to the good feelings and trust that teammates share with one another.

Destructive conflict can be particularly toxic to the development of team cohesion and can have negative effects on team dynamics. This is because the conflicts aren't usually simply a one-time occurrence. The individuals involved, as well as their poor conflict patterns, are experiencing and causing difficulties with multiple people on the team, including the coaches. Multiple relationships are affected. In this case, a leader who doesn't understand the difference between productive and destructive conflict can cause an enormous amount of damage quickly, because his interactions aren't limited to one or two members of the team. Everyone is affected, whether they choose to be or not.

One of the primary causes of the destructive approach to conflict is when individual egos run amuck and become more important than the team. When this occurs, individuals — even the leaders — are out for themselves and focus primarily on their own individual self-importance and accolades. The team, teammates, and coaches become secondary to the ego and selfishness of the individual person. Destructive conflict and management of that conflict becomes detrimental to the overall goals and success of the team.

Coaches, leaders, and teams must learn to address conflict in productive ways. One of the most powerful roles we play as sports psychologists working with teams is to provide a safe environment for coaches and players to speak their minds. We manage the intensity of these moments and assist the team in working through possible destructive conflict occurring on the team. Maintaining these consistent behaviors and providing space for open discussion is critical. If you're a coach or player on a team fraught with destructive conflict, consider working with a sports psychologist to identify ways to restore peace to your team.

Chapter 16

Developing Teamwork

- -

In This Chapter

▶ Coming up with a mission for your team

▶ Fostering teamwork as a coach

▶ Contributing to teamwork as a player

- -

A person doesn't really become whole until he becomes a part of something bigger than himself.

—Jim Valvano, college basketball coach

You've probably heard about the importance of teamwork over and over, from every coach you've ever played for, at every level of sports. In fact, teamwork is so important that it's discussed outside the world of sports — businesses use the concept of teamwork to achieve their goals, too.

Teamwork is a group of individuals working together to accomplish a common mission that's more important than any individual achievement alone. Individual effort, discipline, and hard work are important components of teamwork, but they aren't enough on their own. In order for individuals' hard work and discipline to translate into teamwork, they can't be in it for their own individual gain.

When a team doesn't have strong teamwork, it's obvious. Teammates bicker; players don't perform well, tend to hog the ball, or lack motivation; coaches and players are angry with each other; and everyone is eager for the season to be over. On the flip side, when a team does work well together, the opposite is true: They enjoy each other's company, play their best, and put the team first.

In this chapter, we start by helping you and your team develop a mission — because without a mission that all the players and coaches are working toward together, you have no foundation for teamwork. Then we give coaches and players concrete advice on what they can do to improve teamwork.

Developing a Team Mission

A *team mission* is a statement about who you are as a team and what you hope to accomplish. It isn't enough for a team mission to be "to win." Of course you want to win — what team doesn't? Instead, the mission should talk about *how* you're going to win.

In this section, we walk you through the process of creating your team mission and getting the buy-in of all the players and coaches.

The team mission is the foundation on which all your effort and hard work are based.

Coming up with your mission statement

To develop the team mission, you need to ask several key questions. The answers to these questions will provide the framework around which you'll build your season:

- ✔ What goal(s) are we dedicated to?
- ✔ Why are we dedicated to these goals?
- ✔ How are we going to reach these goals?

As a coach, you'll want to first talk about these questions with your coaching staff. Remember that effective mission statements are simply guidelines for what your team is going to do and how your team is going to behave while doing so. Too often, mission statements are simply pretty pieces of paper framed on the wall of the coach's office. Instead, mission statements should be the personality of your team, evident in every player's behavior on a daily basis. Coaches, as leaders of teams, need to start with the end in mind, and help craft a vision for their team from the very beginning. So, get your assistant coaches together for a meeting, and take the time to answer these questions. When you do that, you can move on to the next step, which is to take the mission statement to your team captains.

With your team captains, review what you and your fellow coaches have come up with for your team mission statement. Ask your captains for their thoughts and feelings, because their input provides you with a pulse for the team's needs from the athletes' point of view. Make adjustments as needed, and then schedule a time to present the new mission to the entire team.

When you present the mission statement to the team, make sure they understand that a mission statement is not simply a piece of paper to be framed and put on the wall. It's a template and a guide for what your team is dedicated to and how they'll achieve their goals, from off-season practice and lifting to game-day decisions. The mission statement requires commitment from everyone — coaches and players alike.

The beginning of the season is the perfect time for coaches and players to talk about and develop their team mission. If you're reading this chapter midway through your season, don't worry — you can still develop a temporary team mission to carry you through the rest of your season.

Getting the buy-in of everyone on the team

Coming up with an effective mission statement isn't enough. You need to make sure that every player and coach is onboard with the mission — and stays onboard throughout the season.

Whether you're a player or a coach, here are some things you can do to help other players and coaches accept and commit to the team mission:

- ✔ **Talk the talk and walk the walk.** If you want buy-in, you not only have to *talk* about the mission, but you have to live it as well. Everything you say and do, on and off the field, needs to be an example of your ultimate commitment to the team mission.

- ✔ **Inspire.** Great leaders are inspiring and can help others see the vision of what success looks like. They have the ability to rally the troops around this common vision. Your players will be motivated when you show them how their actions will help accomplish the team's mission. Help your athletes see that their hard work is paying off — show them stats that prove that they're getting stronger and faster. Reinforce their hard work at every turn. Point out their small daily successes.

- ✔ **Make sure each player and coach feels valued.** Everyone has a part to play in the mission and in the team's ultimate success. For that to happen, your players and coaches need to feel valued. One way to do that is to take any blame for negative results, and credit others for any successes. Another way is to make sure to personalize your relationships with your coaches and players as much as possible. Show interest in their lives outside of sports. Get to know them, and let them see your personal side from time to time. Point out the small successes they have and the positive moments they bring to the team.

- ✔ **Focus on principles, not personalities.** Keep your eyes on your team mission, and avoid getting distracted by the drama and personal issues that arise on every team. Deal with misconduct quickly and decisively, and remind the team that the mission remains the same and that misconduct of any kind falls outside of that mission. Focus on the principles of what it takes to be successful, not on how a certain personality may do it slightly differently from the way you would do it.

For Coaches: Helping Your Players Come Together as a Team

One of the most difficult aspects of being a coach, at any level, is bringing your players together as a cohesive, productive team. Although much of sports is science, coaching is more art than science. Coaches are taught X's and O's, strategy and tactics, rather than the art of motivating, defining roles for their players, and helping them to take ownership of their success. In this section, we give you some specific ways to be a better coach and motivate your players to work together as a team.

Defining your players' roles and responsibilities

Defining roles and responsibilities for a team is one of the most important things a coach can do to develop teamwork. These roles and responsibilities can change from game to game, and during different parts of the season, but it's essential to be crystal clear about your expectations.

Every athlete needs to know his or her responsibilities on the team. These responsibilities are critical for the success of the team and must be executed correctly. For example, an athlete's role on a certain basketball team may be to guard a certain player the entire game and be more defense-oriented. Another athlete's role might be to distribute the ball to the scorers on the team ("pass first, shoot second").

Your job, as the coach, is to ensure that your athletes understand what you expect from them. You can do this by communicating your expectations to the team as a whole and to each person individually.

 Make sure your assistant coaches know exactly what you're expecting from your athletes, so that the coaches can communicate clearly to the athletes, too. The more unified your coaches are on communicating your expectations, the quicker your athletes will fulfill them.

Even though your assistant coaches may not see eye to eye with you, you all need to be on the same page when it comes to communicating with the athletes. You can disagree behind closed doors, but present a united front to the athletes in both words and actions.

In addition to knowing his role, the athlete must accept it. Athletes may not necessarily like their roles (or even agree with them), but they have to be willing to accept those rules for the betterment of the team. For example, when Alex Rodriguez went to the New York Yankees, he had to accept that his role would be at third base, not his usual position of shortstop. His team needed him at third, and this took priority over his own desire to stay at his usual position on the field.

If you have an athlete who's having difficulty accepting or understanding his role, sit down with him and have a talk. Listen to the athlete's concerns, and then communicate clearly what you want his role to be and why you chose him for that role. Emphasize that you've put thought into this issue, and that you feel that he would be ideal to fulfill this role. A discussion like this will go a long way toward helping the athlete accept his role on the team, even if he disagrees with it at first.

Finally, athletes have to believe they have the ability to fulfill their roles on the team. Often, athletes don't believe they can fulfill a certain role, even though their coaches believe otherwise. Your job as a coach is to maximize your athletes' confidence in their ability to play the roles you've assigned to them. You can do this by consistently communicating to each athlete why you chose her for this role. Emphasize the strengths that she brings to the sport, and how those strengths formed the basis of your decision. Point out moments when she fulfilled her role exactly as you envisioned.

Be patient for your athletes to embrace and learn new roles. Spend extra time with players who are having trouble believing that they can fulfill the role you've chosen for them. The more they realize that *you* have full confidence in them, the easier it'll be for them to have confidence in *themselves*.

Getting the team to take ownership of their success

Good teams take ownership of their own success. They hold themselves accountable to higher standards, and understand that they need to rely more on themselves to get the job done than they do on their coaches, who are there to help guide and direct the team and make executive decisions. In fact, good teams are those that have the ability to police themselves. They can take care of issues such as tardiness and misconduct. By doing so, they allow you to do what you do best: coach. Teams with ownership view their coaches more like consultants — there to help them be successful.

One way to help your athletes take ownership of their success and mission is to take frequent steps back on everyday issues, such as player personality conflicts, tardiness, lack of effort, or personal issues that affect the team chemistry. Lean on your athlete leadership (your team captains) and let them handle these issues. Let them decide the consequences for these types of minor issues. Make sure your team understands that this is the way that most issues will be handled — this reinforces your captains' credibility.

There's no "I" in team

The Ryder Cup is a golf competition between the best players in Europe and the best players in the United States. It's such a big deal that even people who don't normally watch golf get swept up in the national pride and become temporary fans of the sport. In the Ryder Cup, individual scores aren't the measure of success; instead, how the team is doing as a whole is what counts.

In 2008, the United States was competing for the coveted Ryder Cup, something they had failed to capture from the Europeans for the previous nine years. Captain Paul Azinger had spent years in advance thinking about the need for the U.S. Ryder Cup players to be a solid team. In his book *Cracking the Code,* Azinger discusses how critical it was for the U.S. to be a team rather than just a group of individual players. One of his primary goals was to get a bunch of highly successful ego-driven golfers who play an individual sport to put team first and themselves second.

Azinger had a number of insights in his planning as a coach, but one interesting one came from watching a documentary on the Discovery Channel about how the Navy turns recruits into SEALs through having them work together as small units. Azinger's insight was that a lack of team on Team USA was a primary reason for European dominance for almost a decade. Azinger spent a lot of time working with the individual players and explaining the importance of the team concept. He even hired an outside consultant specializing in creating successful teams to help him. He got players like Phil Mickelson and Anthony Kim to buy into the fact that "we" is always going to be better than "me" in this type of competition, a concept foreign to most golfers (because they usually compete individually).

Azinger was successful at explaining the importance of the roles he wanted each of them to play and explained why he was doing so. It was difficult for some of the players, because part of being a professional athlete is having a large ego. But he got them to buy into, accept, and embrace the individual roles that were best for the team, even though it may have been a role they weren't accustomed to playing. He helped them to realize that the USA logo on their shirts was far more important than any of their names individually.

As you may know, the United States went on to dominate the Ryder Cup that year. And many of the players and captains said that the team development that Paul Azinger headed up was crucial.

Another way to enable your athletes to take ownership is to make sure that you're generous with spreading the wealth when things are going well. Doing so promotes pride and confidence among your athletes. It reinforces their success as something that they've worked hard for and deserve to experience.

As a coach, view yourself as a consultant. You have a specific knowledge base, but your athletes have to take responsibility and execute. The more you put the responsibility on them to get better, the more ownership they'll take. They'll realize that their success is ultimately up to them. Emphasize to them that all the staff — coaches, trainers, strength and conditioning coaches, sports psychologists — are simply consultants to help them get better at their jobs, but that *they're* the ones who determine their ultimate success.

Require your athletes lead the warm-up exercises from start to finish, not even having to remind them to get things started. You can also ask your athletes to design and lead practices and take primary responsibility for getting things accomplished; this puts them in the role where they more directly take responsibility for the results.

A final way to assist your athletes to take ownership is to ensure that most activities are done as a team. You may be tempted to divide your team into offensive players and defensive players, but the more you do that, the more you risk fielding a team that's made up of cliques. Emphasize, at all times, that your players will either hang together, or hang separately, as Benjamin Franklin said.

Building a "we" mentality instead of a "me" mentality

In today's sport culture, building a "we" mentality can be a challenge because of the continuous focus on individual success. Younger athletes are encouraged to do what they need to do to be the star of their team so that they can earn that college scholarship. In many high school sports, the emphasis is not on the high school team, but more on the travel and club teams because those are forums where the athletes can get individual attention from college coaches. It isn't easy making a commitment to a team in this sort of competitive, "me first" environment, but it's ultimately the true determinant of long-term success.

Here are some ways you can help build a "we" mentality with your athletes:

- ✔ **Reward efforts that support the team, not the individual.** Give team awards for effort, teamwork, character, and academic success.

- ✔ **Discipline the team as a whole, whenever required.** Doing so builds accountability and responsibility in the entire team to take care of each other and to hold each other to high standards of behavior.

- ✔ **Allow your team and players to have input on the choosing of captains, practice schedules, and roles.**

- ✔ **Encourage team activities in the off-season.** Arrange barbecue dinners, bowling nights, or any activity that the team can do as a whole.

✔ **Design practices and drills where successful accomplishment requires that the team works together, not individually.**

✔ **At least twice a month, discuss with your team the importance of "we" and how you assess them on this quality.** Cite examples of when you've seen the "we" mentality and praise them for it. Have them discuss their own perception of their "we" mentality — where they see it happening and how they can improve it.

Managing egos

Being part of a team means that players have to do what's best for the team, not necessarily what's best for them, and this is an important but sometimes difficult lesson that team sports teach athletes. What's best for the individual may coincide with what's best for the team, but this isn't always the case.

As a coach, you need to teach your athletes to check their egos at the door. Your players have to accept that they may not have the exact role and responsibilities they want, but when they're a part of a team, they have to follow and do what's best for the team — and, as the coach, you're the one who makes that call.

As a coach, how can you better manage the egos on your team? Here are some suggestions:

✔ **Make sure you model for your athletes a team ego.** Punctuate your discussions with *we* statements instead of *I* statements.

✔ **Reward selfless and team-oriented behaviors.** For example, when a player makes the extra pass or stays late to help teammates, make sure to praise him for it — in front of the whole team.

✔ **Take the names off the backs of your team jerseys.** This approach emphasizes to your players that they're playing for the name on the *front* — the team.

✔ **Don't be afraid to punish players — even the best ones — for selfishness.** When an athlete blatantly display a "me" mentality and is selfish, you may have to enforce consequences, such as pulling that player from a game or not starting her next time.

There's nothing wrong with having a big ego. Just make sure that it's a big team ego rather than a big "me" ego.

For Players: Putting Your Team above Yourself

In today's athletic world, it's far too easy to fall into the "me first" mentality. Society rewards great individual efforts, and it feels good as an athlete to stand out and receive the attention you think you deserve for all your hard work. But this attention can distract you from your main reason for competing in the first place: winning championships.

In this section, we offer some tips and tricks you can use to become a better team player. We explain how to be a better teammate and how to accept your role on the team. Finally, we cover the importance of personal accountability and responsibility on the path to becoming a better athlete, as well as better teammate.

Getting to know your teammates

Part of the prevailing belief in team sports is that you're here to compete and win — and getting to know your teammates is beside the point. But the reality is that human relationships are the fuel that supports the team mission. When you know and care about your teammates, teamwork will improve.

Think about it. If you were walking down the street and saw a stranger with a flat tire (and plenty of other people were walking around), you might not be inclined to help. If, on the other hand, you saw that a friend or family member had a flat tire, you'd immediately help. Why? Because you know and care about this person. In the same way, the better you know your teammates, the more you'll care about and be committed to them.

Developing strong ties with your teammates is the essence of chemistry and teamwork. In the words of the immortal Vince Lombardi, "Teamwork is what the Green Bay Packers were all about. They didn't do it for individual glory. They did it because they loved one another." In order to love someone, you have to know him on a deep, personal level. And when you know him, greater teamwork will result from that bond.

You can get to know your teammates better by

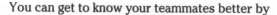

- ✔ **Making sure you give your teammates credit when you're placed in the spotlight:** This will increase the trust that your teammates have in you and help lay the groundwork for you to know each other better.

- ✔ **Spending time with them outside of your sport:** Go bowling, catch a movie, or attend concerts together.

- ✔ **Hanging around before and after practice:** The more time you spend with your teammates, the better you'll know one another.

- ✔ **Talking to your teammates:** Ask questions about their families; their boyfriends or girlfriends; their likes and dislikes; the classes they're taking; their favorite movies, music, and food. If you lead the way, your teammates will probably ask many of the same questions of you, and as a result, you'll get to know each other beyond sports.

Knowing and embracing your role on the team

Your role on the team is defined for you by your coaches. Knowing and embracing this role is important, not only for your own individual success, but for your team's success.

If you aren't clear on your role and responsibility on your team, ask your coaches for clarification. Some coaches are new to the process of defining roles and responsibilities, and they won't know you're unsure unless you tell them. When you know your role with perfect clarity, you'll be more confident, you'll perform better, and you'll improve your team's chances of success.

When you know your role and responsibilities, you need to accept them. It's really tough when you don't like or agree with your role on the team. One of the hardest tasks for athletes at any level is to accept and embrace their role when that role isn't what they want it to be. Here are some examples of situations that athletes have to face:

- ✔ Not starting
- ✔ Being asked to play a different position
- ✔ Not getting as much playing time as they want or think they deserve
- ✔ Not being placed on the travel squad
- ✔ Being asked to lead and not wanting to

How you respond to these challenges can have an enormous impact upon teamwork and your team's success. Setting aside your ego and doing what the coach believes is best for the team can be difficult. But if you've made a commitment to the team and its mission, you don't have a choice.

It's unacceptable, and seldom helpful, to pout or mope or give less than your best. Doing so breaks your commitment to the team. If you gossip or get angry or do things that hurt the success of the team, your teammates and coach will notice. You can't allow your individual ego to get in the way of the overall team success.

If you're not happy with your role on the team, you can do some positive things in response:

- **Ask your coach what you can do to improve individually and also improve your chances of helping the team.** If you feel like you're stuck playing left field when you really want to play third base, you can mope around out there in the outfield — or you can work to be the best left fielder your team has ever seen! The choice is yours. And if you prove yourself to be a hard worker, who knows? You may even be moved into the position you covet.

- **Make a conscious decision to put the team first.** If you find yourself getting upset, odds are that's because you're thinking of yourself and what you want. You need to trust your coach's judgment and put your team's success before your own.

- **Commit to your team's mission.** Remind yourself of that mission when you feel your motivation flagging. Think about how much it means to you to be a part of this team, and focus on doing everything you can to make that mission a reality.

- **Accept your current role, even if you aren't satisfied with it, and work toward changing it.** The reality is, your coach has the final say. You can be the kind of player who moans and groans whenever things don't go her way — or you can be the kind of player who's willing to help in any way possible. Which kind of player would *you* rather play with?

Recognizing that you're responsible for your own success and failure

As an athlete, you're responsible for your own success and failure. If you're blaming your teammates or opponents when you screw up or when the team loses, you're only dodging responsibility.

The key is to define what success and failure look like to you. Your success should be measured by how good you become and how close to your potential you get. A team's win-and-loss record is just one measure of its success, and it's a variable that isn't always under your control. You *can* control your effort, your work ethic, your attitude, how well you communicate, your coachability, your preparation, how much you sleep, what you eat, and numerous other factors. If you do these things to the best of your ability and you're disciplined, you *will* be successful — regardless of what position you play, how much playing time you get, or what the scoreboard says when the final buzzer sounds.

When *every* player on a team takes ownership and realizes that everyone on the playing field is responsible for both her own and the team's success, strong teamwork occurs and great things happen.

ANECDOTE

Following Gamble's lead

It's hard to argue with Jim Tressel's success as football coach at The Ohio State University. He won a National Championship in 2002 and has appeared in two more championship games since then. He also won four Division I-AA National Championships at Youngstown State. For almost his entire tenure at Ohio State, his teams have been at the top of the rankings in college football, and he's beaten rival Michigan many times, second only to legendary Ohio State Coach Woody Hayes.

Given how many players there are on a football team, it's only natural that many of them will see limited playing time. Some players never see the playing field their entire four years — their primary role is to prepare the starters for the games that season. They absorb all the bumps and bruises without any of the glory. All these players have to accept their role; otherwise, it can be a long four years for them.

It can be even harder when a premier player is asked to switch positions, especially when he came to that school to be a premier wide receiver, with the long-term goal to make the jump to the NFL and become one of the top receivers there as well. In Coach Tressel's book, *The Winners Manual,* he describes this very situation with Chris Gamble, a great example of an athlete who was committed to the team first. Gamble accepted an initially undesired role because it was the right thing to do for his team.

When Chris first came to Ohio State, he was a great wide receiver and had dreams of becoming a star wide receiver in college and then in the NFL. In the 2001–2002 season, however, Coach Tressel asked Chris to play some defense

in addition to playing wide receiver, because Ohio State was weaker in that area because of injuries. Coach Tressel asked Chris if he was okay with this move and Chris said yes. As the season continued on, Chris was playing both offense and defense — and enjoying it. Toward the end of the season, however, Chris was asked to play defense full-time because he was having such a great year at cornerback, and he wasn't needed as much at wide receiver. When Coach Tressel again asked Chris if he was okay with this decision, Chris again said yes.

Chris accepted his new role on the defensive side of the ball and was a critical part of the 2002 National Championship game against Miami. Even though he came in as a receiver, and still wanted to be a receiver during his time at Ohio State, he accepted the role asked of him by the coaching staff. As Coach Tressel said, "If he could have written his own script, he would have chosen to be a receiver, and he would have been a good one. But for the good of the team, he went over to the defensive side and then realized that though he could be a good receiver in the NFL, he could be a great cornerback. The moral of Chris's story is that if you do what the team needs and let your dreams and desires be shaped as you give to and support others, things will work out well for the team and for you."

At the time *The Winners Manual* was written, Chris Gamble was entering his fifth year as a starter for the Carolina Panthers. So remember, just because you might have to take on a role that you aren't necessarily that interested in, it just might work out for you and the team in the end.

Coaches, trainers, parents, fans, physicians, and psychologists are just supporting players in your success. They can't perform for you. You and your teammates have to execute. Those other people have a role in winning, but they don't determine your team's success — you and your teammates do.

Building and maintaining teamwork requires that you ultimately take ownership of your mistakes as well as your successes. You need to work to improve so that those mistakes don't become bad habits. By taking ownership of your mistakes, you're displaying maturity, which builds teamwork, cohesion, and success. You're showing respect for yourself, your teammates, and your coaches, and sending a message that you're committed to winning. By admitting your mistakes and not blaming them on other people, you're creating an atmosphere in which others can be honest with you and respectful of you — and the chances of you and your team enjoying success dramatically improve.

If you don't take ownership of your mistakes, you can't improve, and if you don't get better, your team can't improve either.

Part V

Sports Psychology for Coaches and Parents

The 5th Wave   By Rich Tennant

"The first thing you need to know about coaching is that it takes understanding their limitations, and allowing them to feel like they're participating. And that's just the parents..."

In this part . . .

Although most people think of sports psychology as being solely for athletes, coaches and parents can benefit from what sports psychology has to offer, too. In fact, whether you're a coach or a parent (or both), you can apply principles of sports psychology to help your team or your kid achieve higher levels of success.

Coaches have all kinds of responsibilities, many of which go beyond the X's and O's of simply teaching sports skills. You may know your sport inside and out. You may even be talented when it comes to teaching athletic skills to your athletes. But these traits aren't enough to translate into more wins and athletic success. You need to know how to motivate your athletes, as well as how to teach them to perform and focus under pressure, play as a team, and become strong leaders. In this part, you find out how to implement sports psychology principles in your next practice, to help your athletes improve their mental mechanics.

Parents of athletes spend an enormous amount of time watching their kids play. If your kid is an athlete at any level, you need to know how to navigate the deep and difficult waters of sports. In this part, we explain the difference between being a supportive fan and parent and being a pushy and demanding influence on your kid. We also help you recognize burnout, assess your kid's motivation levels, and even balance your own motivations for having your kid in organized sports.

Chapter 17

Coaching Today's Athlete

As a coach, you probably haven't given much thought to how often you already use principles of sports psychology in your own life. You probably wish, though, that you had better resources available to teach you how to transfer those skills to your athletes. Applying sports psychology in your coaching (and with yourself as a coach) can be one of the most critical factors to your athletes' success.

Coaches and players alike are learning that winning depends on a lot more than just talent and hard work. Coaches at all levels know that the mental game has more to do with success than any amount of technique does. How many times have you seen certain players who possess incredible talent, but lack motivation? How about athletes who work hard and are extremely focused, but can't seem to execute when the pressure is on? What about those incredibly gifted athletes who lack confidence in their abilities?

These mental areas of competition are where you can begin to make a bigger difference in the success of your athletes. If you want to be consistently on top of your sport as a coach, you can't afford to *not* mentally train your athletes. Not only will these skills improve your odds of being a successful coach, but they'll make the journey much more effective and enjoyable.

In this chapter, we focus on four key areas of the mental game that every coach needs to address: focus, pressure, motivation, and teamwork.

Improving Your Athletes' Focus

Your athletes' level of focus the week before competition will typically be their level of focus on game day. If you want your athletes to maximize their focus in competition, you have to make sure that you're training their minds by making certain they're practicing with consistent focus. If your athletes are engaged in highly focused practice sessions, the quality of their training will be better, and, as a result, their execution on game day will improve. This improved execution will result in more success and more wins.

The quantity of time your athletes spend practicing is not nearly as important as the quality. Focused execution in practice means focused execution in competition. If your athletes practice with 80 percent focus, they'll compete with 80 percent focus.

You can use a variety of simple techniques to improve your athletes' focus, as well as your own. We start this section with some techniques for getting your athletes ready for practice. Then we offer tips for helping your athletes stay focused throughout practice. Finally, we explain how to evaluate your athletes' focus over time.

Preparing athletes for practice

You may have noticed that athletes often come to practice with things on their minds other than their sport. They may have school concerns, financial worries, homework, or personal stress on their minds. So, you need to develop ways for your athletes to become focused *before* practice begins.

Think of this preparation as part of the actual practice. Taking time to prepare your team is critical. If they're focused, the quality of practice will be better and their performance in competition will improve.

Here are some easy ways to prepare your team for practice:

- ✔ **Blow a whistle or horn to let your players know that they have five minutes before practice officially begins.** This signal indicates that they need to begin preparing mentally for practice and that they need to wrap up social conversations and/or meetings with trainers. Blow the whistle or horn five minutes later to let them know that the practice is beginning.

- ✔ **Have them complete a journal entry.** Give your athletes five minutes at the beginning of practice to write in their journals about what they want and need to accomplish in practice that day. Journaling helps them focus on what they're there to do. In the journal entry, they should address the following questions:

- What are my primary objectives for this practice? In other words, at the end of practice, what do I want to be able to say I accomplished today?

- How am I going to accomplish these objectives?

- What mindset will I bring to practice?

Give them at least five to ten minutes to complete their journal entry. It doesn't matter how *much* they write — it's more about clarity and quality.

✔ **Have your athletes discuss their objectives with a teammate.** When your athletes verbalize their personal goals, their focus improves. Verbalizing creates clarity and accountability.

✔ **Tell them your specific expectations and purpose for each practice.** By letting your athletes know what they'll be doing and why, you help them focus on the tasks for that day. You're helping them concentrate on the practice objectives — and you're helping yourself, as a coach, be clear and deliberate about your goals.

✔ **As your players are warming up and stretching, require silence.** They should use this time to think about their practice goals or visualize themselves achieving their goals.

✔ **Develop routines.** Routines increase focus. Most athletes have routines before competition, but having routines before practice is just as important. *Remember:* How you practice is how you perform. (See Chapter 10 for more on routines.)

✔ **Spend time at least once a month in which your athletes discuss and make a list of the things over which they have control.** Athletes need to understand and begin to develop the mental habit of focusing only on what they have control over — such as how much they practice, their attitude, their lifestyle choices, and how they prepare. They don't have any control over coaching decisions, teammates, opponents, referees, what other people say, and so on. When they focus on the things they can't control, they're wasting energy — and their performance will decrease.

Todd was working with a Division I college golf team and noticed that the team was consistently slow to begin practice. He also noticed that they consistently started slow in tournaments. After Todd talked with the coaches and players, the coaches began setting aside the first 15 minutes of practice for the players to get mentally prepared and focused. Some players wrote in their journals; others spent time visualizing. At first, the coaches were somewhat hesitant to give up this time, but they also knew that their approach wasn't working so they gave it a shot. At the end of the year, the team made it to nationals, something they hadn't done in over five years. The coaches and players said that this focused 15 minutes at the beginning of practice was a critical part of their success.

Keeping athletes focused

Preparing your athletes to practice (see the preceding section) is one part of the equation. But you also need to help them maintain their focus throughout the practice.

Here are some ways you can help your athletes to stay focused better, for longer periods of time:

- **Stop in the middle of practice and address your team's focus.** This pause will bring your athletes' attention to how focused they are at that moment. It only takes five to ten seconds to do this. If practice lasts an hour and a half or two hours, stop at least two or three times and remind them to focus. If you don't, you'll notice a decrease in focus.

- **Remind your team of the goals for the day.** Throughout practice, remind your athletes what you're trying to accomplish in that session.

- **Create and develop shorter skill drills.** The human attention span is short, so you want drills that are sharp, clear, and to the point. By keeping practice moving along and interesting, your athletes are able to better focus for extended periods of time.

- **Make practice interesting.** Sometimes practice will be routine and humdrum, but it doesn't have to be that way all the time. Inject competitive, pressure-filled situations and games to break up the monotony and keep athletes' minds sharp and alert. For example, instead of just practicing free throws, assign a percentage they have to reach in order to win. Talk to other coaches and ask them how they make potentially boring topics and drills more interesting.

As a coach, you may think that your athletes should be focused all the time. But focus isn't an all-or-nothing phenomenon. Instead, there are several zones of focus (see Chapter 6). Not only is maintaining the highest level of focus for hours on end impossible, but even if athletes *could* do it, their energy would be drained. The key is for your athletes to be as focused as they need to be for the situation.

Tracking and evaluating your athletes' focus

You track and evaluate numerous facets of your athletes' performance, and focus is no different. Tracking focus improves concentration and fosters discipline. Here are some methods for tracking focus:

✔ **Begin and practice with journaling.** Before practice, have your athletes write and think about the importance of focus for the practice ahead. Have them rate their focus on a simple scale of 1 to 5, with 5 being most focused. If they rate themselves before practice, they're more aware of what they need to do to improve. Then they should end practice by doing the same. Over time, they'll begin to see trends emerge, and they'll feel a sense of accomplishment as their focus improves.

✔ **Build focus into your practice discussions.** As you begin and end practice, have an open discussion about their levels of focus that day. You can have them quantify their focus with a number, as a team.

✔ **Create a focus board.** This can be a simple white board where the team rates their level of focus in practice that week. The focus board should be displayed someplace where the athletes can see it and make it part of a weekly routine. This technique is great for bringing focus to the forefront of their attention.

Teaching Your Athletes to Perform under Pressure

The ability to perform under pressure is one of the most critical aspects of athletic participation. In fact, it's the most common issue that brings athletes to see sports psychologists. As a coach, you've probably been frustrated and disappointed when your athletes — individually or as a team — failed to perform up to their capabilities. You've seen them execute and perform well in practice, only to watch them fail to deliver in competition. This is the damage that pressure can do to your athletes.

You, as a coach, have both the ability and the responsibility to help your athletes practice under pressure so that they can perform under pressure. Being able to execute in practice (without pressure and consequences) is much different from doing so when the game is on the line or when performance really matters.

In this section, we fill you in on some simple yet extremely effective ways to run your practices so that your athletes get better at performing under pressure. If your athletes don't practice with pressure, they won't be able to compete with pressure. So, your goal is to design your practices with as much pressure and competition as possible.

Simulating competition

One of the best ways to prepare your athletes to perform under pressure is to simulate competition in practice — the more, the better.

If your team has an important tournament this coming weekend, hold a practice game the week before the competition, but be sure to control as many variables as possible, keeping them as similar to game day as you can. These variables can include

- **Time of day:** If your game is in the evening, schedule an evening practice game.

- **Length of competition:** Make sure your practice game is exactly the same length as the real one will be.

- **Quality of opposition:** You can bring in former players to provide better, newer challenges to your team.

- **Weather conditions:** If the game will be outside, practice outside. If the game will be in the heat, practice in the heat.

The more you can simulate game-like conditions, the better prepared your team will be.

Using imagery before, during, and after practice

Another way of helping your athletes perform better under pressure is to teach them to use imagery (see Chapter 7). There are many uses for imagery, but its main purpose is for athletes to put themselves in the field of competition long before the game itself. In other words, they create upcoming competitive situations in their minds so that when they step into actual games, they've already been there (in their minds). The more they see and feel themselves competing successfully when it counts, the better their ability to perform when competition actually arrives.

Here are some ways you can work on this skill with your team:

- **Journal before practice.** Have your athletes write about their performance in the upcoming practice. This gives them the opportunity to see themselves succeeding and prepare their minds before going into practice.

- **End practice with imagery.** At the end of every practice, take your athletes through a short imagery about the upcoming competition. Have them see the competition in their minds, and imagine themselves competing with great skill and composure.

✔ **Teach athletes to use imagery during breaks in competition.** They can see themselves executing perfectly in a high-pressure drill or when a competitive situation is set up in practice. They can use imagery on a water break or when they aren't directly involved in a drill and they're just observing.

✔ **Have your team discuss how they need and want to perform in the upcoming competition.** Having them verbalize the image of how they want to compete with one another forces them to think about and visualize what they want to happen. This way, they'll be less affected later, in competition.

✔ **Go to the competition site ahead of time.** If possible take your team or have them go on their own to the competition site in advance. Visiting the venue can reduce nerves and help them imagine their upcoming performance more vividly. If you can't go to the actual site, see if you can get a picture of it online, or have someone else who's been there describe what it's like (how big it is, what the surrounding area looks like, and so on).

✔ **Have your athletes write an imaginary newspaper article.** Create a headline that will appear in the local or national magazine the day *after* competition. For example, the headline might read, "Amherst Cardinals Begin Season with Huge Victory!" Then have your athletes write their own article. This exercise helps them focus on what's going to happen, so that when they compete, they feel that they've already been there. In turn, pressure becomes less of an issue.

A high school soccer team was preparing to play in the state semifinal tournament game. They had never reached the final four of the tournament. The coach had asked Todd to come and speak with the team about performing in unfamiliar situations. He had them write an imaginary newspaper article with the following headline: "Team Reaches State Final for First Time in School's History!" The date on the newspaper he had created for the players was the day *after* the actual game. This exercise allowed the players to write and think about what was going to happen as if it already did. At first, the players thought it was silly, but as they discussed it with each other, they became more confident and calm. They went on to win the game. Later, they repeated this exercise and went on to win the first boys' soccer state title in school history.

Creating pressure-packed drills

Try to create drills in practice that put pressure on your athletes. The drills don't necessarily have to be game situations — they can be tasks and experiences where competition and consequences are present. Keep in mind that you're simply trying to provide opportunities where your athletes are exposed to pressure prior to stepping out on the field of competition.

As a coach, your job is to be creative and think of ways that you can bring pressure into everyday practice. For example, if you're a soccer coach, you may create five-on-five drills with goals where the losers have to run or clean up the locker room. If you're a basketball coach, you may force players to make a certain number of free throws and, if they don't, practice continues. If you're a tennis or golf coach, you may provide the "magic ball" — you give your players one ball to make the shot, and they earn a reward of some sort if they succeed or a penalty if they don't.

Sports: Not a life-and-death situation

One of the ways to help your athletes manage pressure is to keep sports in perspective and educate them about the true meaning of fear. Although athletes may feel pressure and fear when it comes to performing well in practice, trying to make the starting lineup, or having to make that final shot when the game is on the line, this isn't nearly the highest level of pressure a person can face. These moments may *seem* like life-or-death situations, and they may think that their lives will be ruined if they don't get the starting position, get a college offer, or win the national title, but that isn't the case.

Most athletes' sense of urgency, fear, and panic is disproportionate to reality. Athletics are important, and sometimes they can seem like the most important thing in the world, but the reality is that life will go on and the sun will come up tomorrow regardless of any sporting event or performance today. Todd learned this lesson up close and personal and has shared this perspective with athletes and coaches throughout the world.

In 2006, Todd was chosen as part of a team of people to consult to the Green Berets, the highest level of the Army. The Green Berets are involved in some of the most dangerous missions in the world, where the result can be life or death. Although Todd was there to help the Army understand the reasons for a high dropout rate that they were experiencing in a certain military program, he learned more about what real fear and pressure is. During his days down at Fort Bragg, North Carolina, Todd interviewed and talked with numerous brave and highly decorated Green Berets. He heard their stories — stories about coming face to face with death in some of the most war-ridden and dangerous places in the world. These men saw some of their fellow soldiers get killed, and they still had to survive and fight on themselves.

This is real fear. This is real pressure. Their lives are actually on the line. That just isn't the case in sports. As a coach, you need to make sure that you keep sports in perspective yourself, and help your athletes do the same. Sure, sports are important and highly stressful. We've made it our mission to help athletes manage this stress and pressure. But at the same time, you can help your athletes manage the pressure of sports better when life and the role of sports in life are kept in perspective. Sports aren't life and death — the next time your athletes are having difficulty with pressure, remind them of that.

Motivating Your Athletes

Motivation is the topic of many conversations among coaches. You hear things like "Alex has all the potential in the world — if only he were motivated to achieve" or "If the entire team had the motivation Sheryl has, we'd win the championship." Although motivation ultimately begins within each individual, you can do things as a coach to improve and enhance motivation in your athletes.

Numerous factors affect levels of motivation, including the following:

- Family environment and upbringing
- Previous athletic experiences
- Physical health
- Personal history and life experiences
- Individual goals
- Social experiences or issues

This list isn't meant to be all-inclusive — other issues can affect motivation. As a coach, your goal is to understand how to best help your athletes to motivate *themselves* for competition.

Intrinsic motivation is where an athlete is inspired to practice for the sheer love of the sport and getting better. He or she may be able to practice for hours and hours without getting bored or tired. *Extrinsic motivation* comes from the outside world, in the form of incentives like trophies, money, awards, or praise. Intrinsic motivation is more important for long-term athletic success, while extrinsic motivation works on a short-term basis.

In the following sections, we offer some strategies for enhancing the motivation of your athletes.

There are no quick fixes for motivation. Improving motivation is a complex process — your job is to try different ways to motivate your athletes, as well as offer ways they can learn to inspire themselves.

Recognizing the signs that motivation is lagging

Motivation seldom remains constant. You probably remember this from your days as an athlete. It rises and falls throughout a season and through any athlete's career, regardless of age or skill level.

Here are some common symptoms to look out for:

✔ Showing up late for practice

✔ Decreasing effort in practice and games

✔ Increased mental errors and penalties

✔ Changes in attitude toward team activities

✔ Decreased performance and hustle

Directly discuss with your athletes any decreases in motivation that you notice. If you see a drop in motivation, address it from a position of concern and observation. Share your perceptions of their behaviors (for example, "I've noticed that you've been late to practice three times the past two weeks . . .") and see if you can assist them in any way. Your concern for your athletes' well-being may be the thing that actually raises their motivation.

Showing them the big picture

Often, as a coach, your job is to help your athletes maintain proper perspective. You can do so in two different ways:

✔ **Explain how what they're doing today is directly connected to the success they'll achieve during the season.** When athletes see this connection, their motivation levels rise because they feel like they're doing something worthwhile — not just what the coach wants. Let them know the goal of the drills you run. They may not always agree, but they'll be more motivated if they can see the connection between today's practice and the bigger picture — being successful and winning.

✔ **Focus on life skills.** Sports are a terrific metaphor for life. They teach people how to work hard for goals and how to fight through adversity. Sports also teach lessons on dealing with the inherent unfairness of life, and how to work together with others for a bigger cause. Your athletes need to appreciate the fact that sports teaches these life lessons, because most of them will be doing something other than their playing sports when they hit the professional world.

During and after practice, remind your athletes that what you're doing applies not just to sports, but to life. Ask them how they can use what they learned in practice in their schoolwork, their relationships, or their eventual careers. In this way, even though they may not see the direct connection of the practice to their sport, they can find motivation in the fact that it's going to help them in life.

Plus, by providing this perspective, you take pressure off the athletes because they see the bigger picture. They realize that the focus isn't just on just winning.

REMEMBER

Your goal is to teach perspective to your athletes all the time — not just when they're going through adversity. They need to know how to win with class, and how to understand that today's wins don't guarantee tomorrow's wins. They also need to understand that, although sports are an important part of life, they aren't the single most important part of it. There is life outside of sports. And part of your job as a coach is to help your athletes recognize that fact.

TIP

The key to proper life balance is perspective. If you can teach your athletes to keep proper perspective in the heat of battle or during a long, difficult season, you'll find that your athletes become better, more balanced athletes.

TECHNICAL STUFF

Mastery versus ego

As a coach, a key part of your job is motivating your athletes. One of the best ways to motivate is through positive reinforcement — rewarding and praising effective and positive behaviors. For example, compliment an athlete when she shows a great work ethic in practice or mental toughness after having a rough game.

There are two ways to reinforce your athletes, and they have a different result when it comes to motivation:

✔ **Mastery-oriented motivation:** Rewarding and reinforcing the process of sports rather than the outcome. For example, when you praise an athlete for giving his best effort, for accomplishing the task in front of him, or for having mastered a skill or play that he's been struggling with, these are examples of mastery-oriented motivation. This type of reinforcement and focus will bring about more motivation among your athletes.

✔ **Ego-oriented motivation:** Rewarding and reinforcing athletes for winning and out-performing others, and punishing them for unsuccessful performance. Ego-oriented motivation pays little or no attention to effort, process, or the improvement of skills. Here, you're focusing on how your athletes compare to others and only praising them if they win. If you use this type of reinforce-ment, you'll create a *decrease* in motivation among your athletes. Why? Because there will always be someone better and your team won't always win. If you base your judgment of success only on these things, an athlete's motivation can't help but drop.

Great athlete success is about getting better, about mastering skills and situations, regard-less of whether you win or lose. If you focus on mastery, and not on ego, you'll find that your athletes' motivation continues to grow.

Designing fast-moving practices

One of the most effective strategies for increasing motivation is to design focused and fast-paced practices that require a lot of mental and physical energy. This strategy keeps your athletes from getting bored and helps them stay motivated to improve.

Here are some ways you can pick up the pace of practices:

- **Keep your own energy level high.** When you're running practices, you need to demonstrate you own motivation by being excited and displaying lots of energy. Your own personal energy goes a long way toward modeling intensity for your team. If you're yawning on the sidelines, what are the odds that your players will be motivated to push themselves on the field?

- **Focus on quality, not quantity.** You can raise motivation and focus among your athletes when you keep practices shorter, efficient, and effective. These types of practice help maintain motivation. Long, ineffective, and inefficient practices — just for the sake of saying you were practicing — decrease motivation.

Most coaches believe longer is better when it comes to practice. Nothing could be further from the truth. Focus instead on designing high-quality, effective practices. You'll achieve far greater results without as much wasted time.

- **Keep each task short and focused.** Develop a well thought-out practice plan. Make sure each task is no more than 30 minutes in length. The ideal time increment is 10 to 20 minutes. Employing a variety of drills keeps the mental and physical energy high.

- **Cultivate variety.** Practice routines can easily get boring and monotonous. But you can increase motivation by creating a variety of ways to teach and get your points across. You'll need to do some brainstorming and planning, and have some creativity, but the work you put in will pay positive dividends.

Ask other coaches for ideas, and share your own ideas with them. Coaches can be great resources for each other.

Finding inspiration

Motivation is directly linked to inspiration. The more inspired you are, the higher your motivation. When teams and athletes play and compete with inspiration, they play with sustained motivation.

Think about teams who've gone through some source of despair, such as the death of a teammate. They find deep inspiration to compete to their highest levels. Their inspiration goes beyond just winning — it involves a meaningful sense of purpose.

Although major life events do inspire athletes, your team doesn't have to suffer a tragedy in order to be inspired. Your job as a coach is to help your athletes find their inspiration. Spend time at the beginning of the season discussing what inspiration is and what it means to your athletes. Ask them to write and journal about what inspires them to compete — it might be a person, an experience, inner drive, or something else. You can do this before one practice early in the season, or before the first competition. Make sure they connect to this source of inspiration throughout the season by putting pictures or words to their inspiration. They can do this individually — taping pictures and quotes in their lockers, for example.

Athletes need to access this source of inspiration, especially when things are hard, because it'll help them dig a little deeper to perform when they need it most.

Inspiration comes from the heart. Discuss with your athletes how inspiration is a "heart" experience, not a "head" experience. Explore with each individual and the entire team what inspires them to succeed.

Battling burnout

A long-standing effect of lack of motivation is burnout. With the obsessive nature of sports today, athletes commonly play sports year-round and specialize in one sport very early in life. Because of this, coaches see burnout among athletes at younger ages, sometimes as young as 12. You can combat burnout in your athletes in a variety of ways, including the following:

- **Randomly schedule off-days throughout the season.** If this isn't possible due to training demands, decrease training times across the board.

- **Change up the order in which you do things at practice.** This variety will help to keep your athletes interested and on their toes.

- **Alter the actual training activities.** Occasionally, include well-known games, such as kickball or tag, to mix things up while remaining competitive.

- **Have athletes learn new positions.** Not only will this provide for variety, but athletes will have a newfound respect for their teammates.

- **Provide for some sort of off-season.** Most coaches these days only pay lip service to the idea of an off-season, scheduling "voluntary" workouts that are really mandatory. Don't be one of those coaches. Allow your players to take needed time away from the sport, so that they can return to it refreshed and ready to kick butt.

- **Have your team engage in activities that aren't related to their sport.** This could mean having a cookout, going bowling, doing community service projects together, and so on. You'll help build a "we" mentality among your athletes.

Tune into inspiration throughout the season. Motivation ebbs and flows throughout a season. Make sure to address and remind your athletes (and yourself) of their sources of inspiration. This consistent reminder and focus on inspiration helps keep motivation high.

Getting Your Athletes to Play as a Team

As a coach, you've probably always wondered whether there's a secret formula for creating a team with great chemistry. If you've been coaching for a while, you've experienced teams that seemed to gel naturally, and other teams that seemed to be made up of completely opposite personalities, always fighting and bickering. You've had games where you knew that if the team just played *together,* they'd be successful. You've also had teams with less talent that overcame great odds because of the commitment and camaraderie they shared.

Teamwork and chemistry are two of those complex issues that sometimes leave coaches scratching their heads, wondering what went wrong.

The good news is that you can do things to improve teamwork and commitment among your players. As you know, there is so much more to success than just talent, and teamwork is a key component. Players need to function as a team in order to reach the goals they've set.

There is no truer statement in sport than that famous acronym of TEAM: Together Everyone Achieves More.

Discussing the common mission everyday

A basic definition of a *team* is a group of people brought together to achieve a common mission. You need to build and develop the mission of your team, as well as maintain focus on it throughout the season. Here are some ways to do that:

- ✔ **Make sure that your team mission is just that: a *team* mission.** Everyone has to have some role in developing that mission. When this happens, you automatically have greater buy-in with the mission because everyone was involved in its creation.

- ✔ **Make the mission of your team clear, concise, and simple.** Understand that goals are different from a mission. Every team has the goal of working hard and getting better, but your mission is more about who you are and what you stand for in your sport.

✔ **Make the mission visible to players throughout the season.** Often, mission statements are written down and then never referred to again. Make yours a mission that is weaved into your everyday sport experience. You can do this by posting the mission statement (or at least part of it) around the locker room and other places where your players congregate. Remind them of the mission as they're warming up for practice, as well as during and after practice. Put written reminders in their lockers, e-mail or text the mission to them, or put it on the team Web site if you have one.

✔ **Determine how you'll achieve and live by the mission.** Give clear details of how athletes should perform every day so that they have a good chance of accomplishing the mission by the end of the season. For example, they need to be on time and prepared for every practice, make good off-the-field decisions for the team, be disciplined with their mental training, give 100 percent in practice, and so on. Talk with your athletes about the core beliefs and attitudes that they'll have to live by in order to make the mission a reality.

The greatest example of your mission statement is *you*. What you do, what you say, and how you say it goes a long way toward modeling for your players the behaviors you're seeking from them. Be sure to be a solid example of your team's mission statement.

Demonstrating how "we" is better than "me"

Although, as a coach, you may talk a lot about teamwork, you need to be active about emphasizing the importance of this concept to your team. Provide experiences and activities that help with team building and make teamwork and the "we" concept concrete for your athletes.

Here are several of the most popular and effective team-building exercises that we recommend in our work with hundreds of coaches across the United States:

✔ **Team autograph:** In this exercise, you take a piece of equipment from your sport — such as a hockey stick, a soccer ball, a basketball, a baseball, or a bat — and have everyone on the team sign his name, but only after committing himself to the team mission for the season. Place this autographed item in a place where all players see it every day.

✔ **Roped together:** Buy a rope that's long enough to have each team member take a hold of it. Have your team get in a circle. Give the rope to one person and ask her to state what she's committed to doing for the team's success. She passes the rope to another player — not the person next to her — and that person does the same. Each person in the circle catches and holds onto the rope, states her commitment, and then passes it on. When everyone has done this task, you'll see that the rope has formed a web. Make analogies that we're all connected, that someone is on either side of you for support, that one player's attitude can pull another person's attitude in another direction (positive or negative), and so on. Additionally, if one person lets go of the rope, everyone else on the team is affected. After the activity is finished, some teams like to cut the rope into smaller pieces, and then use the pieces as wristbands for the season.

✔ **Video highlights:** When your team has performed well and you were able to have it videotaped, put together a highlight reel to show your athletes. This puts in their minds the importance of teamwork, shows them proof of its success, and let's them see it in action.

✔ **Balloon train:** In this exercise, each player on the team blows up a balloon and ties it off. When each player has a balloon, split up the team into two or three groups. The object is for each team to place the balloons between them and "carry" them over a certain distance without dropping any of the balloons. The hard part is that players can't touch the balloons with any body part except their stomachs. In others words, they have to make a train, with the balloons keeping them connected, at the same time walking or running through a path set out by you. Make observations about leadership, teamwork, communication, and integrity as they proceed in this exercise.

✔ **Movies:** Have your team watch a movie together. Some movies that have good sports psychology themes include *Rudy, Hoosiers, Any Given Sunday, Remember the Titans,* and so on. The goal is to find a movie that addresses teamwork in some way, whether it actually shows players working together or players and coaches discussing what teamwork means to them.

Don't just play the movie and expect your players to get the message. Instead, watch the movie, or certain scenes in the movie, and then discuss how the movie or those scenes apply to your team. Ask your players whether they have the kind of teamwork shown in the movie. Talk about how they can continue to build greater teamwork or what gets in the way of their teamwork. The movie should be a springboard to a conversation about teamwork.

Giving teamwork more than lip service

Teamwork can't be taught — it must be modeled. In the preceding section, we fill you in on some team-building activities. In this section, we offer ways you can make a difference in how well your players work together.

Here are some ways you can lead your athletes toward becoming a closer-knit, hardworking group:

✔ **Be consistent with your rule-enforcement.** Make sure that your players know the rules ahead of time; distributing team-policy manuals is a good way to do that. When the rules are clear, have the players agree to follow them or sign off on them. Then be consistent with enforcement. One of the greatest ways to destroy team cohesion is to enforce rules inconsistently. No player or athlete on your team — star player or not — is above the law.

When developing rules for your team, keep in mind that, the more rules you have, the more potential problems you're creating. Less is more. Develop rules that provide guidance on how you want your players to act ("We agree to display good sportsmanship during competition" or "We agree to be on time for all practices and competitions"), but don't make them exhaustive. The more rules, the greater the chance that your athletes will break the rules, and the more potential work and stress you're creating for yourself.

✔ **Address team conflicts or rule violations immediately.** The team needs to be focused on improving their skills as athletes and accomplishing their team goals, not on bickering and "he said, she said" discussions. Deal with violations of team rules immediately, and move on.

✔ **Address and manage egos.** Athletes need to have healthy egos, but athletes who get too big for their britches can create dissension and distraction on your team. If you see that any of your athletes is acting in a way that seems selfish or counter to the team mission, address it quickly. You're better off developing a strong *team ego* — in which everyone has pride in the actions of the entire team — than you are in allowing a culture to develop on your team in which individual egos rule the roost.

O captain! My captain!

Leadership by captains or co-captains can have a major impact on the success and enjoyment of a season. A team can be successful without strong leadership, but your odds are greatly improved when your team is led by strong captains.

The actions and words of captains influence the team's motivation. If captains have the respect of their teammates, those athletes will want to follow the captains' lead. On the other hand, when players don't respect the captains, motivation wanes in practice and, as a result, in competition.

More disciplined teams have greater leadership, both on and off the field. Captains who show up early to practice, stay after practice to work on individual technique, and balance healthy living outside of sports have a positive impact on team success.

In the same way, positive attitude and belief are enhanced by excellent player leadership. When captains have a bad attitude or don't believe in the team's potential, you see a ripple effect throughout the team.

When you have strong captains, you can spend more of your time actually coaching. When

(continued)

(continued)

your captains are doing the right things on and off the field, there are fewer obstacles in your team's way.

Talk to your team about what qualities you're looking for in a captain: maturity, years of experience, past positions of leadership (for example, student council president), communication skills, the ability to lead by example, commitment and loyalty to the team, a willingness to hold other players accountable, respect for and from teammates and opponents, and a strong work ethic. Then allow the players to vote. If you've educated them well on what you're expecting from your captains, you shouldn't be surprised by the results — most teams will choose the same two or three people that you would've chosen yourself.

Chapter 18

Parenting an Athlete: How to Be More than Just a Fan

*B*eing the parent of an athlete can be complex and challenging. Youth athletics are different today — more serious, more complicated — than they were when you were a kid.

Your goal, first and foremost, is to be the best possible parent for your kid, and that starts with making sure you know why your kid wants to play sports. You also need to know how to encourage your kid without pushing him — the distinction is subtle, but in this chapter we make it crystal clear. We also fill you in on how to help your kid prepare for competition and how to conduct yourself as a fan. And we wrap things up by letting you know what to do if you think your kid may be burning out on her sport or even want to quit.

Having a kid in sports can be a real joy, as long as you keep your priorities straight. In this chapter, we give you the information you need to do exactly that.

Differentiating Between Your Motivation and Your Kids'

As a parent, you may have all kinds of reasons for wanting your kid to be involved in sports. Maybe you were (or still are) an athlete yourself, and you want your kid to experience the thrill of competition and the camaraderie of being on a team. Maybe you were a star athlete and you want your kid to feel the adulation of the whole school. Or maybe you never quite realized your own athletic dreams and you want to live vicariously through your kid.

You're entitled to your own motivations — and you should be as honest with yourself about them as you can be. But you also need to understand your *kid's* motivation for being involved in sports, because that motivation is what matters most. Your job as a parent is not only to recognize that your motivation may be different from your kid's, but also to respect that difference and let your kid approach sports on his own terms.

You've probably witnessed or heard about parents who push their kids in sports. You may even worry that you're doing a little of that pushing yourself — or your spouse or partner may have told you that you are. When you're pushing your kid, that just means that *your* motivations are taking priority over your kid's motivations. (For more on how you can encourage your kid instead of pushing her, see the next section.)

We're seeing more burnout among kids in sports — and at younger ages. Young people — even those with the talent to play at the college level — are quitting sports because of burnout. Some kids even develop a hatred of the game they once loved. Burnout has numerous possible causes (see "Understanding and Managing Athletic Burnout," later in this chapter), but a large one is parents pushing their own desires and dreams onto their kids. If your kid remains involved in sports more for you than for herself, she's never going to reach her highest potential — and she probably won't stay involved in sports as long as she would have otherwise.

The good news is that you can help make your kid's athletic experience a positive part of her life by routinely asking yourself whether you're respecting your kid's motivation. Here are some pointers to keep in mind:

- ✓ **Motivation is individual.** The motivation to play or compete in sports is different for everyone. Some kids play sports to compete and win, but many kids play simply because they have fun with their friends and they feel good about themselves when they participate in sports. All these reasons are good reasons to play.

✔ **Make sure that you understand your kid's motivation.** Ask him open-ended questions like "Why do you want to play baseball?" or "What do you like about swimming?" Don't ask yes-or-no questions like "Do you want to win?" and then use a positive response as reason to push him harder. Every kid likes to win, but competing and winning may not be your kid's top priority. The answers you get to the open-ended questions can be very revealing, and they should be what you focus on in your role as a parent.

Your kid's motivation may change, so talk to her throughout the year about why she likes to participate in sports. A good time to have this conversation is between seasons or sports so that she has some perspective on her motivation. You can also talk to her before the season starts and then again after the season ends. Pay attention to changes in motivation — and remember that those changes are completely natural. Your kid may start out ultra-competitive and ease up a bit on that intensity, or vice versa — she may decide, as she plays the sport longer, that she wants to compete in a tougher league to get better. She may want to try a different sport or pursue a non-athletic hobby or interest. All these possibilities are completely valid — the key is for you to know how your kid feels and help her achieve her own goals for herself, not your goals for her.

✔ **If possible, match your kid's motivation to the league and the coach.** When you understand your kid's motivation for playing sports, you can explore the best fit for him in terms of a league and/or a coach. If your kid is highly competitive, he'll be better off in a league or with a coach where competition and winning is highly embraced. On the other hand, if your kid enjoys the social aspect of sports more than the competition, you'll want to find a league or coach that emphasizes effort and improvement, and where everyone has opportunities to play.

Sometimes you may not be able to match your child's motivation with his coach or league. For example, competitiveness can vary dramatically in high school sports, depending on the school, the conference, and the coach. If your kid wants to play for his school, then he has to accept the coach. If there is a major mismatch between your kid's motivations and the coach's approach to sports, your kid will have a choice to make. He can either drop off the team if it's causing him a lot of stress and frustration, or he can stay on the team and deal with it. Either way, you may be able to help your kid get his needs met by playing on a club or travel team instead of or in addition to the high school team. Or maybe he'll have just as much fun playing intramurals if he's not as into the competition as the high school team is.

✔ **Ask yourself the tough questions, and be honest with your answers.**
Throughout your kid's entire athletic experience, you need to continually ask yourself if you have your kid's best interests in mind. This question is a tough one to ask and an even tougher one to answer. After all,
what parent *wouldn't* want to think he has his child's best interests in
mind? If you have trouble seeing yourself objectively, ask people you
trust (your spouse or partner, your closest friends) to give you honest
feedback. And if you're having trouble believing what *they're* telling you,
talk to a sports psychologist who has experience with parents and youth
sports — she'll be able to provide an honest assessment of your behavior.

Don't rely on your kid to tell you how you're doing. He may be hesitant to
tell you the truth, especially if the truth isn't what you're wanting to hear.

Encouraging Your Kids Instead of Pushing Them

There is an ongoing debate among parents, coaches, and everyone else with
an opinion about how parents and coaches should treat young athletes. On
one end of the spectrum are those who believe that adults should treat all
young athletes equally — every kid should get an award, whether they win
or lose. At the other end of the spectrum are extremely demanding coaches
and parents who believe that playing to win is the only reason for competing. Most parents find themselves somewhere in the middle, not knowing
whether their kids need a hug or maybe a kick in the pants.

When we say that you should encourage your kid instead of pushing her, we
aren't suggesting that you should treat your kid with, er, kid gloves. We realize that athletics is competitive by nature, and sometimes kids do need to be
held accountable — that's a very important and necessary component of your
child's development. The key is in finding balance between encouraging and
pushing. So what's the difference between the two? We believe that encouraging has the best interest of your kid in mind and is done in a positive, calm,
and mature manner. Pushing has more to do with your *own* motivations, not
your kid's, and it's done in a negative, harsh, or immature manner.

As a parent, encouraging your kid without pushing him is a challenge.
Participating in sports is an emotional experience — sometimes it's intense
and painful, and other times it's positive and exciting. Because of the emotional
volatility, you — as the adult — have to make sure to keep your emotions in
check. You're only human, so you will make mistakes with your kid — acciden-
tally yelling at her or maybe even not demanding more from her. But the key is
to do your best to be consistent in the messages you communicate to your kid.

A major factor in how well you succeed at encouraging instead of pushing is your willingness to be open to feedback from others about your behavior. If you're always striving to become better as the parent of an athlete, and you're aware of your thoughts, behaviors, and emotions when it comes to your child's participation in sports, you'll have the greatest chance of success.

Here are some tips to keep in mind as you work to encourage your kid without pushing him:

- **Put your kid's needs first.** Remember that encouraging has the best interest of your kid in mind, while pushing has your own best interests in mind.

- **Be generous with positive feedback.** Most young people don't hear enough positive feedback. Adults are quick to point out their mistakes, but slow to compliment them on their achievements. You don't need to be falsely encouraging toward your child (for example, telling her she did great when she struck out), but you should be more intentional about giving positive feedback when it's appropriate.

Think about how good you feel when you get positive feedback from your boss, your spouse, or your partner. Doesn't it make you want to work even harder to impress that person? Do the same for your kid, and you can bet he'll work hard to impress you, too.

- **Focus on the lessons you can teach your kid through sports — but do it in a positive way.** Participating in sports is a great way for kids to learn about things like discipline, hard work, effort, accountability, pushing through adversity and pain, resilience, and bouncing back after mistakes. Your goal should be to teach these lessons in a positive, motivational way, not in a harsh, condemning one.

Getting Your Kids Ready for the Game

Many parents have asked us how they can help their kids get ready for games and competitions. As sports psychologists, we discuss this issue with young athletes when we see them in our offices — but you're with your kid every day, so you have an important role to play in helping your kid get ready to play. In this section, we give you our best advice on ways you can help your kid prepare for performance.

You're teaching your kid skills that will help him off the playing field, too. If he learns how best to prepare for a competition, those skills will transfer over to performing better in the classroom and in life.

Asking what they need

The first step in helping your kid get ready for athletic competition is to know what works for your kid — and what doesn't work. Start by asking your kid what you can do to help her prepare before games. Here are two questions to start with:

- ✔ What can I do to help you get ready for a competition?

- ✔ Is there anything you *don't* want me to do before a competition?

Many young athletes just want their parents to be positive and excited, maybe even talk about other things besides the game. Other kids want their parents to help them go over the final game plan or strategies.

Every kid is unique. What one of your kids needs probably differs from what your other kids — or your friends' kids — require. Also, your kid's needs may change down the road.

Providing pre-game reminders and encouragement

If your kid wants to be left alone before a competition, respect her wishes. But if she wants your support, you can encourage her and help her get ready to perform. Remind your kid to

- ✔ **Focus on the process of competing rather than the outcome.** He has control over the process (for example, staying relaxed, swinging smoothly, or giving maximum effort the entire game). He may also have a skill or technique he can focus on — a golfer might say "Turn the hips" or a tennis player might say "Relax the arm" as his process reminder. (For more information, see Chapters 6 and 10.)

- ✔ **Ask herself, "What's my goal?"** This question helps kids focus on what they want to accomplish in each competition. The goal should be something they have control over — such as having fun, staying focused, communicating with teammates, scoring a goal, or swinging smoothly. The simpler the goal, the better they'll perform. *Remember:* Your kid may perform extremely well and still not win.

- ✔ **See himself accomplishing his objective.** He can use imagery to see exactly what will happen long before he ever arrives at the competition. Remind him to use imagery the night before a game or even when traveling to a game. (For more on imagery, turn to Chapter 7.)

> ✔ **Pick two to four songs for her phone, iPod, or MP3 player to listen to on the way to competition.** These songs become part of her routine and help her focus on the upcoming competition. Her music choices should reflect the mental state she wants to achieve (for example, rock for excitement, slow jazz or classical to relax). (For more on routines, turn to Chapter 10.)

Have fun and keep it light. The more relaxed athletes are before competition, the better they perform. Keep things simple so that your kid doesn't run the risk of overthinking and overanalyzing his performance.

Don't comment on how your kid needs to improve a certain skill or add a new play to the playbook right before a competition. As competition gets closer, simpler is always better.

Tell your kid you love her no matter what. Sports is a part of life — *only one part of life* — and your love should never be based on your kid's performance or whether she wins or loses. You can still give feedback, hold her accountable, and address negative behaviors, of course. But you need to make sure your kid knows that you love her no matter what happens on the playing field. When your kid is confident in how you feel about her, she'll be able to relax and do her best — and let the results take care of themselves.

Emphasizing effort

To be good at anything, you need to put in the effort required. When it comes to helping your child get focused for competition, emphasize effort as the most important factor. He may not win, but the fact that he's giving his best effort and getting back up after he falls is the most important thing.

Offer specific examples of when she's given outstanding effort in the past, so she knows exactly what *effort* looks like. For example, you might say, "Remember in your game last week, when you made an error in the field, but you came right back with the very next hitter and made a great play? That was awesome, and I was so proud of you! You did a great job of sticking with it!"

Focusing on fun

Today, more young athletes are facing burnout in sports than ever before. Our society is more focused on results and winning than on how we play the game. In many ways, the fun has been taken out of sports. When you attend competitions, you may see angry and frustrated parents, fans screaming at each other with hostility, police being called to break up fights, and parents and kids not talking with one another on the way home because of the tension they feel. This isn't what sports are meant to be.

Keep the role of sports in your life and your kid's life in check. For example, before going to games, remind yourself to enjoy the competition. Have fun and your kids will, too — plus, they'll perform better! Remind yourself that how your child performs is not a reflection of you as a parent. And finally, make sure to focus on the right things — effort, discipline, sportsmanship, integrity — not on winning and losing.

Cheering on Your Kid the Right Way

Before you had kids, you may have liked watching sports, but no professional competition can compare to the games your kid plays in — whether he's 5 or 25. Being a parent of an athlete is an emotional roller coaster — you feel the thrill of victory and the agony of defeat right along with your kid. And that's normal. After all, you want the best of everything for your kid, and sports are no exception.

But how can you be your kid's biggest fan without going over the edge? How do you balance your role as a parent with your role as a fan? In this section, we give you concrete suggestions you can use at your kid's next game.

Cheer, but don't yell

Lots of parents who think they're cheering for their kids are really yelling at them. So what's the difference between the two? When you cheer, you're positive and supportive of your kid — you show him that you're happy for his success. When you yell, you criticize and judge — you show him that you're only happy with him if he does well. Yelling has a bitterness to it, a biting and ugly side that often sounds like an irrational rant.

Your goal is to cheer for the team and for your kid's individual success rather than yell, scream, and berate your kid, the coaches, or the officials. If you're upset with your kid's performance, keep quiet instead of yelling or screaming; later, you can sort out if your being upset was something you need to address. If you see your kid do something inappropriate (say, shove another kid or otherwise break the rules), you can talk to her about it in private, after the game. You may become emotional at these times, but do your best to keep your emotions in check and know you can discuss it more rationally later, when the intensity has dissipated.

Cheering creates a positive, fun environment. To remember the difference between cheering and yelling, think of cheerleaders — they're all about smiling and encouraging. When was the last time you saw a cheerleader yell, "What's wrong with you? Are you blind or something?"

Follow the 24-hour rule

Because sports are emotional and because you have a strong emotional bond with your kid, athletic events can be like a keg of dynamite with a fuse ready to be lit. Regardless of the situation — whether you're upset with your kid, his coach, another parent, or an official — wait 24 hours before addressing your concerns. This cooling-off period helps you have a productive conversation with the person, instead of screaming and yelling in his face. Besides, screaming and yelling may help you blow off steam, but you probably won't get your point across because no one can hear you through all that anger.

The only time when you should step in right away, instead of waiting 24 hours, is when it involves your kid's physical safety. Even then, do your best to keep your emotions in check so that your words accomplish something positive.

Let the coach coach

Let the coach do the coaching. You may not agree with how the coach is running the team, but she's the coach and you need to respect that. If you have concerns, you can talk with the coach at appropriate times and places — in private, when you're not upset. If you feel that the coach is truly not helping your child, then you may decide to put your kid on a different team or change leagues next season. Or you may decide to coach yourself.

No matter what, never yell from the stands for your kid to play one way when the coach is requiring the opposite. This puts your kid in an impossible situation — trying to please both of you. Plus, it teaches her that she doesn't have to respect the coach.

Have a sense of humor

Sports are supposed to be fun, exciting, and positive. Make sure to keep your kid's athletic participation in perspective. The winning or losing of a game won't change the way the earth rotates on its axis — it really is just a game. Try to laugh and have fun at your kid's games. It may not be one big laugh riot, but talk with other parents and if you feel yourself becoming too intense, walk away for a while. When your kid sees you having fun in the stands, he'll be able to relax and perform better. Plus, he'll be better able to handle defeat when he sees that it's not the end of the world.

Be patient with officials

Officials at youth athletic events have a very difficult job, and they don't get paid much to do it. Most of them officiate because they love the sport and they want to be a part of it. The last thing they need is a half-crazed parent walking up and down the sidelines screaming at them.

Even if you can't muster any sympathy for officials, remember that you're setting an example for your kid and everyone else's kids. If you throw a tantrum like a 2-year-old every time the official makes a call you don't agree with, what does that teach your kid about how to conduct himself on the field?

Officials are only human — they make mistakes, just like everybody else. If you see an official make a series of wrong calls — calls that obviously violate the rules of the game as opposed to just being the result of human error — you can talk to the coach or the league's management later. But nothing excuses yelling at an official during a game.

Don't play the blame game

Numerous factors determine how successful a person is in sports, especially in team competitions. So when your kid is competing on a team, make sure you don't blame any individual athlete — whether your own kid or someone else — for the team's loss. If you refuse to play the blame game, you teach your kid that she's never entirely responsible for a loss, and you help her loosen up and relax when she's playing. For example, even though a batter may strike out in the bottom of the ninth inning to "lose" the game, every player on that team could have done something in the previous eight innings to help the team win. If your kid knows that, he won't be as nervous when he walks up to the plate in the bottom of the ninth.

Keep age and skill level in mind

When you're watching your kid play, never lose sight of her age and skill level. No matter what level she's playing at, she'll make mistakes — even the best athletes in the world screw up daily. And when your kid is young and just learning, she'll make even more mistakes.

Every time she makes a mistake, she's learning and getting better! Even if it's a skill that you have been working on with her, remember that she's never intentionally screwing up. Be patient and understanding and make sure you're paying attention to the right things — effort, discipline, resilience, and attitude. The younger your kid is, the more important it is that he's having fun out there. Especially for little kids, socialization should be a higher priority than winning.

Be a role model

Just like Kim Clijsters, Peyton Manning, and Annika Sörenstam are role models for kids, you're a role model as well. In fact, you're the most important role model your kid has. You may not realize it, but your kid is watching you and learning from you all the time. Kids are like sponges — and what your kid absorbs is largely dependent on the example you set.

Consider this question as a good gauge of your own behavior: If my kid were acting the way I'm currently behaving, would I be upset with him? If the answer is yes, then you're setting a poor example.

Teach, don't lecture

Sports are full of teachable moments, and you want to make the best of them when they arise. But keep in mind, when you try to use these teachable moments, that you're better off sharing stories than you are lecturing. Kids have a way of tuning out if they think an adult is lecturing them. So, for example, you can say "I remember how Michael Jordan handled a situation like this. He had difficult times, too." Or simply ask them questions about how great athletes might handle situations that they recently encountered. For example, "What would a great hockey goalie do when he lets in three goals?"

Nobody likes a lecture, especially when it involves a mistake they made. Keep in mind that your ultimate goal is to teach, not lecture.

Understanding and Managing Athletic Burnout

Burnout involves two main aspects, and both are important:

- ✔ **Physical:** The physical side of burnout involves overtraining and can often result in physical exhaustion and injury.
- ✔ **Psychological:** The psychological side of burnout involves emotional exhaustion, loss of motivation, diminished interest in the sport, less involvement, apathy, and even depression.

Twenty years ago, nobody used the term *burnout* when talking about kids and sports. Today, though, the reality is that more and more young athletes are burning out — and at a younger age.

Why are we seeing higher rates of burnout in younger and younger athletes?

- ✓ **Young athletes are training and competing year-round with no or minimal breaks or downtime.** In the past, young athletes would have breaks, even for a short time, between seasons or sports, but this window has closed over the years.

- ✓ **Young athletes are specializing in one sport at younger ages than in the past.** Whereas, in the past, a high school kid might have played football in the fall, basketball in the winter, and baseball in the spring, today it's common for young athletes — especially ones who want to compete at the college level — to specialize in *one* sport.

  In fact, many parents falsely believe that if their kids don't specialize by middle school, their chances for competing at the college level are minimal. The reality is that many athletes at the college level today did not specialize year-round at a young age. In fact, many college coaches like to have two-sport athletes because of the skills and attitudes learned from the different sports, coaches, and teammates.

- ✓ **The expectations placed on young athletes today is higher than it was in the past.** Kids are expected to condition year-round, compete year-round, and spend more time learning about and practicing their sport. The training and preparation today — because of the greater pressure and emphasis on winning and obtaining college scholarships — is more intense and involved. For example, young athletes are expected to watch film, study playbooks, and keep journals. These are all good things, but when you add them to the already demanding athletic schedule, it can be much more than even an adult can handle.

In our practices, we see more and more athletes begin their high school careers with the high hopes of competing at the college level, only to have those hopes wane over the years because of the intensity and time required. They have trouble balancing the demands of sports, academics, and a social life. We see many young student-athletes lose their desire by the time they reach their junior or senior years. It isn't so much that they lose the passion for their sport, but that they burn out because of playing, competing, and practicing for so many hours, and for so long, beginning at too young an age. Plus, the pressure isn't limited to sports — kids face intensity in academics; a long, drawn-out, complicated recruiting process; responsibilities at home. . . . It can be too much pressure in too many areas over too long a period of time.

We advise parents, coaches, and athletes to maintain balance in their lives. Being good in anything takes a lot of work and discipline, but if you're in it for the long haul, you need balance. We make sure that young athletes take short breaks from competing, play other sports (even if just recreationally), and make sure not to overtax their bodies and minds to a degree where burnout can begin to occur.

Here are some warning signs that burnout may be developing:

- ✔ Loss of interest in practice

- ✔ An expressed lack of desire to play

- ✔ Not doing the extras (practicing on their own, going to the gym on their own, and so on)

- ✔ A deterioration in athletic performance

- ✔ Symptoms of depression, such as sadness, loss of interest, being tired frequently, a change in appetite, a change in sleep patterns, frequent feelings of guilt or worry, and isolation

- ✔ Lack of preparation

- ✔ Not wanting to talk about sports as much as they used to

- ✔ Frequent feelings of anger, rage, or irritability

As a parent, you can take steps to prevent or intervene if burnout is occurring:

- ✔ Talk to your kid before and after every season about his motivation to remain in his sport. Does he still enjoy it? Is he happy at practice and in games?

- ✔ If you see some of the warning signs of burnout, address them directly by asking your kid if she's okay. Is she struggling with her sport? Are there other things going on? Show concern for your kid's well-being. Don't worry that you'll put anything in her mind by asking her about it. She'll be glad you care.

- ✔ Talk with your kid's coaches, teammates, or others who know her to see if she's struggling with her athletic involvement.

- ✔ Take your kid to a qualified and experienced sports psychologist who can help assess whether burnout is present. Often, kids feel more comfortable talking to someone else than they do talking to their parent. Try not to take this personally — sometimes it's just easier to talk to someone with an outside and objective perspective. The sports psychologist can also help you with more direct ways to communicate and help your kid.

- ✔ Continue to accept and love your kid unconditionally — love her no matter her interest, skill, or motivation in sports.

- ✔ Make sure he takes breaks, even if just for a few days, especially after a long season or part of season. Sometimes all athletes — especially kids — need a timeout from their sports.

- ✔ Be supportive of your kid's social life. Make sure she stays connected to friends and has fun doing things other than sports, such as going to movies and dances, on family vacations, or to summer camp.

- ✔ Encourage your kid to play other sports if he expresses an interest, even if it's not in any formal, organized way.

Talking with Your Kids When They Want to Quit

At some point, your kid may want to quit playing her sport. She may come right out and tell you she wants to quit, or she may exhibit signs of burnout (see the preceding section) and tell you she wants to quit only after she struggles for a while.

Either way, the realization that your kid wants to quit her sport can come as a complete surprise. You may have a wide range of emotions, from disappointment (if you've enjoyed her sports participation) to anger (if you stop to think about how much money and time you've invested in her development).

What you should and can expect from your kids in sports is directly related to life skills — hard work, effort, discipline, motivation, and the like. You can't expect results in the form of wins, college scholarships, or a lifelong desire to compete.

In the following sections, we walk you through this situation, helping you to be there for your kid, so that he can make the best possible decision.

Exploring the best decision for your kid

When your kid discusses quitting sports, keep in mind the following:

✔ **Listen, but don't judge.** Listen to what your kid is saying, and ask her why she wants to quit. Ask if something specific happened or if this decision is something she's been contemplating for a while. Even though you may not agree or understand her reasons, what she's saying is real for her and you need to respect that.

Part of what you need to do at this stage is make sure your kid isn't running away because she's

- **Scared:** Some athletes decide to quit sports right before the season starts — they dread the grueling conditioning or the physical and mental pain that they know is right around the corner.

- **Anxious:** She may be anxious because she's afraid of making mistakes, being an inferior player, or not getting along with teammates.

These feelings are common and very real for many young athletes and need to be discussed openly. But quitting is not the answer — instead, you want to help your kid work through her fears and anxiety.

This issue can be a tricky one to sort out, so if you talk to your kid and think that fear or anxiety is at the root of her desire to quit, make an appointment with a sports psychologist to get some help. Make sure your kid knows you respect her feelings and you aren't trying to change her mind. Tell her that you want to help her work through these feelings so that fear and anxiety don't get the better of her.

✔ **Find out whether your kid just wants to take a break or quit for good.** You may find that your kid simply wants to take a break from his main sport and play something different or join another team or league. Again, talk with him to find out what he's thinking and feeling.

✔ **Help your kid find something else she'd like to do.** If she quits playing a sport altogether, she'll need to get involved in something else. One of the dangers of quitting a sport occurs when a kid has too much down-time or no other interests outside of sports. The key is to help her find something she *does* enjoy, whether that's volunteering at a local animal shelter, taking pictures, reading, or playing another sport.

Separating yourself from the process

Your kid will probably be anxious or nervous about telling you that he wants to quit — he doesn't want to disappoint you, especially if he knows how much you enjoy watching him compete. You can make this process easier on your kid by allowing him to tell you what he's thinking and feeling without judging him. Even though you enjoy watching him, and even though you may have spent a lot of time and money on his development, you have to remain as objective as possible. The ultimate decision for your kid to play sports is his, not yours. Talk with him about the pros and cons of quitting (not just one conversation, but a short series of them over a period of time), but, in the end, support his decision.

Your kid's decision to play sports — or not play sports — is about him, not you.

If you're too close to the situation and you're having a hard time separating yourself form the process, you may want to ask your spouse or partner, your sister or brother, or your parents to play the role. Don't take your kid's decision to quit sports lightly, especially if he's played for a long time, but if you're too emotionally attached, you may not be the best person to help him sort through this decision. If you don't feel comfortable asking for help from family or friends, you may want to have your kid talk to a sports psychologist, who can objectively listen to what he's thinking and feeling and help him make the decision that's right for him. A sports psychologist can also help you understand what your kid is thinking, as well as provide some tips for managing the situation.

Finding the right time

You may not be thrilled when your kid comes to you and says she wants to quit playing her sport. But there are better and worse times for your kid to quit. In this section, we give you advice for how to handle this decision, whether it comes during the season or in the off-season.

During the off-season

If your kid has decided that he doesn't want to play for a certain team and/or coach (or that he doesn't want to play anymore at all), let the coach know as soon as possible. The coach can then do what he needs to do to replace your kid before the pre-season or season begins.

The coach may want to talk with you and/or your kid about the decision. If your kid is comfortable talking to the coach about it, the coach may be able to give your kid valuable feedback and help him explore whether the decision is for the best. No matter what, the coach shouldn't try to convince your kid to play. You may want to sit in on that conversation just so you can step in if the coach starts pressuring your kid.

During the season

If your kid wants to quit during the season, it's a different story. You can talk to her about the reasons she wants to quit, explain that you understand what she's saying, but make sure she knows that she has to honor her commitment to the coach and team. This applies from the very beginning — once tryouts are over and the team has formed, even if they haven't played a game yet. Sticking with the sport will be challenging, but kids need to learn the value of honoring commitment — this is a very important and valuable life lesson, regardless of whether she ever plays sports again.

After an injury, your kid can and should still stay on the team for the remainder of the season. She can still find a role on the team — it just may be a different one than she originally thought she'd have. If your kid has serious physical or emotional issues, however, you have to put her physical and emotional well-being first.

TECHNICAL STUFF

Trust us, you have more influence on your kids than you realize

Research has shown and continues to show that parents' behaviors and attitudes have clear influences on their young athletes' motivation levels and psychological development. The feedback and behaviors that you demonstrate can influence how long your kid plays sports, how he defines success (for example, winning versus improving), his perception of his own abilities, and his anxiety about sports participation.

Here are some important things to keep in mind when it comes to raising your kid in sports:

- **What you focus on affects your kid's motivation.** When you focus mostly on rewards and outcomes, you give your kid a higher extrinsic motivation (such as winning and scoring critical points). When you emphasize skill mastery and getting better, you provide your kid with more intrinsic motivation (playing for the love of the game and pure enjoyment). When your kid is intrinsically motivated, he's more like likely to stay involved in sports longer and to enjoy his experience more. (For more on extrinsic and intrinsic motivation, turn to Chapter 4.)

- **Your kids, whether you realize it or not, look to you for judgment about their abilities.** When you're encouraging and emphasize your kid's skills in sport, she takes this information to heart and is more likely to continue playing and practicing. If you don't comment at all, or you make lots of negative comments, she's more likely to find less enjoyment in sports and eventually leave sports altogether. Your nonverbal communication also sends messages about how you're judging your kid's ability. You want your kid to see you laughing and socializing with other parents — this leads to positive psychological development for your kid. On the flip side, if you're scowling all the time, you're sending influential messages as well.

- **Parents are the main influencers in kids' motivation and attitudes toward sports.** Your attitudes and behaviors have an extremely strong influence on your kids' motivation and development, much more than their teammates and coaches. Research shows that fathers have the most influence, but both mothers and fathers have a strong influence on their kids' involvement in sports, through what they say and how they behave.

- **Kids report much more enjoyment with sports when there is lower parental pressure.** Your kids will experience less anxiety, enjoy sports more, and probably play better when they feel less pressure from you. In fact, one of the main factors young athletes cite in the research as a cause of pre-game stress was parental pressure. So, the more pressure you place on your kid, especially to win, the more stress she'll feel. And as you already know, higher stress doesn't lead to better performance.

- **The more positive interaction and involvement you have in your kid's athletic career, the more positive his experience will be and the more he'll enjoy the season.** If you're enjoying your kid's athletic involvement and you're having positive interactions with your kid, her coaches, and other fans, she's going to enjoy the experience more as well.

(continued)

(continued)

✔ **Fear of failing and negative evaluation have an impact on kids' athletic anxiety.** Remember that your evaluation of your kid, how you handle his failure, and how you define failure (losing a game versus lack of effort) will influence his attitude and motivation in sports. Research shows time and again that kids want to please their parents. So, remember that even though you may not think your kid cares what you say, think, or feel, you have a tremendous influence on him.

✔ **Some of the more negative parent-child interactions that have caused problems include overemphasizing winning, having unrealistic expectations, and criticizing kids too much.**

You have a very powerful influence on your kid's involvement in sport, both negative and positive. When you're aware of the power of your role, you'll be better able to remember how much of a positive influence you can have.

Exiting gracefully

After you and your kid have talked, you've weighed the pros and cons, and he's made the final decision to quit, he needs to exit gracefully. That means being honest with his coach and teammates about his intention and decision to quit.

Precisely how this happens depends on the age of your kid and how long they've been a part of the team. In general, if they're 12 or older, and they've been part of the team for several years, they should talk to the coach and the other players directly. If they're younger than 12, this step probably isn't necessary.

You have to use your best judgment in terms of your kid's age, how long he's been with the team, the impact his quitting will have on the team, and so on. If you're not sure how to break the news to the team (or whether you need to be so formal about it), consult a sports psychologist for advice on your kid's unique situation.

Part VI
The Part of Tens

The 5th Wave   By Rich Tennant

"I was giving them a rousing motivational speech from my college football days, at the end of which everyone jumped up and butted heads."

In this part . . .

This wouldn't be a *For Dummies* book without a Part of Tens. We start this part by offering ten ways you can apply the principles of sports psychology at the office. Then we give you ten techniques you can use to become a more ferocious competitor in your sport. We fill you in on ten ways to manage stress, so you can have more fun on (and off) the field. Finally, we give you ten tips for parenting an athlete.

Chapter 19

Ten Ways You Can Use Sports Psychology at the Office

*P*rofessional athletes' jobs are their sport. And in order to perform their best in their job, athletes prepare their minds and bodies, set goals, tune out distractions, achieve balance in their lives, and more. Your co-workers probably don't line the halls and give you high fives as you walk into the workplace, but you can adopt some of the mental skills of professional athletes in order to succeed at your job just as they succeed at theirs.

In this chapter, we give you tips from the world of sports psychology that you can apply to your career. You may not hear the roar of a stadium full of fans when you nail that presentation, but you'll have the satisfaction of knowing you did great work.

Preparing for the Workday

Just as athletes prepare for competition, you need to prepare for work. Your job is likely more demanding mentally than it is physically, but physical preparation is key to your mental performance. A weak body results in a weak mind. So, start by making sure you're well rested and fueled for your day. You may imagine that professional athletes live that jet-setting, party-all-night lifestyle, but if they do, it's not before a game. Athletes pay close attention to what they eat and how much they sleep, and you need to do the same.

Strive for eight hours of sleep per night. Don't take your work to bed with you. Try to allow at least an hour between the time you stop working and the moment your head hits the pillow. Avoid eating for at least two hours before bedtime. And have a healthy breakfast before work in the morning. Grabbing a doughnut on the way to work and shoving it in your mouth in the car or on the train doesn't count. You want something that'll carry you through your morning meetings.

At the end of every workday, go over your game plan for the next day. Athletes and coaches have a plan for every practice and every game, and you need a plan for every workday. Your game plan should cover the following:

- Anything that happened (or didn't happen) today that you need to address tomorrow.

- Tomorrow's main priority.

- A short list of tasks for tomorrow. The smaller the tasks, the better. Get these done early in the day to build momentum.

- The mindset you're striving for tomorrow — in a particular meeting, on a specific phone call, and about a certain task.

Defining Career Success

Every athlete defines *career success* differently. Some athletes, like Robert Smith of the Minnesota Vikings, retire early; others, like Brett Favre, keep coming back for more.

When it comes to defining *career success* in your life, you're the only one whose definition counts. Everyone's priorities is different — the key is to know what yours are. For example, you may value being top in your field, becoming a partner at the law firm, or making millions from your work. Or you may define career success as having time for leisure pursuits and family.

Sit down with a paper and pencil (or at your computer) and imagine yourself at the end of your career, looking back on your life. What do you hope to have achieved? Write your own retirement announcement. What do you want to be remembered for? The quality of the relationships you have with your clients and co-workers? The fact that you always gave 110 percent? The way you balanced your personal and work life? How quickly you climbed the corporate ladder? Determine your nonnegotiable career variables — those things that you're unwilling to compromise on. Maybe it's a certain salary, the amount of business travel you're required to do, how much time you have to spend with your family, not working on the weekends . . . you name it. There are no wrong answers here, so be honest with yourself. And then use your answers to help set goals for the next three to five years.

One of the keys to success — regardless of your chosen career path — is doing something that you're passionate about. Seek a career that excites and motivates you. Successful coaches and athletes are passionate about what they do. What career would you pursue if salary didn't matter?

If you're not in that career right now, don't give up! Instead, start looking for ways you could transition to that career eventually. For specific advice on how to do that, check out *Changing Careers For Dummies,* by Carol L. McClelland, PhD (Wiley).

Balancing Work and Your Personal Life

The most successful athletes are ones who achieve and maintain a balance between their athletic pursuits and their personal lives. Sure, they love what they do — but they also enjoy the off season. The same is true for the rest of us. Successful people — in any line of work — have family and friends who love and care for them. They work hard, play hard, and rest hard.

Here are some ways to achieve that kind of balance in your life:

- ✔ **Get enough sleep.** Strive for eight hours per night on average.
- ✔ **Take vacations every year, even if just at home away from work.** Make this time away from work mandatory.
- ✔ **Develop close relationships with others outside of work.**
- ✔ **Make sure to program fun into your schedule whenever possible.**
- ✔ **Develop hobbies, such as sports, gardening, boating, and so on.**
- ✔ **Volunteer.** When you help other people, you maintain perspective about what's really important in life and don't take yourself too seriously.
- ✔ **Schedule time away from work — and stick to it.**
- ✔ **Ask for help.** If you can, delegate some of your work responsibilities to relieve stress.

Think of your family — whether it's just you and your partner or you, your partner, a slew of kids, and a passel of pets — as a team. Communicate with your partner and your kids regularly. Go over schedules, be clear about roles and responsibilities, discuss your values, and address conflicts. You all need to be on the same page of the playbook to be as successful as possible. The most successful teams meet these same criteria — they communicate, know roles and responsibilities, establish routines, and address values and conflicts. When your family works together as a team, you'll be unstoppable!

Concentrating Amidst Distractions

Every day, we work with athletes on how to concentrate under pressure, especially when so many distractions get in their way. You have similar distractions in your own life. When you walk into your office, you don't leave behind all the family pressures, financial challenges, health issues, and other distractions that are competing for your attention.

So how do you concentrate on the task at hand?

- **Make sure you get enough rest and proper nutrition.** Your physical state affects your ability to focus.

- **Strive for emotional well-being.** Stress at home makes it challenging to concentrate at work, and vice versa. We work with athletes and coaches to help them keep their emotional lives in order, precisely because their success will be limited if their emotions are running rampant. You can manage your emotions by

  - Talking about your feelings

  - Asking for help

  - Seeking coaching or counseling

  - Addressing your fears and anxieties

  - Praying

  - Meditating

  - Exercising

- **Know your personality and the types of environments where you're able to focus best.** For example, you may concentrate best in the morning or with music in background.

- **Be clear on your objectives for the day or hour.** When you know specifically what you want to accomplish this hour, this morning, or this day, outside distractions will have a harder time affecting you.

Taking a Timeout from Stress

When things aren't going well, athletes can call a timeout and regroup. We encourage coaches to take water breaks during training as a way to help athletes refocus. Taking timeouts is a healthy practice that you can implement as well. You may not be able to call a timeout in the middle of a presentation, but you can find ways to recover and re-center on the job.

To manage stress, you can

- ✔ **Walk away from the situation.** Regardless of what's causing you stress — whether it's conflict with a co-worker or a difficult project — sometimes just walking away for a few minutes can help you to take a deep breath and clear your mind.

- ✔ **Talk to or call a good friend or family member.** Some people find that talking out their feelings with a friend or family member helps them move on. If you're someone who likes to talk things out, close your office door (or head outside with your cellphone if you don't have a private office) and vent for a few minutes.

    Put a time limit on the venting so that you don't spend all day talking about what's bothering you. Talking a stressful situation to death can backfire by adding fuel to the fire, so just keep it in check and make sure your venting is productive.

- ✔ **Get out of the building and get some fresh air.** Just stepping outside for a few minutes can reduce your stress level. Take some deep breaths, walk around the building, and walk back in ready to tackle any challenge.

- ✔ **Journal about your stress to get it out of your head.** Some people find that writing about their feelings helps them let those feelings go. Take a few minutes to open a Word document, write about your stress, and then move on.

    If you're concerned about co-workers finding your journal, consider keeping it on a USB flash drive on your keychain. That way, it won't be sitting on your desktop where a nosy person could come along and read it.

- ✔ **Spend ten minutes doing visualization to re-center yourself.** Do some deep breathing to get yourself relaxed, and then begin to see and feel yourself with the mindset and emotional state you desire. You can remember a peaceful time to help you relax or simply imagine your thoughts quieting as you begin to regain perspective.

- ✔ **Address the stress directly and then let go.** If you can, address whatever is causing you stress. If you need to make a worrisome phone call, talk with a co-worker, or address a conflict, do so. If you can't do so at the moment, it is okay to compartmentalize — put the stressor in a box, so to speak, and leave it there until the next day. But don't keep it in the box very long — you do need to address it so you can move on.

Never underestimate the power of focused breathing. When you're stressed, your breathing tends to become more shallow and rapid, your heart races, your focus drops, and your muscles tighten. All these things are detrimental to performance on the job. To counteract these symptoms, try to do some deep belly breathing. Sit in a chair, get comfortable, and begin taking deep and slow breaths, filling your belly and then your chest, and then exhaling out of your mouth. When you focus on your breathing, your body feels more relaxed and stress takes a back seat.

Prevention is better than intervention. Work to identify what causes you stress, and try to manage it before the stress occurs. Situations do not create stress — it's how you *perceive* those situations that makes them stressful (or not).

For more information on managing stress, check out *Stress Management For Dummies,* by Allen Elkin, PhD (Wiley).

Performing Well Under Pressure

Athletic competitions have ups and downs, but one thing remains constant: pressure. Whether it's a batter coming up in the bottom of the ninth with two outs and the tying run on third base, or a basketball player having to make a free throw to send the game into overtime, the pressure can be intense and an athlete's job is to perform well in the face of it. You face times of intense pressure at work, too — for example, when your boss calls you into her office after you made a major mistake or when a deadline is moved up.

To perform well when the pressure is on, think about previous experiences when you handled pressure well. These positive memories will give you a mental boost and a higher level of confidence.

Focus on breathing and relaxing your muscles. Breathing and muscle relaxation won't get your project done, but they will help you conserve energy, which you can use to concentrate.

When the pressure's on, people tend to panic, which only creates more problems. Instead, keep things simple. What needs to be done right now? Narrow your focus to the task at hand. Break tasks down into small parts — this strategy will help you improve your chances for success. When athletes are faced with tremendous pressure, we encourage them to simplify everything and get back to basics. You can apply the same advice to your job.

Developing Effective Work Routines

Athletes implement routines before, during, and after training and competitions. Why? Because routines help them consistently perform well. Picture routines as the top of a funnel, guiding you down the funnel to the base. By staying in the funnel, you increase your chance of success. If you don't have the funnel, distractions will creep up and get in the way of focusing on your chances for success.

Create your own effective routines in your work environment. Some possible routines that you can develop include

✔ Getting up at a certain time

✔ Having a certain type of breakfast

✔ Working out

✔ Getting to work 30 minutes early to return phone calls or e-mails before your day begins

You may have routines in the later part of the day that help you get prepared for the next day, such as

✔ Going over your goal list for the next day

✔ Printing paperwork you'll need to start the next workday

✔ Returning phone calls or checking administrative tasks off your to-do list so that you don't worry about them at home

Find the routines that work best for you and stick to them. They'll help keep you on task and enhance your productivity — two important aspects of success in the business world.

Make sure your routines are consistent, but not compulsive. Be flexible in how you implement your routines, but not so flexible that the routines fall by the wayside.

Focusing On Tasks rather than Outcomes

Most athletes have trouble not focusing on outcomes (in other words, wins). It's tough when, often, their contracts are based on the number of wins and losses they account for. The problem with focusing on outcomes is that you can't control them — all you can control is the process. For example, a golfer may play his best golf and shoot a 65 but still lose the tournament.

The same is true in the business world. You might be the leading salesperson on your corporate team, but still find that the team's overall sales revenue has declined this quarter. You may put together a dynamite presentation, but the buyer may not have the budget to support your interests. When you focus on outcomes, you create anxiety and, as a result, you lower your chances for success. So, when you find yourself worried about outcomes, focus instead on the *process* (how well you're performing) — that process has the potential to lead to improved outcomes, and that's all you can control.

How can you keep your eye on the process instead of getting distracted by outcomes? We advise athletes to focus on the process by creating *process cues* (words, phrases, and/or images, such as "Stay with the process," "Be in the moment," or "Good effort") that allow them to stay focused during competition. Your own cues can keep you focused on the present moment and process, and as a result, keep you more emotionally centered and help you perform better on the job. When we're giving a presentation to a large audience, we tell ourselves "Relax and have fun." You can do the same.

Your goals are important and can keep you motivated, but the process of achieving them is what matters most. The more focused you are on the process, the more likely you'll be to achieve your goals.

Coping with Conflict and Adversity on the Job

Athletes deal with conflict and adversity all the time. One of the essential differences between successful athletes and not-so-successful athletes is how they manage conflict and adversity.

The same is true in the workplace. Your *resilience* — your ability to successfully face and manage conflict and adversity — is one of the most critical aspects of success in the workplace.

Your work life is made up of dozens of relationships — relationships with your supervisor, your employer, your co-workers, your subordinates, your clients, your suppliers. . . . Conflicts crop up in all relationships, and they can be caused by everything from lack of communication or inappropriate behavior, to differences in personalities or work styles.

When you face a conflict with someone at work, address the conflict honestly, professionally, and directly. If you stew about the conflict, your resentment will grow; eventually, it'll negatively affect not only your individual performance but your company's performance. Nothing good comes out of sweeping conflicts under the rug — face conflicts as soon as you're aware of them.

Focus on principles, not personalities. Throughout your career, you'll meet people you just don't click with. This is natural — you won't become best buds with everyone you work with. But if you allow personalities to get in the way of your success, it's your fault, not theirs. Focus on the principles of success — staying focused on getting the job done well, and not letting your ego get in the way of that objective. These principles remain the same regardless of personality.

Athletes face adversity all the time — for example, when they don't start, when they don't get a scholarship or an offer to play at the professional level, or when they're injured. It's how they respond to this adversity that determines their success. The same applies to you with your job: The level of career success you achieve is directly related to how you handle adversity. You'll face challenges and disappointments throughout your career — some minor, others major. How will you tackle these challenges?

When you face adversity (and you will), keep in mind the following:

- ✔ **Take it one moment and one day at a time.** If you can't slow down and focus on the task at hand, you'll panic or feel anxious — and that's a recipe for disaster. Take things one day at a time and don't look too far down the road or worry about all the possible negative outcomes.

- ✔ **Don't go it alone.** No successful athlete got to where he is alone. Develop strong emotional connections with family and friends — they're key to helping you through adversity.

- ✔ **Focus on solutions, not problems.** The adversity is a fact, and you can't change it. Instead, focus on how to *solve* the problem, rather than how you feel about the problem itself.

Enlisting Your Own Support Team

Athletes have family and friends who offer emotional support; coaches who offer guidance and strategy; and support staff, such as trainers, physicians, and sports psychologists, who assist them with their physical and emotional health. You need a support team of your own in order to be successful in your workplace.

You need the following people on your team:

- ✔ **Family, friends, and close co-workers:** These people can all provide emotional support. They're the ones who'll be on your side when you face adversity. You can count on them to have your back — and you'll get satisfaction out of doing the same for them.

- ✔ **Supervisors or managers:** You won't likely have to seek out a supervisor or manager (any more than a football player has to seek out a coach); your company will assign one to you. But just because you don't get to choose your supervisor or manager doesn't mean that you can't learn from that person and view him as part of your team.

    Keep open communication with your supervisor, try to learn more about your field from her, and seek both positive feedback and improvement areas from her. Use your supervisor to help resolve workplace challenges or conflicts.

Your supervisor is in an evaluative role, so be sure to maintain professional boundaries and respect.

✔ **Mentors:** A *mentor* is someone who can help you along your career path. Every successful athlete has people who mentor them in their sport and you need the same in your career. A mentor is someone who has an area of specialty or expertise and from whom you can and would like to learn. The mentor may or may not be someone within your company. In many ways, seeking a mentor outside the company is a great idea because he can provide honest and objective feedback without bias. Regardless, the key is to find someone you trust and respect, someone who truly wants to see you succeed.

Chapter 20

Ten Ways to Be a Better Competitor

▶ Knowing why you're playing sports

▶ Setting goals and a plan for achieving them

▶ Training your body and your mind

*A*re you ready to take your game to the next level? If so, read on. In this chapter, we fill you in on ten ways you can immediately improve your ability to compete. Apply these tips in your own training, and you'll find that they pay immediate dividends.

Evaluate Where You Are

In order to figure where you need to go, you first have to know where you are. In the same way, if you want to become a better competitor, you have to evaluate yourself in four key areas:

✔ **Physical:** You need to consider the physical components for your sport — speed, strength, balance, posture, sleep, diet, flexibility, and so on — and get objective feedback from trainers, coaches, teammates, family, and other specialists.

✔ **Skills:** Evaluate the most important skill sets for your sport and seek feedback from others who are experts in those areas.

✔ **Tactical:** Evaluate the amount of time and brain power you spend preparing for games, watching films of yourself and your opponents, and so on. Elite athletes do this more than anyone, because they're always looking for an edge over their opponents.

✔ **Mental:** With or without a sports psychologist, evaluate yourself on important mental and emotional components in your sport. Assess your attitude, work rate, mental toughness, imagery ability, mental preparation, persistence, leadership, coachability, focus, ability to manage your emotions, ability to handle pressure, and so on.

The more "data" you have, the better your chances for becoming a stronger competitor, so ask others to assess you as well. Talk to your coaches, teammates, and trusted friends and get their take on where you are.

Know What Motivates You

You need to know what motivates you so that you can get through the challenging times. Why do you play your sport? Is it because you love the thrill of competition? Do you do it to be part of something larger, to be one of the best at something, or to prove the naysayers wrong? (Turn to Chapter 4 for more about motivation.)

Motivation levels ebb and flow throughout the season. At the end of every season, evaluate your *intrinsic motivation* (the motivation to compete that comes from within). Although external rewards are nice, they aren't enough to get you through the hard work and pain it takes to be a top competitor.

Define Your Goals

Your goals should inspire and drive you to get better on a daily basis. Make your goals specific, and track and evaluate them consistently. Place written reminders of your goals in numerous places — in your locker, in your bedroom, on the bathroom mirror, wherever you'll see them often.

Often, athletes spend a lot of time developing their goals, only to forget them. They don't take the time to assess their progress toward these goals. Goals motivate you, keep you accountable, and ensure that you're on track to success. If you take the time to set goals, make the time to evaluate your progress consistently.

Your goals must be realistic but challenging. Review your goals with coaches, parents, or mentors. Get feedback about your goals. Set up a plan to accomplish them. And, most important, dream big — don't let anyone deter you from accomplishing and going after something that's important to you.

Set an Action Plan

Your dreams and goals are important, but without an effective plan, they'll remain dreams and goals rather than accomplishments. Part of the reason that many athletes don't accomplish their goals is because they don't have an effective plan. When you set a plan, you dramatically improve your chances of success.

For example, say your team wants to win a conference championship. This goal is important and motivating. But that championship is 6 to 12 months down the road and you need to have the road map on how to get there. What are you going to accomplish in six months, in two months, in one month, in one week, or today? This sort of plan (you'll need to adjust it along the way) provides your team with a clear path of action for reaching those goals.

You need to set action plans in all the areas you evaluate yourself in — physical, skills, tactical, and mental (see "Evaluate Where You Are," earlier in this chapter). When you know your current state in each area, set goals that are critical for success, and then set a written, detailed plan of action toward the achievement of those goals.

Keep a journal in which you track and evaluate your progress along the way. Stay connected to your action plan each and every week — it's the road map to accomplish your success. Think of your action plan as your mental GPS.

Improve Gradually and Consistently

Success in sports can be a long time coming. Think about how good you are now compared to your skill level a few years ago. You've made tremendous progress, but there's always room to grow and improve. Success in any endeavor takes time and hard work. If you're looking for immediate gratification, sports aren't for you. Sure, things can go very well, but you may go months without seeing improvement or rewards for your effort.

Top athletes and coaches know this, and they still work every day to become their best. They take daily steps toward reaching their long-term goals. If you can simply work to get a little bit better today, and then a little bit better tomorrow, and so on, you'll notice dramatic improvements over time.

Train Your Mind Daily

Daily mental training is one of the most ignored parts of becoming a better competitor. Why? Because most athletes and coaches don't know *how* to train their minds. They know how to improve their athletic skills and fitness levels, but they were never taught to train their mental "muscle."

Your mental "muscle" is like every other muscle in your body — the more effectively you work it, the more effectively it works for you.

Keeping a journal is one of the best ways to train your mental "muscle" every day. You take the time to evaluate, monitor, and improve your athletic skills and mental abilities. But don't just complete a journal entry for the sake of completing an entry. Make sure to spend time working on the mental area or areas most important for you right now. For example, if you need to improve your focus, then write in your journal about your focus before practice (making a commitment to be consciously aware during practice and improving it) and evaluate yourself afterward. Use the specific chapters in this book to address the area you feel is most important and make sure to practice at least one of the strategies for that skill on a daily basis.

Improve Your Physical Skills

You already know that improving your athletic skills is necessary to become a better competitor, no matter your current level of fitness and skill. That's why you practice and drill so often. Your mental abilities might be sharp, but they certainly don't replace the specific skills you need for your sport — your mental skills only complement your physical skills.

Training physically is where you spend the majority of your time, and rightly so — but make sure you're improving in the areas most important and necessary for your success. Get feedback from coaches and others and be honest with yourself about where your strengths and weaknesses lie.

Focus on your strengths, and make them your competitive weapons. Develop your weaker areas enough that they are a strong part of your arsenal, but put most of your attention and focus on improving your strengths.

Don't spend too much time trying to develop your weaknesses into strengths — it'll take too much effort when compared to building your existing strengths. Plus, your natural motivation will be higher when you're working on your strengths than it will be when you're working on improving your weaknesses.

Tweak Your Methods

If you want to be a better competitor, you need to be able to evaluate and adjust your methods as you go. As a competitor, you want to stay ahead of the pack, which requires you to seek out every opportunity to get better.

You can stay ahead of the pack by seeking out new mentors, new coaches, and a sports psychologist, as well as by learning new skills in your sport. Adjust your action plan every so often to accommodate obstacles and changes in your life that occur along the way.

The most successful athletes, coaches, and leaders are ones who are always seeking to learn, grow, and improve.

Develop and Maintain Your Fitness

Your fitness level — your strength, speed, power, endurance, flexibility, and so on — is linked to your level of competitiveness in two ways:

- **The more fit you are, the better you'll perform.** You need to start the season in top shape, not try to get in shape when the season is starting.

- **The more fit you are, the more confident you'll be.** Confident athletes compete better and more fiercely! If you feel good about your body and know that you can physically outlast your opponent, you'll feel more confident. On the other hand, if you aren't sure you'll be able to perform your best, your confidence will take a hit.

If you want to be a better competitor and a more confident athlete, keep yourself in great shape.

Seek Out Pressure

A key aspect of being a better competitor is the art of performing when it counts. One of the main reasons that some of the top athletes in the country come to see us is because — even though they have amazing skills and can perform well in practice — they struggle to perform when it really counts. We help them develop mental skills and teach them ways to train their mental "muscle" in order to better handle pressure. Some of these strategies include journaling about how you want to perform under pressure, evaluating and tracking your progress, tracking how you feel when under pressure, practicing breathing and muscle relaxation strategies, and using mental imagery. (We cover these techniques throughout this book.)

Actively seek out pressure whenever and wherever you can. Put yourself in a position in which you have to perform when something is on the line, where performance matters and has real consequences. If you practice under pressure, you'll perform under pressure. Compete against your most skilled teammates in simple drills, create more pressure with inter-squad and pre-season games, and have fun!

Professional golfers wager with each other on who can make the most putts. Soccer players see who can hit the crossbar from a certain distance. The more situations you can find to put pressure on yourself to perform, even in non-sport situations, the better you'll perform under pressure.

Chapter 21

Ten Ways to Manage Stress Better

● ●

In This Chapter

▶ Setting priorities and achieving balance

▶ Meditating and using imagery to counteract stress

▶ Taking charge of your thoughts and emotions

▶ Giving your body what it needs

▶ Building a safety net of people to help you along the way

● ●

*I*n this fast-paced world, you're being pulled in numerous directions. You're needed at home and at work, by family and friends, at your church or temple, by community organizations and your kids' T-ball team. . . . And though the T-ball team, under other circumstances, would be pure fun, when you're driving at breakneck speed across town to make it to practice after your meeting at work ran late, it's just one more stress on a heaping pile of them.

Stress is a normal part of life. The key is how you respond to that stress. What can you do to cope with the stress of your hectic life? We have plenty of ideas, and we share them in this chapter.

For even more information on managing stress, check out *Stress Management For Dummies,* by Allen Elkin, PhD (Wiley).

Prioritize

When you have a to-do list a mile long — and who doesn't these days? — you can end up feeling frantic (and stressed). One of the keys to combating this stress is to set priorities on a weekly basis.

Every week, on the same day of the week (every Sunday night, for example), sit down with a calendar and a list of all the tasks you need to accomplish, all the meetings you need to attend, and all the deadlines you have to meet in the week ahead. Rank these items in order of importance. Maybe you absolutely can't miss that meeting at work on Tuesday afternoon, but you can reschedule your haircut to another day. Maybe you know you need to be at your kids' school every weekday at 3 p.m., but you can put off going to the grocery store until Saturday.

Be honest with yourself about how much you can reasonably accomplish on a given day. If you know you won't be able to get it all done, look for ways to shuffle things around or ask for help from a friend, your partner, or someone at work. There are only so many hours in the day — make sure you don't commit yourself to doing more than is humanly possible.

Some of your priorities are big-picture priorities — ones that will remain the same week after week. At the top of that list should be your emotional and physical health. The more stress you're feeling, the more important it is for you to nourish your body and mind. Make time to work out, spend time with supportive family and friends, pursue hobbies, and get enough rest and relaxation. When you're emotionally and physically healthy, you'll be better able to balance out your stressful schedule — and to handle whatever unexpected stresses come your way.

Strive for Balance

Good things come to those who are balanced. When you strike a balance between work, play, and rest, not only do you perform better, but you're better able to withstand the pressures and stresses of everyday life.

Muscles are grouped in pairs — the biceps contract while the triceps relax. Similarly, when you're actively engaged in play, you aren't stressing about work. When you're actively engaged in and enjoying your work, you aren't focusing on needing to play. And when you're resting, you're able to put both work and play out of your mind for a while. This sense of balance among work, play, and rest allows for better focus and concentration. Plus, you can pursue each activity with more focus and energy.

When you're setting your priorities for the week ahead (see the preceding section), make sure that you have a balance between work, play, and rest. If all your priorities are work-related, your level of stress will increase.

There is no such thing as "perfect" balance. Your goal is a healthy, low-stress lifestyle. Some weeks your life will be out of balance because of deadlines at work or family responsibilities, but make sure these times are the minority.

Meditate

Meditation is a wonderful tool that many people use to combat the stress in their daily lives. Research has shown that regularly engaging in some form of meditation can reduce levels of stress hormones in the blood, lower blood pressure, and improve mental functioning. The benefits of meditation are enormous. And the best part is that the *form* of meditation you choose to practice doesn't really matter — what matters is that you do it regularly.

Most forms of meditation require you to sit quietly and focus on two things:

- ✔ **The pace of your breathing:** While meditating, your goal is to slow your breathing by focusing on steady, smooth, and deep breaths, in and out.

- ✔ **A cue word or phrase:** Cue words or phrases (such as *relax, one,* or *ohm*) serve to help you maintain focus on one thing.

When you first start practicing meditation, you'll notice that your mind wanders very quickly. When that happens, bring your attention back to the cue word or phrase immediately. Let go of the distractions that enter your mind, and simply listen for the answers to your daily stressors as you sit quietly, contemplating and focusing on your cue word or phrase.

Start with 5 minutes of meditation, and try to work yourself up to longer time intervals, such as 20 to 30 minutes.

Another concept similar to meditation is *mindfulness,* which is the practice of being present in everyday life, from the trivial tasks such as washing dishes or eating to the more complex, such as working on a project or having an important conversation. Mindfulness also involves non-judgment — avoiding negatively evaluating yourself for mistakes or uncomfortable feelings.

If you're new to meditation and you aren't sure where to start, check out *Meditation For Dummies,* 2nd Edition, by Stephan Bodian (Wiley). It comes with a CD containing more than 70 minutes of guided meditations.

Use Imagery

You already use imagery, whether you realize it or not. Every time you try to remember where you put your car keys, every time you think back to your last vacation with a smile on your face, you're using imagery.

You can use imagery to reduce the stress in your life by mentally imaging how you *want* your life to be, and by consistently creating positive, healthy, stress-free images in your mind.

When you hold positive images in your mind, they cause your body to release *endorphins* (hormones that reduce pain) and chemicals (neurotransmitters like serotonin) that make you feel good.

In your daily life, try to form vivid images (the more vivid, the better!) of what you want your life to look like. The more you can imagine your life as you want it, full of joy and happiness, the more likely you'll be to actually create that life for yourself in the future. But don't just do this practice for the big picture. Imagine what you want your mind, body, and attitude to be like for an important conversation with your boss, a classmate, or a friend; when you're stuck in traffic; when you're working toward an important deadline; or when you're at the gym. Imagery works for big and small things. (For more on imagery, turn to Chapter 7.)

What your mind perceives, your body achieves.

Manage Your Thoughts and Emotions

Your thoughts directly correlate to how much stress you experience. All your emotions flow from your thoughts. So, the key is to proactively manage how you look at the world.

Basically, you have two ways to look at every situation: up or down. You can see the positives in the situation, or you can focus on the negatives. These two paths result in opposite emotional reactions. When you choose to see the positives, you'll experience more positive emotions, such as happiness, joy, and curiosity. When you choose to focus on the negatives, you'll endure more negative emotions, such as sadness, anger, and despair.

We aren't saying that things should always be rosy, or that you have to bury your head in the sand when you face challenging situations. We just want you to know that you *do* have a choice in how you manage your thoughts and emotions and, in turn, your level of stress.

Situations are not stressful in and of themselves. It's what you think and feel about a situation that makes it stressful or not. No matter who you are, you're guaranteed to face difficult times — any athlete knows this — but those difficult moments and experiences don't have to completely take you off the playing field of life. Manage your thoughts and emotions, or they'll manage you!

Exercise

Exercise is one of the best ways to manage your health. Plus, it's a natural remedy to stress. If you want to beat back the negative effects of stress, make sure you're engaging in some sort of regular exercise. You don't have to work out like you're training for the Olympics to see the benefits of exercise. The key is simply to get your muscles pumping, your blood flowing, and some sweat forming. Even something as simple as a daily walk with your dog at a slightly increased pace will provide cardiovascular benefits and decrease stress.

Start small and build your way up in terms of frequency and intensity. If you can't remember the last time your gym shorts saw the light of day, going for a 20-minute brisk walk once or twice a week is a great start. Then, when your body has adjusted to this routine, increase the number of days per week and the amount of minutes per walk.

The key is to choose an exercise that fits into your lifestyle. Walking is one of the best forms of exercise because anyone can do it, just about anywhere and anytime.

If you're feeling ambitious and thinking about starting a more elaborate and intense workout routine, get a medical checkup before you start, just to make sure that all systems are go.

If you're having trouble sticking to your exercise routine, partner up with a friend who can hold you accountable. If you know that your neighbor is going to be standing in your driveway at 6:30 a.m., ready to walk with you, you'll be more likely to drag yourself out of bed. If you work out at a gym, pack a gym bag and exchange bags with your partner — that way, if you don't show up for your workout, not only are *you* missing out on the workout, but your partner is, too!

Don't beat yourself up if you miss a workout once in a while. Just figure out how you went off track, and get back on track the next day.

Get Enough Sleep

Sleep is a key component to health. In fact, research has linked sleep deprivation with decreased immune system functioning, increased blood pressure, decreased mental focus, and even increased odds of on-the-job mistakes and car accidents! Sleep deprivation also reduces the mental and physical energy you need to manage stress. It even increases the release of stress hormones like adrenaline and cortisol in the brain.

The problem with sleep deprivation is that its onset is unnoticeable and seemingly harmless. It usually starts with staying up late to take care of some pressing task. One night of reduced sleep turns into a week, and that lack of sleep begins to pile up. If you miss one hour of sleep a night from your normal sleep schedule, over the course of a month, you'll have missed *four full nights* of sleep. Over a year, you'll have missed almost *50 days* of restful sleep!

When you know that increased stress is headed your way (for example, around the holidays, when your workload is particularly heavy, during finals week if you're in school, and so on), or when you feel a cold coming on, adjust your schedule so that you get more sleep. The best way to do this is to go to bed half an hour to an hour earlier. This shift won't impair your normal night-time routine too much, and it'll be easy to implement.

For some people, sleep deprivation is a result of their choices — they choose to stay up late to work or hang out with friends or watch TV — and simply choosing differently will alleviate the sleep deprivation. But for many people, sleep deprivation is a result of *insomnia* (the inability to sleep), often caused by anxiety and stress. And, unfortunately, lack of sleep can compound that anxiety and stress, which results in a vicious circle.

If you're suffering from insomnia, we recommend *Sleep Disorders For Dummies,* by Max Hirshkowitz, PhD, ABSM, and Patricia B. Smith (Wiley). Also, talk to your doctor. Sleep deprivation is a serious issue, and you owe it to yourself to treat it.

Cultivate a Support Network

Humans are social creatures by nature. We need each other. Don't believe us? Consider this: What's the most inhumane way to punish someone? Solitary confinement. Those old clichés about being a "lone ranger" or "going it alone" may sound romantic, but the truth is, they don't work.

A key part of being able to cope with stress is having a strong support network. When you have family and friends who are there for you, you'll be much better able to survive life's challenges — and your level of stress will be reduced.

You don't want to surround yourself only with people who agree with everything you say. You need people on your side who will challenge you to be the best version of yourself.

Get in the habit of making one or two phone calls every day to connect with someone. If you live with people — whether roommates or family members — try to have a meaningful conversation with one of them every day. These conversations don't have to be long — just a few short minutes can be beneficial. If you develop this habit of reaching out to people when things are going well, you'll be able to reach out to them when times are tough.

You might be thinking, "I can't call so-and-so. He doesn't want to hear about my problem." But the truth is, most people are grateful you called for their help. Just think about how good you feel when someone calls on *you* for help. Do the same for someone else — help yourself and help them! You'll thank yourself down the road.

Laugh

One of the problems that can accompany success in any endeavor is that you can develop an over-inflated sense of yourself. You start to believe your press clippings, as they say in the sports world. Eventually, you start thinking you're bigger than life, and you take yourself too seriously.

The problem with taking yourself too seriously is twofold:

- ✔ Life is full of ups and downs. When you set yourself on such a high pedestal, the fall is steep and inevitable.

- ✔ You lose all perspective on what life is really about. You lose sight of the fact that nobody who experiences success does it without the help of others.

Research shows that laughter is one of the best medicines — it provides greater mental and physical health. You need to enjoy the simple things of life and laugh whenever you have a chance. Laughter is like a booster shot to your mental and physical health — every dose brings much more peace and happiness. Learn to laugh at yourself as well — you *will* make mistakes, sometimes dumb ones, but you don't have to take them seriously.

Practice Gratitude

One of the best ways to manage stress is to practice gratitude on a daily basis. You have to train your mind to practice gratitude, but it's worth the effort, because practicing gratitude is one of the best and most effective stress busters.

When you lack something you believe you need or something you want and can't have, you feel stress. Think about it — how many times have you though about wanting more money, a nicer car, a better job, more vacation time, a new iPod, or a flat-screen TV? This constant *wanting* creates stress because you're in a constant state of anxiety over what you don't have.

At the end of every day, make a list of 25 things you're grateful for. Try it for 30 days, and you'll be amazed at how your stress level drops!

Are you thinking that there's no way you have time to come up with 25 things you're thankful for every single day? Here's a list we made in less than three minutes:

- ✔ Warmer weather
- ✔ A hot cup of coffee in the morning
- ✔ A hot shower
- ✔ A good run
- ✔ Sunshine coming into the office window
- ✔ A tasty sandwich at lunch
- ✔ Almost no traffic on the way home from work
- ✔ A phone call from a friend
- ✔ The arrival of spring
- ✔ A great basketball game on TV
- ✔ Good health

- A good job with salary and benefits
- Money in the bank
- A new friend made this week
- Children playing in the park
- Funny text from coauthor
- Another chapter written
- A delicious dinner
- An hour of downtime without the kids
- Supportive family
- A short nap
- Flowers blooming in the yard
- Ice cream
- A new TV series to watch tonight
- An interesting article in the newspaper

Chapter 22
Ten Ways to Parent an Athlete

*P*arenting an athlete in today's fast-paced, results-oriented world of sports is one of the most difficult tasks you'll face as a parent. Today's young athletes are stronger, smarter, and more specialized than the young athletes of previous generations. They're also under more pressure than ever before, and young athletes are becoming stressed out and burned out on their sports at much higher rates than they did when we were kids.

In this chapter, we provide some ways you can maximize the benefits of your kids' participation in sports, allowing them to have fun, reach their athletic potential, and learn life lessons, all while minimizing stress and burnout.

Deciding Whether to Specialize

Today's kids begin the process of specialization almost from the very beginning of their athletic participation. The question many parents ask is whether specialization is a good thing for their kids.

Unless your kid enjoys only one sport, you're better off allowing him to play multiple sports as long as possible, particularly because some kids develop more slowly physically than others do. If they someday play at the college level, they can and will specialize at that point.

In general, try getting away from the idea of specialization. Think more in terms of primary and secondary sport participation. In other words, your kids need to be encouraged to have a primary sport, but also to play one or two other sports on some level. They may want to play these additional sports competitively, and that's great. But the choice of which sport is primary and which ones are secondary will depend on your kids' motivation and whether you have the time and money for them to play those sports.

There are numerous disadvantages to playing only one sport continuously for years, especially from an early age. As professionals, we see high school student-athletes who once had the desire to play at the college level decide not to pursue their dream because they're burned out on their sports. They've spent too much time, with far too much pressure, playing that sport, and now they want to quit. You can never know for sure whether they would've decided not to play college sports even if they hadn't specialized all those years. But it does appear that athletes who are more balanced don't quit as early and/or have more successful and rewarding college athletic careers.

Kids who participate in multiple sports

- ✔ Learn a variety of athletic skills that can enhance their overall movement and coordination in all sports

- ✔ Are exposed to different types of coaches and athletes and learn how to manage and deal with these different personalities, rules, and systems

- ✔ Learn from the experience of participating in individual sports versus team sports — self-reliance as well as teamwork, for example

- ✔ Lower their chances of developing physical overuse injuries

- ✔ Lower their chances of becoming physically and emotionally burned out because of constant pressure associated with one sport

- ✔ May look better in the eyes of college coaches, many of whom prefer cross-trained athletes

Some sports demand more time (and specialization) at an earlier age. For example, ice skating and gymnastics are sports in which many athletes start competing at younger ages and have to do so because of the nature of the sport. A 22-year-old gymnast is considered well toward retirement. Tennis and golf — two individual and technically oriented sports — require years of training to be competitive in today's world of youth golf and tennis. This doesn't mean, though, that these athletes can't find balance with other sports or interests. Even intramural sports are great outlets for athletes who are involved in time-intensive individual sports at early ages.

Choosing the Right League

Choosing the right league for your kid to play in can make a big difference in both her level of enjoyment in competition and how quickly her physical skills improve. Start by evaluating your kid's skill level in comparison to her peers. What are your kid's strengths athletically, and what are her areas for improvement? When you have figured that out, you can go about choosing the right league.

If you're having trouble assessing your kid's skill level, talk to any coaches she's already played for. They should be able to help you identify your kid's individual strengths.

The right league for your kid will strike a balance between being a bit difficult but yet not *so* difficult that she's always frustrated. You want the level of the league to be slightly above where your kid is athletically. This will encourage her to push herself to learn new skills, while not posing a tremendous challenge in the meantime.

Make sure to choose a league that fits your kid's desires and motivation, too. Is competition her main reason for playing sports, or is she doing it more for social reasons and to have fun? Does she want a balance between these two things? Know the mission of the league: Is it primarily to be competitive and train skills, or to enhance the social and life skills of sport? Few leagues are either entirely competitive or entirely social, but many leagues lean one way or another. You want a league that matches your own interests and beliefs for your kid in combination with your kid's preferences.

Knowing What to Say after a Loss

The more competitive your kid is in his sport, the harder it will be for him to take losses well. Here are some general guidelines to follow when talking to your kid after a loss:

- ✔ **Wait until your kid engages you to start the conversation.** If you try to force the conversation, you'll just be a source of frustration for your kid.

- ✔ **Validate your kid's feelings about the loss, no matter what they are.** Frustration, anger, annoyance, and fear are all common emotional reactions to losses. Listen to your kid and express empathy for what he's going through.

- ✔ **Let your kid dictate the length and depth of the conversation.** He'll let you know when he wants to talk, and how much he wants to discuss. Trying to force a lesson into the discussion when he's not ready to learn is simply counterproductive.

✔ **Focus on the positives whenever possible.** Losses are tough to deal with, but there is always a silver lining in every loss if you're willing to look hard enough for it. Teach your kid how to do that.

Choosing the ideal time to do so is important on this matter. If your kid isn't too emotional, go ahead and talk to him about the lessons he can learn. If he's still emotional, wait a day or two. When emotions are high, he'll have difficulty hearing you anyway.

Being a Fan, not a Coach

When you're the parent of an athlete, you need to figure out how involved you'll become in her athletic life, especially when you're attending games and practices.

Make sure you're a *fan* — let the coaches do the coaching. They've accepted that role, and you agreed for your kid to be placed under the coaches' mentorship. This doesn't mean you can't question or discuss something with the coaches, but you need to avoid trying to coach your kid at games and practices. Doing so sends a confusing message to your kid and puts her in an awkward position — she won't know whether to listen to the coach or to you, especially if the messages are conflicting.

If you want to "coach" your kid, you can do so at home, away from her organized practice schedule. Make sure to discuss with her your methods and approach, especially if you're teaching something different from the coach. You can explain that coaches sometimes see things differently and that she should follow her coach's directions.

Avoid bad-mouthing the coach or encouraging your kid to disregard what her coach is teaching or saying. If you do engage in bad-mouthing, it creates problems for everyone, especially your kid. It's okay to encourage your kid to ask the coach for clarification, but remember that the coach has the final say. If you don't like the coach, you can switch teams or leagues at the end of the season, but while your kid is playing under that coach, encourage your kid to be respectful and honor what her coach is trying to teach her.

Cheering, not Yelling

It's very natural to become emotionally charged at your kid's game. Sometimes you may feel extreme joy; other times, extreme anger and disappointment. Your role as an adult and parent is to manage your emotions when you're at practices and games, as well as when you're talking with your kid about his sport. One way you can keep your emotions in check is to make sure you're cheering and not yelling at games and practices. You may *feel* like yelling — youth sports can be frustrating for numerous reasons (errors, poor officiating, or questionable coaching). But yelling and *feeling* like yelling are two different matters.

The difference between cheering and yelling lies in your words and your tone of voice. Cheering is made up of positive words, such as pointing out when your kid or his team does well — for example, "Great job!" or "Nice hustle!" Cheering also has an encouraging and positive tone to it.

A good measure of tone is how others fans perceive you. Do they think you're enjoying yourself or do they think you sound angry and upset? If you're enjoying yourself, your tone will be more positive. If you're not enjoying yourself, your tone may be angry or biting.

Yelling, on the other hand, is more negative in nature and is expressed with anger or hostility. Phrases such as "That was awful!" or "I can't believe you did that!" are examples of yelling. Yelling can also be far worse, such as degrading kids and coaches, using profanity, and even physically assaulting parents, coaches, or officials. With yelling, tone is crucial — you might express the right words, such as "Hustle!" or "Get the ball!", but they're expressed with hostility and venom in your voice.

If you're having a tough time controlling yourself, simply walk away. It's far better to say nothing at all than it is to yell at your kid while he participates in sports.

Talking with Your Kid's Coach

If you want to support your kid, you need to know what to say when you talk to her coach. Here are our recommendations:

- ✔ **Err on the side of talking less, not more, with your kid's coach.** Many times, your engaging in dialogue with the coach can backfire, even with the best of intentions.

- ✔ **If you must talk with your kid's coach, know your role.** Your role is to ask the coach how you can best support your kid in her athletic development.

- ✔ **Never, ever try to tell the coach how to do his job.** Just think about how you would feel if someone came to your office and engaged in the same behavior — you'd be offended! Don't be that parent. Simply seek to understand the coach's viewpoint, decisions, and methods with your kid.

✓ **If you choose to talk to your kid's coach, choose an appropriate time.** After practice, when you're picking up your kid, is usually a good time. Before or after games are usually bad times, because the coach has a lot on his mind at these times.

✓ **Be sure to seek your kid's input on whether she feels comfortable having you talking to her coach.** You don't want to embarrass or humiliate your kid.

Rewarding the Things That Matter

Athletes can control very little outside of their own attitude and effort on the field. This lesson is an important one to teach your kid. If your kid doesn't get this key point, he'll face all kinds of disappointment and frustration, because winning and losing are completely beyond of his control.

Reward your kid for giving good effort, displaying good sportsmanship, managing his emotions, handling pressure, focusing during the game, hustling, communicating well with teammates, and being a team player. These are the things over which your kid has control. When you reward him for the things he can control, you'll see an increase in his self-esteem as an athlete.

Budgeting Your Time and Money

As a parent, you'll likely want and need to have a budget for the time and money you'll devote to your kid's sport. Some sports, like soccer, require less individual attention and travel time than other sports like golf or tennis. Some sports, like track and basketball, are less expensive than other sports, like golf and hockey, because of the equipment, coaching, and travel requirements.

The key is not to spend more time or money than you have. You want to make sure that your kid's sports participation doesn't impinge upon your family's resources. If you have more than one kid playing sports, you'll really have to budget your time and money carefully.

Before your kid starts playing sports, decide how much money you can spend this season. Be realistic and reasonable, and keep yourself to that budget. If you're constantly stressed out because of financial costs related to sports, it will affect your family and can be quite damaging to the home environment.

Be sure to talk to your kid about the cost of sports, too. He may have friends who are doing a lot more when it comes to sports, such as getting private instruction or the latest equipment, and those expenses may or may not be a feasible option for your family.

When it comes to the amount of time you devote to your kid's sport, be fair to yourself and your family. Playing multiple sports during a single season or playing on a school team and a travel team simultaneously may not be realistic. If you're like most parents, you have multiple obligations — from your job to your partner to other kids and extended family not to mention your own activities and interests. Your kid's athletic participation isn't the only thing on your plate, and it shouldn't get all your attention.

Be upfront with your kid. If he wants to play in a second sport or league in a single season, you may have to say no. You're better off setting and sticking to boundaries than you are agreeing and feeling bitter, angry, and stressed all season.

You can expect your kid to be disciplined, show effort, practice hard, and take improvement seriously, especially if he's involved in a sport that requires a substantial investment of time and money. But you can't expect results. You can't expect that your investment of time and money will pay off in a scholarship or fame.

If your kid isn't putting in the necessary effort, ask him how important the sport is to him. If the sport isn't that important long term (for example, he doesn't want to play in college) and he plays for social reasons, then you don't have to invest as much time and money. For example, we tell parents of golfers and tennis players that they don't need to take their kids to national events if the kids aren't motivated enough to work hard to be at these type of events. Local events will do just fine.

You can always change your mind throughout the season, either cutting back or investing more in your kid's development as you see fit.

Focusing on Learning Life Skills

Organized sports teach kids important life skills — skills that they'll need later in life, on and off the field. Some of these lessons include the following:

- **Life isn't fair.** Why expect it to be? Sometimes the referee makes a terrible call, and sometimes the coach plays the less talented kid or the kid who doesn't work as hard. Often, the better teams don't win.

- ✔ **Hard work pays dividends.** In general, you get out of sport what you put into it. The harder you work, and the smarter you work, the better the results you'll experience.

- ✔ **Teamwork is important.** The iconic image of the Lone Ranger doing great things by himself is simply a myth. Great teams accomplish much more than great individuals do.

- ✔ **Everybody has a role to play.** Like parts of a car, everybody on a team has an important role to play in order to help the team experience success.

- ✔ **People are counting on you.** If you fail to do your part, your team or your own individual performance (or both!) will suffer.

- ✔ **Anything worth having requires discipline.** Discipline is one of the keys to greatness and success in anything — sports, music, teaching, medicine, or parenthood. With discipline comes results.

Living Your Own Life instead of Living through Your Kid

One of the most important and frequent issues we see as sports psychologists working with children and adolescents is the tendency of many parents to live out their own personal athletic dreams through their kids. Sometimes, the parent was a successful athlete himself back in the day; other times, the parent didn't get to realize all his athletic dreams. Either way, parents invest lots of time and energy into developing the skills of their kids. They hope for a return on their investment, similar to the way they would if they invested in a growth stock. The problem is, kids don't work like the stock market, and neither should you.

Your kid is a separate person from you. She may have half of your genetic material, but she's her own individual person, and she deserves to be treated as such. There's nothing wrong with wanting your kid to experience the success you either had or didn't have as a kid, but there is a lot wrong with demanding that she carry the burden of your high expectations with her.

If you find yourself living and dying by your kid's wins and losses, try to take a step back and get some perspective. Your kid will more than likely have a difficult time telling you that you're being overbearing or irrational with your expectations. The burden falls on you to be self-aware.

Sports are a training ground for life, and the emphasis should be on the lessons your kid learns — lessons that will serve her well throughout the rest of her life.

Index

Notes

Notes

EDUCATION, HISTORY & REFERENCE

978-0-7645-2498-1 978-0-470-46244-7

Also available:
- Algebra For Dummies
  978-0-7645-5325-7
- Art History For Dummies
  978-0-470-09910-0
- Chemistry For Dummies
  978-0-7645-5430-8
- English Grammar For Dummies
  978-0-470-54664-2

- French For Dummies
  978-0-7645-5193-2
- Statistics For Dummies
  978-0-7645-5423-0
- World History For Dummies
  978-0-470-44654-6

FOOD, HOME, & MUSIC

978-0-7645-9904-0 978-0-470-43111-5

Also available:
- 30-Minute Meals For Dummies
  978-0-7645-2589-6
- Bartending For Dummies
  978-0-470-05056-9
- Brain Games For Dummies
  978-0-470-37378-1
- Gluten-Free Cooking For
  Dummies 978-0-470-17810-2

- Home Improvement All-in-One
  Desk Reference For Dummies
  978-0-7645-5680-7
- Violin For Dummies
  978-0-470-83838-9
- Wine For Dummies
  978-0-470-04579-4

HEALTH & SELF-HELP

978-0-471-77383-2 978-0-470-16036-7

Also available:
- Borderline Personality
  Disorder For Dummies
  978-0-470-46653-7
- Breast Cancer For Dummies
  978-0-7645-2482-0
- Cognitive Behavioural
  Therapy For Dummies
  978-0-470-01838-5
- Depression For Dummies
  978-0-7645-3900-8

- Emotional Intelligence For
  Dummies 978-0-470-15732-9
- Healthy Aging For Dummies
  978-0-470-14975-1
- Neuro-linguistic
  Programming For Dummies
  978-0-7645-7028-5
- Understanding Autism For
  Dummies 978-0-7645-2547-6

HOBBIES & CRAFTS

978-0-470-28747-7 978-0-470-29112-2

Also available:
- Crochet Patterns For
  Dummies 97-0-470-04555-8
- Digital Scrapbooking For
  Dummies 978-0-7645-8419-0
- Knitting Patterns For
  Dummies 978-0-470-04556-5
- Oil Painting For Dummies
  978-0-470-18230-7

- Quilting For Dummies
  978-0-7645-9799-2
- Sewing For Dummies
  978-0-7645-6847-3
- Word Searches For Dummies
  978-0-470-45366-7

Available wherever books are sold. For more information or to order direct: U.S. customers visit www.dummies.com or call 1-877-762-2974. U.K. customers visit www.wileyeurope.com or call 0800 243407. Canadian customers visit www.wiley.ca or call 1-800-567-4797.

HOME & BUSINESS COMPUTER BASICS

978-0-470-49743-2 978-0-470-48953-6

Also available:
- Office 2010 All-in-One Desk Reference For Dummies 978-0-470-49748-7
- Pay Per Click Search Engine Marketing For Dummies 978-0-471-75494-7

- Search Engine Marketing For Dummies 978-0-471-97998-2
- Web Analytics For Dummies 978-0-470-09824-0
- Word 2010 For Dummies 978-0-470-48772-3

INTERNET & DIGITAL MEDIA

978-0-470-44417-7 978-0-470-39062-7

Also available:
- Blogging For Dummies 978-0-471-77084-8
- MySpace For Dummies 978-0-470-09529-4
- The Internet For Dummies 978-0-470-12174-0

- Twitter For Dummies 978-0-470-47991-9
- YouTube For Dummies 978-0-470-14925-6

MACINTOSH

978-0-470-27817-8 978-0-470-58027-1

Also available:
- iMac For Dummies 978-0-470-13386-6
- iPod Touch For Dummies 978-0-470-50530-4
- iPod & iTunes For Dummies 978-0-470-39062-7

- MacBook For Dummies 978-0-470-27816-1
- Macs For Seniors For Dummies 978-0-470-43779-7
- Mac OS X Snow Leopard All-in-One Desk Reference For Dummies 978-0-470-43541-0

SPORTS & FITNESS

978-0-471-76871-5 978-0-470-73855-9

Also available:
- Exercise Balls For Dummies 978-0-7645-5623-4
- Coaching Volleyball For Dummies 978-0-470-46469-4
- Curling For Dummies 978-0-470-83828-0
- Fitness For Dummies 978-0-7645-7851-9

- Mixed Martial Arts For Dummies 978-0-470-39071-9
- Ten Minute Tone-Ups For Dummies 978-0-7645-7207-4
- Wilderness Survival For Dummies 978-0-470-45306-3
- Yoga with Weights For Dummies 978-0-471-74937-0